DATE			

How Labor Markets Work

Richard Lester   John Dunlop   Clark Kerr   Lloyd Reynolds

The bottom line they seek is fidelity to reality.

How Labor Markets Work

*Reflections on Theory and Practice
by John Dunlop, Clark Kerr, Richard
Lester, and Lloyd Reynolds*

Edited by

Bruce E. Kaufman
Georgia State University

Lexington Books
D.C. Heath and Company/Lexington, Massachusetts/Toronto

Library of Congress Cataloging-in-Publication Data

How labor markets work.

Includes index.
  1. Labor supply — Congresses. 2. Wages—Congresses.
3. Dunlop, John Thomas, 1914–   —Congresses. 4. Kerr, Clark, 1911–   —Congresses.
5. Lester, Richard Allen, 1908–   —Congresses. 6. Reynolds, Lloyd George, 1910–
— Congresses. I. Kaufman, Bruce E. II. Dunlop, John Thomas, 1914–   .
III. Kerr, Clark, 1911–   . IV. Lester, Richard Allen, 1908–   .
V. Reynolds, Lloyd George, 1910–   .
HD5701.3.H68 1988   331.12   86-46227
ISBN 0-669-15126-2 (alk. paper)

Published simultaneously in Canada
Printed in the United States of America

Casebound International Standard Book Number: 0-669-15126-2
Library of Congress Catalog Card Number: 86-46227

The paper used in this publication meets the minimum requirements of American National Standard
for Information Sciences — Permanence of Paper for Printed Library Materials, ANSI Z39.48-
1984. ™

88 89 90 91 92 8 7 6 5 4 3 2 1

Contents

Preface

The papers in this volume were originally presented at a conference sponsored by Georgia State University in Atlanta, Georgia, on November 7, 1986. The conference was held in honor of four of the most distinguished and influential scholars in labor economics and industrial relations—John Dunlop, Clark Kerr, Richard Lester, and Lloyd Reynolds. Each of these men has been active in the labor area as both a researcher and practitioner for over fifty years and has published scholarly works that are considered classics in the literature. During the period spanning 1945–1960, the writings and research of Dunlop, Kerr, Lester, and Reynolds, as well as that of several of their colleagues and co-authors, effectively defined the intellectual center of gravity in labor economics. The hallmark of their research was the attempt to combine theory and practice into more realistic models of how labor markets and labor unions actually work. The result was a distinctive view of the labor market process that represented a fusion of the best parts of the neoclassical and institutional schools in labor economics. Their research also led to the development of a number of specific and highly influential theoretical concepts and pathbreaking empirical studies of wage determination, labor mobility, and company employment practices.

The first four papers are written by the honorees. In their papers, the honorees provide a personal reflection on the significant events and people in their careers, a survey of the state of theory and practice in labor economics in the 1930s when they received their Ph.D. degrees, a discussion of the significant theoretical concepts and empirical evidence concerning wage determination and labor markets that emerged from their own research and the research of their colleagues during the 1945–1960 period, and an assessment of the current strengths and weaknesses of theoretical and applied research in labor economics today. The end product is a fascinating review of the evolution of thought in labor economics over the last half-century and a penetrating analysis and critique of the current state of theory and research methodology in the field.

The remaining two papers in the volume are by Bruce Kaufman and Richard Freeman. Kaufman discusses the place of Dunlop, Kerr, Lester, and Reynolds in the history of thought in labor economics, surveys their published work and identifies the key features of what he calls the "postwar" model of labor markets and wage determination, reviews Lester's famous attack on marginalism, and assesses the contributions of the honorees to the advancement of economic science. Freeman in his paper examines the extent to which the findings of recent empirical research support or contradict the basic premises of the postwar view of how labor markets work. After an extensive review of the empirical literature on wage determination, collective bargaining, and labor mobility, Freeman concludes that most of the major conclusions or hypotheses advanced by Dunlop, Kerr, Lester, and Reynolds in the 1950s remain valid today, despite the great changes that have taken place over the last thirty years in both the labor market and the techniques of empirical research.

As editor of this volume and organizer of the conference, I would like to acknowledge the contributions and assistance of a number of people who made this work possible. First, and foremost, I would like to express my appreciation to Michael Mescon, Dean of the College of Business Administration at Georgia State University, who through his commitment of time, financial resources, and enthusiasm made this project possible. Through his office, funding for the conference was also obtained from the chair of Private Enterprise and the Franklin Foundation. I would also like to gratefully acknowledge the cooperation received from John Stepp, Associate Deputy Undersecretary for Labor–Management Relations and Cooperative Programs of the U.S. Department of Labor, and his willingness to contribute financial support for this effort. Thanks also goes to Michael Jedel, Director of the Institute of Industrial Relations at Georgia State University, for the help and assistance he gave me in organizing and coordinating the conference and in preparing the manuscripts in this volume for publication. Last, but not least, a big thank-you also goes to Marian Mealing and Grace Williams for the many hours they devoted to typing the final manuscript.

1

The Neoclassical Revisionists in Labor Economics (1940–1960)—R.I.P.

Clark Kerr

The Low Road of Realistic Studies

How did the explorations whose interests, methods, and results are outlined below all begin? I shall give an answer from a quite personal viewpoint. For nascent labor economists in the early 1930s (I began my own graduate studies in the fall of 1932), the two most important recent books of special relevance were by Lionel Robbins (*An Essay on the Nature and Significance of Economic Science*, 1932) and by John R. Hicks (*The Theory of Wages*, also 1932). They both carried discouraging messages which, if followed, would have aborted any interest in labor economics by any reasonably intelligent person. The central message of the first was that realistic studies were the low road and pure theory the high road. The central message of the second was that all that needed to be known about labor economics was already known, since it was a sub-branch of standard marginal analysis applied to nearly perfect labor markets with few special characteristics.

Robbins was my advisor at the London School of Economics in 1936 (and again in 1939), so I paid even closer attention to his book after I arrived at LSE. He shortly suggested to me, in 1936, that I get my Ph.D. in the United States, on the grounds that placement opportunities (as it turned out to be true) were much better in the States with an American degree and with American professors as sponsors. The subliminal message was that my clear interest in realistic studies was the low road and did not fit LSE at that time—the big influences intellectually in economics were Robbins and Friedrich A. Hayek. Even without Robbins, the message was clear in seminar assignments at Stanford, LSE, and Berkeley, and in the obvious pecking order of faculty members on each campus and at the professional meetings: the best people were interested in pure theory.

Robbins was then an Austrian economist by persuasion (later on, Robbins II became a broad political economist and my good friend, with shared interests in both economics and higher education). His passion in the early

1930s was "economic generalization." He was contemptuous of "quantitative economics," of the "historical school," and of the "institutionalists": "Not one single 'law' deserving of the name, not one quantitative generalization of permanent validity has emerged from their efforts"; "of 'concrete laws,' substantial uniformities of 'economic behavior,' not one"; only "useful monographs on particular historical situations." "It is theory and theory alone which is capable of supplying the solution." (For these and other Robbins' quotations that follow, see chapter 5 of the 1935 edition.) Yet "realistic studies," Robbins conceded, have a place—if, and only if, "undertaken by those who have a firm grasp of analytical principle and some notion of what can and what cannot legitimately be expected from activities of this sort"— which was not much.

Robbins set forth, however, three useful functions for "realistic" or "empirical" studies:

> One was to "check on the applicability to given situations of different types of theoretical constructions."

> A second was to suggest "auxiliary postulates" in elaboration of the general theory in order to fit it more precisely to actual situations.

> A third was to "bring to light new problems."

These three roles may be identified as (1) testing the realism of the assumptions as related to specific situations, as (2) extending the explanatory powers of the theory into the far corners of practice, and as (3) alerting theorists to changed and changing conditions in the real world. These really are important roles. Among modern (post–World War II) labor economists, the neoclassical revisionists, as I shall call them in this discussion (I earlier, 1983, used the designation of "neorealists"), concentrated on the first and the third of these roles. The subsequent and more traditional neoclassical labor economists of the Chicago school—the "restorationists," as I shall later identify them, were, as true believers, more interested in the second role and have been spectacularly successful.

These three roles all assume, however, as did Robbins, that the only purpose of realistic studies is to support theoretical analysis. There are other roles for empirical studies, however, not noted by Robbins, including providing a running history of and commentary upon actual developments in the area under consideration, and exploring and reporting on new and anticipated developments as a basis for public opinion formation and for policy actions. These additional roles only marginally assist economic theorists, if they assist them at all. Realistic studies may, thus, be said:

1. to serve theorists (as Robbins advocated),

2. to aid historians, and

3. to serve, with information and analysis, current participants and teachers in the area under examination, and to enlighten the public in general and policymakers in particular by increasing understanding of what is going on.

Judgments will differ, but it is my own view that the contributions in these second and third areas have, in the post–World War II period, certainly been adequate and perhaps much better than that.

It is the first area, however, which is most important in the long run: service to theorists. To this extent, Robbins is correct. If this service had been more adequate in the past, we might now have the better economic models so badly needed. The failure, however, was not for lack of trying.

While Robbins was saying that realistic studies are of secondary importance and most of them of no importance at all, Hicks was saying that they were not needed in the area of labor economics even if of high quality. The *Theory of Wages* stated, in effect, that everything that needed to be known was known—that this was a well-mapped terra cognita. Hicks, like Robbins, was then in an Austrian phase of his development. In an article in the *Economic Journal* (June 1930), Hicks had even challenged Alfred Marshall, who had written in his *Principles* (8th edition, 1920: 375) that "advantage in bargaining . . . is more often on the side of the buyers" in the labor market, thus creating opportunities for exploitation and indeterminacy. Hicks accepted indeterminacy only under conditions of organized bilateral monopoly; otherwise it was negligible. All, or almost all, was understood. D.H. Robertson, in his "Wage Grumbles" (1931), agreed.

Thus, with Robbins and Hicks among the great councillors, and Robertson playing a lesser role, why would anyone aspire to become a labor economist at all, and, in particular, of a realistic inclination?

Economics might have gone in another direction. Oskar Lange, when teaching at Berkeley in the middle 1930s and knowing my interest in labor economics, had introduced me to F.Y. Edgeworth's *Mathematical Physics* (1881). Edgeworth thought that all was indeterminacy except pure monopoly and perfect competition; only under these conditions were the results fully determinant. In all other situations there were ranges of indeterminacy. He was obsessed with indeterminacy. Perfect competition required full information available throughout the market, large numbers of buyers and sellers, freedom of all buyers and sellers to contract and recontract at any time, absence of combinations on either side, and contracts that were not entered into simultaneously. These are very restrictive conditions. In the area of bilateral monopoly, Edgeworth developed his "contract curve"analysis to try to indicate the most likely range of possible bargains under ideal conditions, and I later found this a most useful concept in trying to understand collective bargaining and to practice mediation and arbitration.

Had more of the attention of economists followed Edgeworth, the understanding of reality might have been advanced. His was, at the time, however, almost a lone voice and seldom heard: purely abstract reasoning is greatly limited in its powers of explanation. In his inaugural lecture at Oxford in 1891, he argued that the "general rule" is of limited usefulness. Few, at the time, followed this advice, but it has echoed down the intervening century, including among labor economists of the revisionist persuasion after World War II. Following Edgeworth in another way, however, might have led (and even did lead) to trouble. John Maynard Keynes says in his *Essays in Biography* (1933: 192) that Marshall worried about Edgeworth as to whether his mathematics would "carry him out of sight of the actual facts of economics"; worried that there was potential danger in his method. Nevertheless, the economics profession might have done better over the past century if it had taken more seriously the view of Edgeworth in his 1889 (p. 125) presidential address to Section F of the Royal Society that: "in pure economics there is only one fundamental theorem, but it is a very difficult one: the theory of the bargain in a wide sense."

The Choice of the Low Road

The group of labor economists who gave dominant leadership to the field in the United States from 1940 to 1960 chose, in the phrasing of Robbins, "the interpretation of reality"—the low road—over the building of theoretical *a priori* models. We turned our backs on the message of Robbins as giving too narrow and too unimportant a role to realistic studies. What seemed to us to be wrong with economics was not poor logic (and too many moralistic value judgments, as in Marshall) but an inadequate grasp of the nature and significance of the real world. We also turned our backs on Hicks with his nearly perfect markets, equilibrium in the overall labor market, lags that were only temporary, negligible ranges of "indeterminateness," and bloodless strikes based upon precise and cold-blooded economic calculations. The Robbins approach seemed too arid, and that of Hicks too defensive of the status quo. All was not really for the best in the best of all possible worlds, or so it seemed at the time.

Let me say, quickly, that we were questioning the main themes of Robbins and Hicks. On reading them once again more than fifty years later, I realize that their qualifications of their main themes were neglected at the time. If they, and we, had highlighted their soft-line qualifications and built on them and had not so concentrated on their hard-line main themes, progress in economic understanding might have been substantially advanced. They were wrong in downplaying their qualifications. We were wrong in not building on them more. I now find their qualifications to be immensely valuable; and both of them built their subsequent careers more on the qualifications than on the major themes. Robbins II, of his Ely lecture (1981) and his autobiography (1971), and Hicks II, of "flex-price" and "fix-price" (1955), both emphasized their earlier qualifications and noted their regrets over their more single-minded youthful enthusiasms for their main themes. But this was after the initial and formative impacts they had in the early and middle 1930s on unsuspecting and totally unsophisticated novices, such as myself.

Knowledge changes under many influences, including:

1. The accretion of studies in the field and in adjacent fields, sometimes slowly and sometimes at a revolutionary pace.

2. The introduction of new methodologies.

3. The confrontation of received doctrine by unsolved problems that appear, or remain, in the real world.

4. The changing mentalities, both normative and analytical, with changing fashions of thought, changing attractive ideologies, et cetera.

5. The changing policies for support for studies by foundations, government agencies, universities, et cetera; or, in some societies, changing efforts at suppression.

Each of these influences has had an impact on labor economics over the past fifty years, as a case in point and as the discussion below will illustrate.

Two explosions in the realm of reality (point 3 above), in the period 1930 to 1945, were dominant in challenging traditional approaches to labor economics: the onslaught, first, of the Great Depression and, second, of World War II, with the latter following right on the heels of the former. In both periods, labor markets were under great stress approaching *in extremis*. These were, however, quite different and, in labor economics, almost antithetical periods—going from great surpluses to great deficits in labor supply; but each was an overwhelming experience for young labor economists. As one of this group, my experience may be illustrative.

Experiencing Reality

I came into contact with the impacts of the Great Depression in very disturbing ways. In our beautiful agricultural valley in eastern Pennsylvania, our hard-working neighbors and friends, through no fault of their own, were sold out, down to the family dog going to a stranger for a dime. These farmers were not seeking leisure nor going on a job search (as some theorists later suggested) from the farms that had been in their families for generations. What happened to them was totally involuntary.

At Swarthmore, and under the auspices of the American Friends Service Committee, I went once a week to a school in a black neighborhood to help prepare breakfast for, and keep discipline among, the ravenous children whom we fed on donated old bread, stale milk, and solidified apple butter. They were really suffering from hunger, and not by their or their parents' choice.

At Stanford, I started a study of the self-help cooperatives of the unemployed (1933 and 1939), where former merchants and farmers and craftsmen were trying to hold body and soul together (more soul than body, for their self-respect was so badly damaged) by exchanging services and by getting and distributing the surplus produce and goods that surrounded poverty. No equilibrium, no clearing of markets—except by scavengers. The transitional lags in necessary adjustments might end, the anticipated turning-of-the corner might come eventually but, in the meantime, individual human endurance and the solidity of a very solid democratic society were both severely tested. The twin phenomena were how slowly and inadequately the economy adjusted of its own accord and how heroically the common people held to their beliefs in the democratic system. It was a time of economic tragedy surpassed only by the triumph of political loyalty.

My first experience with labor problems had been at Swarthmore when, again under the auspices of the American Friends Service Committee, I served as a Peace Caravaner, with my teammate, arguing before any available audience for the United States joining the League of Nations and World Court. Driving into New Bedford, Massachusetts, late one night, we were stopped at a police roadblock. We were young, we had an out-of-state license, we had literature in the back of the car. We were arrested on suspicion of being "Communists" entering town to assist a long and bitter strike of textile workers. Emotions were very high, hatred very deep; violence was on the very surface of police behavior.

My first contact with academic labor economics began quite differently with my graduate education at Stanford in 1932–33. The "big-book" in the field then was Hick's *The Theory of Wages*, and it remained influential until at least the end of World War II. I learned only much later that Hicks had already quietly begun to abandon the book, in his own "personal revolution," when I had just finished reading it (Hicks 1963: 307). My teachers did not abandon it while I was a student, and I did not abandon it as a teacher until well after World War II. *The Theory of Wages* is a well-argued description of a rational world of nearly perfect competition. Some of us added our own weights to the "imperfections" that Hicks discussed, and noted some that he did not, but Hicks, with his full-blown theory, was the base point for analysis. My first article on labor economics (Kerr 1941) related to a situation where an S-shaped supply curve for labor existed, and my first footnote to the economic literature was to Hicks. My first monograph (Kerr 1942), and the first of what later became a long series of modern labor market studies by others, was based on Hicks's framework, although I did put more emphasis on the noneconomic "costs of transference" and on inertia.

My first deep contact with actual labor problems was in the fall of 1933. A bloody cotton pickers' strike took place in the San Joaquin Valley. I assisted Professor Paul S. Taylor of Berkeley, where I was by then a graduate student, in a study of the dispute (Taylor and Kerr 1940). This was not the world of chapter VII of Hicks, where strikes were not really necessary except "occasion-ally" to keep the strike weapon "burnished"; for, with this exception, they were just the result of "faulty negotiations." The San Joaquin Valley was, instead a world of hatred, of exploitation, of ideologies right and left, of the raw power of guns and hunger and damaged crops. It was not only a war between growers and itinerant workers but also between the lay preachers, on the one hand, who led the Okies and who wanted a reasonable settlement so that their people could eat, and the Communists, on the other, who led the Mexicans and who, as Communists, wanted a start on the revolution by showing the workers they could never win under capitalism. And the growers were split also between the vigilantes among the larger growers and the small growers, who did their own work and who were sympathetic to the laborers. Hicks then would have swept all this aside into the unimportant category of aberrations. I found a great gap between the rational world of theory and the real world of group conflict. This dichotomy of theory and reality has been a central feature of labor economics throughout its history. Labor economists individually have chosen to live mainly in one or the other of these worlds; few in both.

My next significant experience with the real world was during World War II. I served, as did a substantial number of the labor economists of the postwar period, with the War Labor Board (WLB). According to Hicks, "the apparent range of indeterminateness [of wage rates] is negligible except for exceptional men"; and, for the "average" workman, the "range of indeterminateness is so narrow that it is not worth considering" (Hicks 1932: 33). This was the result of competition. The board's basic wage policy was to stabilize wages at the "going rate," which we set out eagerly to find with the help of the Bureau of Labor Statistics (BLS). We actually found it only where there was no competition—where union rates universally applied. Otherwise, wage rates for the same occupation varied greatly within the same labor market areas. This was the result of many other forces at work in addition to market competition. As government agents we *set* the going rate according to our best judgment, since we did not *find* it already in effect except in special circumstances. We tried mostly to find a modal spread of rates, but often found two or three, and turned that (or them) into the official going rate.

My experience, still later, as an arbitrator after the war taught me, as many others also learned, how important job security is to workers and thus how important are seniority rules and grievance procedures, as compared with the opportunities for mobility that Hicks emphasized. This phenomenon has been put into the more elegant terms of "voice" versus "exit" by A.O. Hirschman (1970). Clear also was the centrality of institutional (and leadership) security that E. Wight Bakke (1946) so effectively described as "mutual survival," and which Hicks neglected.

Entering into Revisionism

These experiences illustrate how a good many of us then-young labor economists lived with the ghost of Hicks I. Hicks II later called *The Theory of Wages* "a juvenile work" and "a thoroughly bad book" with a "terrible first chapter" (Hicks 1963: 310,311,321). At least two observations can be drawn from this little history: how an elegant and persuasive theory can lead to false expectations in practice; and how the very best of theorists can learn from applied economists despite their original commitment to a prior theory. I shall return to this point later with reference to Hicks, who is, for me, an intellectual hero.

As for Robbins, the real world was so different from the neoclassical theory he defended and so much more exciting than the study of what seemed like old dogmas that I was, as were others, more attracted to the low road of practice than to the high road that went from office to library and back again— thinking only high thoughts all the way. Robbins, like Hicks, also became a hero to me in his late writings and in his many other activities, and for the same reason—he kept on learning, and from reality.

Two lessons that can be drawn from these and similar experiences (if they were not already self-evident) are (1) that theory should lead and not mislead; and (2) that realistic studies (and experiences) can be one very important means to this end. Perhaps a third lesson is that trying to live on the margin between theory and practice gives the labor economist who tries to do so a split personality: he is now a Dr. Jekyll and then a Mr. Hyde; now a high-minded quasi theorist and then a low-minded participant—observer; now secluded on lofty Mount Olympus and then in the busy Agora doing the bumps and grinds.

Other things were going on in the intellectual world that added to the impact of depression and war in helping to influence the approach of the revisionist labor economists. Studies that came closer to reality had been coming out in other fields: Adolph Berle and Gardiner Means (1932) on the separation of ownership and management, Joan Robinson (1933) and Edward Chamberlin (1933) on monopolistic or imperfect competition, and, above all,

Keynes (1936) on the causes and cures of depressions. These were all welcomed as bringing theory and practice closer together.

Key books by the early 1940s in the labor field were Bakke, *The Unemployed Worker* (1940), and Sumner H. Slichter, *Union Policies and Industrial Management* (1941). Robert Aaron Gordon at Berkeley, on the management side, was writing most realistically about *Business Leadership in the Large Corporation* (1945), and E.S. Mason at Harvard along similar lines in a series of famous articles. Both Gordon and Mason were very influential in the development of the views of the labor economics revisionists, particularly at Berkeley and at Harvard. They lent encouragement and inspiration.

However, in retrospect, we may have been too much influenced by the developments of our times—by labor markets in great distress rather than in more normal operation; and we may have overreacted to the Austrian-type economics to which we were exposed and become too obsessed with gods that seemed to have failed, and we were thus too intent on revisionism. We were also prisoners of our times, because we saw a closed labor market economy that lay between earlier and later peiods of immigration. This led to some false predictions, as my own (1958), for prospective reductions of wage differentials—"the new equality." We also came before the great influx of women and of blacks into urban labor markets and neglected the impacts of discrimination. We dealt mostly with labor markets composed predominantly of white males.

In any event, we, the revisionist labor economists, ended up as little foxes knowing many things, not as hedgehogs committed to one all-embracing theory. We looked for small truths, not the one overwhelming truth; or, at least, for the small truths that amended the big truth. We became pluralistic foxes, not monistic hedgehogs. The "fox knows many things," as the ancient Greek adage goes, and for a very good reason: there are many things to know. "The discovery of a pluralist universe is a real discovery; there really are many visions and many ways" (Walzer 1986: Introduction). But many in the intellectual world want simplicity and certainty—the "one big thing" that the hedgehog knows—to guide their thoughts; a central vision that gives coherence to their many perceptions; a single explanation that makes sense out of the many events. There is eternal tension between those who follow the pluralistic path and those who follow the monistic path; and also, as Isaiah Berlin's famous essay (1953) demonstrates so convincingly for Leo Tolstoy—within individuals who are painfully drawn both ways. And some foxes try to help some hedgehogs, even though hedgehogs seldom appreciate the proffered help—which can be sad for both in the intellectual world. The indeterminate (almost) world of Edgeworth and the determinate (almost) world of Hicks I have long stood in conflict and will continue to do so into the long future.

The Choice of the Neoclassical Framework

We, the revisionist foxes, chose as our basic framework the neoclassical pattern of explanation. One proof is the topics we studied. Another proof is the footnotes we employed. This is the framework in which we had been trained and, more importantly, the framework we judged to be most useful in beginning to begin an understanding of reality.

Four alternative frameworks were then available for choice.

The Neoclassical.   Marshall, A.C. Pigou, and Hicks, the key figures in this group, had applied their general theory of competition to an exploration of labor markets. Only much later did I learn that there was more to Marshall than the *Principles of Economics* (1890) as I read particularly his essay on "The Future of the Working Classes" (1873) and *Industry and Trade* (1919) (see my discussion in *Marshall, Marx and Modern Times*, 1969). Marshall knew a great deal about the economic world that does not show up in the caricature of him in the textbooks. As Martin Bronfenbrenner (1966: 15) observed, Marshall may be classed as a member of the "realistic" school, given his effort to formulate abstractions which deviate only marginally from observed facts. Later I also found out how sensible A.C. Pigou (1905) could be on subjects like the range of "practicable" bargains, and was likewise impressed by his much later recognition of the importance of "the many centers" of "employment between some of which, at all events in the short run, labor does not move at all freely" (Pigou 1945: 70). Pigou's range of "practicable" bargains, along with Edgeworth's "contract curve," were the principal analytical concepts that I have found useful in a nearly fifty-year history of labor arbitration and mediation—in fact, the only two, and nothing from game theory.

The antimonopolists were an extreme branch of the neoclassical school. Henry Simons's and Hayek's work is representative of this approach in which unions were presented as economic monopolies that ought to be eliminated. However, it seemed to some of us young labor economists that there was then more monopoly power on the side of employers than on the side of labor, as Adam Smith had long ago noted.

The Marxist.   Karl Marx (and Friedrich Engels) were known mostly through the *Communist Manifesto* and *Capital*; the *Manuscripts of 1844* and the *Grundrisse* were not then available in English. Though there were some political devotees of Marx, particularly among avant garde intellectuals, there were then no academic Marxist labor economists of note in the United States, and few general economists of this persuasion. Few American economists then shared Joseph A. Schumpeter's (1954: 384) view of Marx as a "central sun of social science." The "labor theory of value" seemed like boring nonsense; and

American unions were increasingly intent on bread-and-butter issues and not on revolution. Also, Marxism then meant Stalinism—an onerous association.

I have by now read a great deal more of Marx and have come to understand how his long view of history, his broad view of the social sciences, and his concern for large central issues could make his ideas so influential, even when so often proved wrong. Marx's style of thought (though not its content) and Schumpeter's have many similarities (Paul A. Samuelson 1981), but, in the thirties in the United States, Marx was considered by the vast majority of economists as either irrelevant or wrong, or both—to me, he was both. The work of Schumpeter, however, was then and later greatly respected by many.

The Institutional.   Key figures in this group included John R. Commons, Selig Perlman, Edwin Witte, and Philip Taft. The "Wisconsin school" was strong on history, supportive of unions, and favored ameliorative social legislation. These were very appealing approaches in the twenties and thirties. Perlman's *A Theory of the Labor Movement* (1928) was a central book. *The Economics of Collective Action* (Commons 1950) should have made sense out of this total approach, but it was very opaque. It did have, however, some good but much neglected emphases: on the importance of looking for both "similarities" and "dissimilarities," on the large role played by "working rules," and on the distinction between the "part" and the "whole," for example.

This school might be enlarged to include Beatrice and Sidney Webb in the United Kingdom, George E. Barnett and Jacob H. Hollander in the United States, and, later, Harry A. Millis and Slichter. They were all concerned with the work rules and group relations that had been developed both to govern labor input into industrial production and to determine the distribution of rewards. The classic U.S. book was, and is, Slichter's *Union Policies and Industrial Management* (1941) on "industrial jurisprudence"; and the classic British book was, and is, *Industrial Democracy* (1897) by the Webbs. Among prominent general economists, Schumpeter could be classified as most sympathetic to the institutional approach (see Gordon 1963).

It should be noted, however, that Slichter cannot be clearly listed in the institutional classification, for he also wrote as a more traditional general economist with a special interest in labor problems. Paul H. Douglas, who was also one of the early giants in the field, is likewise hard to classify. His *Theory of Wages* (1934) and his *Real Wages in the United States, 1890–1926,* (1930) are in the hard-line neoclassical framework, but he also wrote about unemployment (1931) as a basic and continuing phenomenon in a way that went beyond neoclassical expectations. He was critical of some assumptions of neoclassical theory, including the assumptions of full employment and of equal bargaining power between capital and labor; and concluded that marginal productivity theory must be "modified" (Rees 1979). Both Slichter and Douglas, thus, were part traditionalists and part revisionists, Slichter more on the revisionist side and Douglas on the traditionalist in their overall impacts. To the extent that the neoclassical revisionists of 1940 to 1960 looked at models, it was more to Slichter and to Douglas than to anyone else (although some looked more to Millis); and that is to say to models who themsleves looked in two directions. Slichter had the greater impact on the views of the revisionists, and Douglas on the quantitative methods later used by the Chicago restorationists.

The Human Relations.   Elton Mayo, Fritz Roethlisberger, and many others composed this group. Only very marginally related to labor economics (but more to industrial relations), the human relations school offered an inward-looking, promanagement approach to understanding working situations. Members of this school saw the factory as a psychological–sociological community that, like a tribe, needs good leadership by the chief. This approach contrasts, in particular, to that of the Wisconsin institutionalists. Lloyd H. Fisher and I once rather unfairly caricatured members of this human relations group as concentrating on a lopsided primitive view of "the elite and the aborigines" (1957). It was true, however, as we pointed out, that they looked exclusively at the internal environment and ignored the great importance of external environments.

The Road Not Taken: Institutionalism

The intellectual world of labor economics and industrial relations was highly segmented at the end of World War II. Each established school stood by itself. The neoclassical revisionists were, however, eclectics. We got our theory from the neoclassicists, our history from Commons and the Webbs, our contact with ideology from Marx on one side and Simons and Hayek on the other, our appreciation of unions from Commons and Perlman and the Webbs and our understanding of the workplace quite separately from Slichter and Mayo. We had placed before us a collage of intellectual snapshots taken by various people from various angles: snapshots of markets, of social classes, of rules and regulations, of institutions, of monopolies, of industrial tribes.

In the pre–World War II and early postwar period, these approaches, except for the neoclassical, were either ignored by mainstream economists or dismissed with occasional gestures of contempt. In turn, members of these other schools sometimes castigated mainstream theorists as prisoners of their own grand illusions.

The great explosion in the number of professional labor economists came after World War II. A series of centers for the study of labor problems was set up, although the original one at Princeton was established before the war. Much research was done from a variety of perspectives. But this period was different from those before and after it, because it was also marked by a core effort, by an attempt to fashion a central strand from what previously had been separate threads. This was one role of the revisionists.

Those who participated in this integrative effort, particularly from 1940 to 1960, are often identified as "neoinstitutionalists" (see, for example, Cain 1976). I think this terminology is inaccurate, even misleading, and certainly sometimes intended as derogatory. Some of whom I have called the neoclassical revisionists shared a degree of sympathy with the institutionalist school—with its concern for history, with its emphasis on real life, even with its sympathy for unions and for ameliorative social legislation. But the people who contributed to the integrative effort were not, as the neoinstitutionalist label implies, a new version of the Wisconsin school. They were not Wisconsin school products and they did not wear the "old school tie" which meant so much to those who did.

Members of the revisionist group had been trained in the theory of the thirties—in Hicks, in Robinson and Chamberlin, and in Keynes. They were more descendants of Smith, Marshall, and Pigou than of Commons and Perlman. They did not reject theory, as did the institutionalists, whose work "was not meant to complement economic analysis as it had always been understood, but to replace it" (Blaug 1978: 713); rather, they respected theory and wanted to make it more useful in understanding practice. Martin Segal (1986: 395) in his broad survey of labor economics concluded, quite correctly, that "the work of the dominant labor economists of the 1940–1960 period has had little in common with the . . . institutional school."

The labor economist revisionists, it is true, stood between the orthodox neoclassical absolutists and the abolitionist institutionalists, but far from either of these extremes. They were, instead, incorporationists, and, as such, much closer to the neoclassical side of the argument. Michael L. Wachter (1974: 641–642) once divided labor economists of the 1970s into the followers of three models: "(1) the 'dual' model, (2) the competitive model that rules out institutional barriers and industrial and demographic segmentation and in which human capital considerations are dominant, and (3) the neoclassical model as defined above." The revisionists fall within his third category as he defined it: those who recognize "the impact of institutions" and "integrate these elements into labor market models in which maximizing behavior and traditional price theory are central."

The followers of both the revisionist and institutional schools in the 1940s and 1950s did have in common, however, very substantial field experience, particularly through the WLB, and a broad social science orientation to economic life, rather than a narrow, strictly economic one, as a result of this experience. Few of either school were strictly "hothouse" graduate school products. The two schools, however, were not compatible. They were, indeed, the two major competitors of that era—one rejecting the received theory, the other wishing to build on it. Representatives of the two schools had an unwritten understanding to respect each other—but to go their own ways. These interpersonal accommodations between the followers of the two schools, however, coexisted within an atmosphere of extremely intense confrontation of school versus school, of center versus center, of individual scholar versus individual scholar. The centers at Madison and Illinois, for example, were on the institutionalist side, and at Yale, Princeton, Harvard, MIT, and Berkeley on the revisionist.

The Neoclassical Revisionists Defined

The participants in the neoclassical revisionist group were interested, first of all, in markets, and they recognized the great role of market forces. At the same time, they were concerned with the social forces that limit the role and affect the influence of competition—with markets in the embrace of custom, of concepts of justice, of rules and regulations, of combined power. The institutionalists showed no interest in markets. The revisionists supported collective bargaining and were interested in its operations more than they supported and were interested in unions per se, in contrast to the Wisconsin school. This led the revisionists to a concern with the activities of management in relation to labor, and to a more neutral stance between labor and management than that of the Wisconsin school. Their interest in how institutions operated and how markets worked led them, however, just as it did the institutionalists, to make contact with political science, sociology, and psychology.

Rather than as neoinstitutionalists, it would be more accurate to identify the members of this core group as realistic neoclassicists, for their grounding was in neoclassical economics, which they wanted to revise; or as neostructuralists (with Slichter and Millis and the Webbs as models) concerned with the detailed practical workings of the industrial order but with a revision of theory as a central concern; or as premature post Keynesians (or Left Keynesians) who, ahead of the times, took an interest in the role of power and of politics, as well as of markets, in the conduct of economic life, and in the role of noneconomic goals and rules of behavior.

A better label, however, if there must be one for identification of a rather heterogeneous group, is the one I have chosen in this essay of "neoclassical revisionists." The members of this group wanted to look at things as they really are, to render the precise details of relationships. They also wanted to connect faithfully theory to practice, since they rejected efforts to present complex relations in an abstract or idealized form.

The effort to connect theory (whether neoclassical at the microlevel or Keynesian at the macrolevel) with practice constituted the essence of the efforts of this core group. But there were other themes as well:

Middle-Level Generalizations and Typologies. The revisionists concentrated on middle-level generalizations rather than on either description of a series of discrete events or on one eternal explanation of all events; on typologies or patterns of actions related to time and place rather than on either idiosyncratic developments or on one central, universal theme; on the specification, description, and analysis of types of situations rather than on rampant exceptionalism or on an all-purpose determinism; on several explanations rather than no explanation or one grand theory.

Interdisciplinary and International Perspectives. The attention to current reality led to an interdisciplinary perspective. Mainline economics abstracted out noneconomic considerations. In reaction to this, wider contact was made with sociology, political science, and psychology, in particular. Most of the new study centers had interdisciplinary staffs, and the new journals started out as interdisciplinary. Within economics, contact was made with organization theory and behavior because of the mutual concern with how organizations make decisions. Little contact was made with game theory, however, because of the abstract nature of the work in this field and its underdeveloped level of sophistication. This was, in retrospect, a great mutual loss.

The main effort at an interdisciplinary perspective was at Berkeley, from 1945 to 1952, when Fisher and I were both active. Fisher was a polymath in the social sciences, although trained in political science, and his mind ranged across disciplines, even into literature, as though academics had never erected their barriers among fields. His insights were sometimes breathtaking.

More attention was also directed to comparative international studies; there was an effort at less ethnocentrism. In particular, Kerr, Dunlop, Harbison, and Myers's *Industrialism and Industrial Man* (1960) generated some support and a great deal of criticism, especially among neo-Marxists, but it was recognized, even among some of its critics, as the "most ambitious and influential attempt" at a non-Marxist "understanding of the emerging pattern of global social development" (Goldthorpe 1984: 315).

Rejection of Ideologies. Fully developed ideologies of left or right were rejected as unrealistic: they put blinders on people. But also, the general stance was a mediating one—among groups, ideas, and methodologies.

Also rejected were the purist approaches of the historical exceptionalists— that each event, each situation, is unique, so that everything must be looked at case by case, and generalizations are not permissible. Instead, lessons were drawn from history to illuminate both the rule and its exceptions.

Policy Concerns. Policy was a central interest, particularly policies that encouraged industrial peace (see Golden and Parker 1955, with participation, in particular, by Dunlop, Harbison, Kerr, and Myers). Strikes were a great public concern at the end of World War II, and several of the industrial relations centers (including Cornell, UCLA, and Berkeley) were specifically set up to encourage workplace harmony; and even earlier this was a concern at MIT. This orientation, of course, stood in opposition to that of the Marxists and also of the antimonopolists. A second concern was governmental policy affecting labor–management relations (see, in particular, Labor Study Group 1961). A third and later policy concern was manpower development, particularly affirmative action and the role of education in upward mobility and in economic growth—how best to use human resources more justly and more effectively.

The Wisconsin school, however, was the one that had the greatest impact on public policy through its influence on New Deal policy, quite beyond that of any similarly identifiable small group of economists in American history. This was their great, unsurpassed triumph.

Great Expectations for the New Labor Economics

The revisionist effort was intended to bring neoclassical theory closer to reality. We approached this effort with enthusiasm and confidence.

The first revisionist to make his mark was John T. Dunlop. Dunlop had the temerity and ability to challenge Keynes' argument in the *General Theory* that money and real wages moved in opposite directions. Dunlop used logic and statistics to demonstrate that, instead, money and real wages "generally rise" together. Keynes quickly acceded (he could afford to do so without damage to his general theory). Dunlop not only made his point but also set forth the central theme of the core group just then beginning to form: that an effort must be made "to bring theory and observation closer together" (1938: 434, 413).

The first general exposition—and an excellent one—of the revisionist point of view was by Richard A. Lester in his *Economics of Labor* (1941). He wrote that "the focal point of labor problems is the labor market," but that "some of our most imperfect markets are labor markets." Their operations result in "wide and illogical variations in the payment for identical work in the same locality," and "in the sale of an hour of labor, no one knows exactly what is sold." He noted that "theoretical economists" want "determinate" solutions, but what is needed instead is an explanation of indeterminacy, and that takes a more "eclectic theory" (1941: 5, 43–44, 186). His footnotes, it may be observed, were mostly to Smith, Marshall, Pigou, and Robinson, among the English economists (fifty-six in total), and to Slichter, Millis, and Douglas, among American labor economists (forty-six in total). Commons was given seventeen footnotes, but all of them were to his historical work on the American labor movement done with his colleagues, and none to his institutionalism. The Webbs had four references, and Marx also four. This listing of authorities is very representative of what other revisionists at the same time also considered to be the main readings for their attention. The Lester textbook quickly became the most chosen text by the revisionists in their undergraduate teaching—I used it throughout my teaching career—later matched by that of Lloyd G. Reynolds (1949).

The most frontal attack by a revisionist on the neoclassical theorists was by Lester in his article on "Shortcomings of Marginal Analysis for Wage-Employment Problems" (1946) where he raised "grave doubts as to the validity of conventional marginal theory." He found that firms did not think in terms of marginal costs and marginal revenues, and had little idea even of what they were; and he quoted with approval the study by R.L. Hall and C.J. Hitch on markup pricing (1939). Consequently, firms did not maximize profits according to the processes set forth by the neoclassical economists, and employment levels were mostly determined by market demand. Fritz Machlup in his reply (1946) concluded that marginal theory "has not been shaken" and that it had great explanatory power by and large and in the longer run. No impact on Machlup had been made. Lester replied sharply (1947) that the neoclassical economists were in "mental ruts" with their "pecuniary marginalism."

The Lester–Machlup debate has led the revisionists to be called "anti-marginalists" (Fearn 1981), and this designation is much closer to the mark than "neoinstitutional," but it was particularly true only of Lester.

Most mainstream economists of the time followed Machlup, but Gordon came to the general support of Lester. He said (1948) that many of the assumptions of the neoclassical economists are only "approximations of reality" and that firms aim more at "satisfactory" profits (thus anticipating the "satisficing" theory of the Carnegie–Mellon school) than at maximizing them. He called for "greater realism," particularly in recognizing the important roles of "ignorance and of uncertainty." And George J. Stigler conceded that "economists have more often made errors . . . in observations than in logical analysis" (1947: 155).

Reynolds chided the neoclassical economists more gently than Lester in saying that they lacked "an adequate theory of wages" (1948). He was particularly critical of the "ambiguities" in basic concepts such as what was meant by "wages" and by the "quantity of labor." He asked for a theory "bearing some resemblance to reality." Little, if anything, was done by the theorists of the time to clarify the definitions as requested by Reynolds.

Most general economists just ignored the labor economist revisionists. A few of the most prominent, however, began to realize the complexities of labor markets and to doubt the more simplistic neoclassical model. Samuelson (1951: 312) wrote:

> But I fear that when the economic theorist turns to the general problem of wage determination and labor economics, his voice becomes muted and his speech halting. If he is honest with himself, he must confess to a tremendous

amount of uncertainty and self-doubt concerning even the most basic and elementary parts of the subject.

Doubts had been raised in the minds of some—including some of the very best.

Modest Results—At Least in the Short Run

To what end did the great expectations of the revisionists at the close of World War II come? One result was a greater realism among some theorists—belated, selective, and not exclusively due to the revisionists' efforts. A more likely proximate cause was the theorists' need to explain stagflation, which is affecting the corpus of economic theory today much the way mass unemployment did in the thirties and forties. The American economy and society changed rapidly before, during, and after World War II. Overall, the economy became based less on atomistic decisions in markets and more on power relations in negotiations. Prices and wages became less flexible in a downward direction and showed more of a long-term upward bias. The first generation of labor economist revisionists tried to serve as an early warning system to the theorists of the impacts of these and other changes in the areas encompassed by labor economics. Some of these developments far predated the postwar period, however, and ought to have been incorporated into economic analysis much earlier.

British revisionists had greater early impact than their U.S. counterparts. Kenneth Knowles and Barbara Wootton, as well as Henry Clay from earlier times, had a major and specifically acknowledged impact on Hicks's gradual realization of the importance of "the revolutions which have occurred in the realm of fact." "We get a better clue to actual behavior," wrote Hicks II, "if we think of wages as being determined by an interplay between social and economic factors, instead of being based on economic factors—and crude economic factors at that—alone" (Hicks 1955: 389,394). This statement reflects an acceptance of one of the revisionists' central points. Not until the late seventies and early eighties, however, did Hicks's concession become a standard tenet of some mainline theorists. Henry Phelps Brown, it should be noted, had by that time become the dominant British labor economics revisionist (see, for example, 1972).

Hicks II became first a Keynesian and then, increasingly, a post-Keynesian. He has continued to write like a revisionist (1974—especially chapter III, and 1985): of the new world since Keynes; of "fix-price" and "fix-wage"; of the different worlds of flex-price and equilibria versus of fix-price and disequilibria; of how wages rise in the absence of "labor scarcity" due to the separation of the wage and the job markets; of the importance of "fairness" from the workers' point of view and of "continuity" of relations from the employers' point of view in the setting of wages; of what are now called segmented labor markets but still using his own earlier designation (in the original *The Theory of Wages*) of "casual" and "regular" employment—a distinction which he earlier thought was not very important; of the centrality of "comparison" in setting wages, and of even more that follows along the revisionist lines. What had once been set aside as unimportant "imperfections" to be noted quickly and then dismissed were now seen to be the essence of reality. The exceptions had become the rule, and the rule had become an exception.

Arthur M. Okun's *Prices and Quantities* (1981) is a landmark book in many ways, for Okun makes revisionist labor economics one central point in his explanation of the economic world. "Career labor markets" are a basic building block for his overall explanation. These career labor markets are the internal markets of the revisionists. Along similar lines, accepting some revisionist views, are the writings of Oliver E. Williamson (1975) and E.S. Phelps (1979).

As it was once said of Keynes, it may yet come to be said that we are all (or nearly all) revisionist labor economists now. The economics mainstream has "discovered that labor economics was like the barren plains of Oklahoma—unattractive on top, but concealing great pools of black gold," and many general economists are now "pumping for profit that black gold" (Perlman 1981: 1084). Having lived so much of its life on the periphery, labor economics now is becoming more central to the study of general economics. And a new generation of labor economists, who use the new methodology, seems willing to try to incorporate more aspects of economic reality which were once swept under the carpet. It has already been said of labor economics that "developments within the institutional [or what I call the revisionist] approach have positively contributed to the understanding of the inflationary process in contemporary Western economies" (Burton and Addison 1977: 367). The revisionists, however, contributed somewhat more than just this.

Why the Modest Short-Run Results?

Why were the early revisionists not more successful—at least in the short run—in persuading the theorists?

1. Effective interpreters between the revisionists and the theoreticians, particularly among them Melvin W. Reder and Albert Rees, were too few; but they played a crucial role nevertheless. Reder and Rees knew standard theory in great depth, but they were also critically sympathetic to the work of the revisionists. What they accepted of this work gave it a Good Housekeeping seal of approval , and they packaged it in a way that general theorists could accept, if they were interested. While they followed the revisionist literature, they also had strong connections with the fast-rising and increasingly influential Chicago school. What they accepted and amended was what came to the

considered attention of interested mainline theorists. Robert M. Fearn, as a subtitle to his *Labor Economics* (1981), notes what he calls "the Emerging Synthesis." This synthesis is between the Reder-Rees version of revisionism and the work of the Chicago school labor economists.

The revisionists were fortunate in having two such tolerant and thoughtful interpreters—but they were only two, and too few theorists listened to the interpretations. They did, however, perform a great service in raising the issues of concern to and presenting selected insights of the revisionists to the economic profession more broadly in a way that could be more easily absorbed into general theory. As Fearn says, they "spearheaded" the "confluence." (For a "confluence" survey of labor economics, see also Annable 1984.)

In particular, Reder and Rees were helpful in interpreting, and in expanding on, an understanding of the nature of trade union wage policy, of labor market behavior, and of differentials within the system of wages. (For Reder, see, inter alia, 1952, 1955, 1957, 1958, 1960, 1963, and 1964; and for Rees, also inter alia, 1952, 1962, 1970 [with George P. Shultz] and 1973.) Their roles, sometimes sadly neglected, were crucial: they evaluated, they explained, they amended, they expanded.

2. As journals multiplied, labor economists began to publish mostly in their own journals, talking more and more among themselves only.

3. Economics, also, was then turning to mathematical models and to econometrics, and these were not the methods of the participant–observers who composed the revisionist school. The two groups spoke in different tongues. Unfortunately, the practitioners of the new methodology too often thought that if it were not in their form of discourse, it was not worthy of consideration. Thus they looked at economics less as a flow of ideas and more as a flow of methodology, and the new methodology was so superior that anything developed by the older was worthy of only minor consideration, if any at all. Thus they "discovered" ideas that had been discovered before. It is as though the New World had not been discovered until the first jet airplane landed at Miami International Airport.

Federal agencies assisting social science research greatly preferred projects that were mathematical or statistical, or both. I served on the Social Science Advisory Panel of the National Science Foundation when social science was first brought within its aegis. Two major, and successful, arguments were made in favor of this approach to the social sciences: (a) it was more "scientific" and (b) it was safer politically—the politicians and the public would never understand the publications! As a result, the mathematical–statistical branch of labor economics was greatly aided.

4. Most theoretical economists, additionally, accepted the then emerging neoclassical–Keynesian consensus, and what seemed like nitpicking by the revisionists was an unwelcome challenge from a lowly "slum field" (Ward 1972). Most theorists were satisfied with their descriptions of the world—

there was no stagflation yet. The more informed views of the revisionists, based upon their direct participation in industrial relations, were mostly ignored or swept aside. One said, at the time, of the revisionists that "if you live with pigs long enough, you become a pig." (I had been talking about wage setting in the meat packing industry with which I was intensely familiar and had, in fact, established the modern wage structure for that industry.)

5. As collective bargaining became less of a novelty, interest in the work of the revisionists declined, just as the Wisconsin school lost position as unions, which they had defended, became a more accepted part of national life and carried with them fewer hopes and fears, and as the welfare state, which they had helped to inaugurate, became established policy.

6. Perhaps the most serious problem, however, was that the revisionists dealt bit by bit with pieces of the puzzle and never assembled them into an integrated statement, let alone into a model or a consistent theory; and it takes a new theory to replace or change an orthodox theory. One labor economist, Mark Perlman, has even argued that this could not have been done, since the field constitutes an area of "true uncertainty" for which "no systematic analysis can be offered *ex ante* and for which no rational explanation can be presented *ex post*" (Perlman 1972: 207). I disagree with this. It could have been, but it just was not done.

Some of what happens in the labor economy is predictable and thus subject to a theory with determinate solutions; more is probable or possible and thus is subject to explanations that allow for indeterminacy within ranges of solutions; and some is unpredictable even within ranges of possibilities and thus is not subject to analysis in advance but may be made understandable in retrospect. The revisionists should have done better in pulling together what they came to know about the probable and the possible into a more structured framework.

7. This major failing might have been corrected if the early revisionists had taken more time at their task. They were mostly activists with substantial accumulated experience and were drawn into public affairs and into university administration early in their careers (this was true for Dunlop, Lester, Reynolds, Shultz, and Arthur M. Ross, among others). To do what was needed would have taken full-time concentration, not occasional papers. On the other hand, given the hostile reaction to their tentative efforts, the revisionists might have chosen not to make additional attempts even had they had the time to do so. Some of them suffered from an inferiority complex vis-à-vis the generalists and from an intellectual timidity before the dominating stance of the pure and increasingly mathematical theorists. The great theoretical effort at the time was to simplify in order to fit (or squeeze) reality into mathematical formulas.

8. Additionally, the revisionists turned their research attention into other fields, variously into the study of the processes of economic development, of reconsideration of the "laws of motion" of industrial societies, of the role of

education in economic advancement, of manpower policy, of comparative industrial relations systems, and of other topics of current concern. As realists, they flowed with the changing topics that drew general attention.

A Revisionist Model of the Labor Economy

There follows an attempt to consolidate the views of the labor economy as developed by the labor economist revisionists in many bits and pieces, as a very partial effort to indicate what might have been drawn together if the revisionists had made a more sustained attempt.

1. The best place to start in an analysis of economic activities is the model of economic man seeking to maximize individual welfare. Economic man does so, however, within an extremely complex environment and in the midst of a substantial variety of goals and considerations.

2. The easiest place to start in an analysis of labor economics in capitalist societies is competitive markets. An understanding of such markets is the beginning, but by no means the end, of wisdom. This view became a central theme of the revisionists: that the basic explanations of traditional economics become useful to full understanding only as realistic observations of them are made in operation and as exceptions to them are comprehended.

3. The fully competitive and frictionless labor market (the structureless or auction market) is at one end of a spectrum. The "marriage contract" or "marriage market" model, so designated by Kenneth Boulding (1951: 254), is at the other end. Fisher (1953) spelled out the conditions of the structureless model for labor markets: no organization on either side of the market, no personal relationship between employer and employee, the work is unskilled, the method of payment is by unit of work, and the operation employs little or no capital. The harvest labor market in California was his illustration. Uniform wage payments per unit of product did result, though not uniform earnings per hour. There are, however, few such markets: "Labor markets seldom, if ever, exhibit these characteristics of the market of economic theory" (1953: 12).

Most labor markets depart in one way or another and to one degree or another from the perfect market, and also from the marriage market. A central issue for labor economists is to study the nature and causes and effects of these departures.

I once tried to categorize external labor markets (1950) as follows: the "perfect" market; the "neoclassical" or not quite perfect market; the "natural" market where, on a substantial basis and not just as minor imperfections, individual lack of knowledge, lack of skills, economic and non-economic costs of transfer, and inertia all enter in with major consequences; the "institutional" market influenced or even controlled by policies and actions of employers, of unions, and of both together; and the "managed" market—managed by government. Only in the first of these, the perfect market, does the "job market," and the job market alone, fully determine wages at equalized rates. Elsewhere an independent "wage market," to one degree or another, exists and exercises its influence. I noted even then that "the overall effect [of institutional markets] may well be to raise the general level of wages" due to the separation of the job and the wage markets.

4. Internal labor markets are, also, extremely important to understand in their diversity and individual complexity, and in their relationships to external markets. One way to understand external markets is to understand internal markets first. Early on (1954a), I divided internal labor markets into "craft" (based on skill) and "production" (based on seniority), each tied to external labor markets mostly at "ports of entry."

I still like the classification of structureless and structured markets (the latter with identifiable internal markets) better than "secondary" and "primary." The nature and intensity and consequences of structure are easier to describe and define, and the terms used are less moralistic and ideological, than are the characteristics of secondary and primary markets as usually employed, with their connotations of "bad" and "good." I recognize that George A. Akerlof (1984) has given a new and more precise definition of primary and secondary markets, but even that definition still, I think, lacks the usefulness of the structureless and structured dichotomy. There are, of course, many degrees of structured, or primary, markets and some of these shade into structureless, or secondary, markets.

These internal markets are where most workers live most of the time. These markets respond less to competition and more to informal and formal work rules and particularly seniority, to the role of customary relationships, to concepts of fairness, to security provisions, and to how to make the relationship productive. Fisher and I wrote about some of the conformations of internal markets in 1950 with particular attention to job evaluation, and Dunlop about others in 1966 with special reference to the importance of "job families." Frederick H. Harbison had explored the forms and importance of the "seniority principle" as early as 1939; and, Reynolds of "intraplant movement" in 1951. Peter Doeringer and Michael Piore (1971) later became the standard source for discussions of internal markets.

5. One effect of the conduct of internal markets is that employers are willing, and sometimes even eager, to pay more than the wages as determined in competitive external markets. Reynolds (1951: 232–233) provided an excellent early discussion of why employers would want to pay more than the market required in what are now called "gift exchanges" under "implicit contracts" as rediscovered in the past decade.

6. Another effect of the strength of internal market bonds and of other barriers to mobility is that movement of workers is restrained; and the less the

movement, the less the external market alone determines wages at a single equalized rate. Early studies of the operation of natural markets, following on experience with the WLB and the new data made available by the Bureau of Labor Statistics, were "Wage Differences in Local Labor Markets" by Reynolds (1946) and "A Range Theory of Wage Differentials" by Lester (1952). They showed substantial dispersions in wages paid for similar work in the same labor market. Reynolds noted that the "highest rate" is "usually at least 50 percent and frequently 100 percent above the lowest" (1946: 366), and Lester that "a range of indeterminacy is natural" (1952: 500) due to the working of "anti-competitive" and "impeditive" factors.

Even earlier, without the stimulus of the WLB experience, Charles A. Myers and W. Rupert Maclaurin had found real differences in wages for similar workers in a small New England factory town. They found that "the movement of workers . . . did not serve to equalize wages and working conditions in comparable jobs," and that the majority of job moves "were forced by layoffs and discharges" (1943: 54, 72). While originally lost in the concentration on the war, their study became a classic in the field and was confirmed again and again by subsequent studies. It was the first really adequate study of labor markets in operation. Myers and Shultz (1951) later collaborated on the "Nashua Study" of a labor market with similar results, and it also has become a classic in the field. Much later, Rees and Shultz (1970) showed that the range of indeterminacy is greatly narrowed when account is taken of differences in worker quality, of seniority provisions and practices, and of the impacts of union contracts; but, even then, full "equalization" of wages does not take place. They also found major geographical variations in wages among submarkets in the Chicago area. The employment of a worker is a very "complicated transaction."

Mobility is what makes external markets work well when they do, but mobility is severely restricted, so it was shown, by lack of information, by heavy economic and noneconomic costs of transference, and by lack of appropriate skills. Additionally, workers move more because they are pushed than because they are pulled. There is great inertia. This was one of my findings (1942) in the very first, but comparatively quite primitive, of the modern labor market studies, and Myers and Maclaurin came to the same conclusion. It takes a major push (such as unemployment) or a substantial pull (such as much higher wages), and a sustained time for consideration and for making arrangements to get most people to change jobs outside their industry or their area or both. It is the young, the unemployed, and those in proximate situations who are most likely to experience the least inertia.

7. Lags in wage adjustments to conditions in external markets can be very long, not only because of restricted mobility, not only because of long-term contracts, but also because workers and employers are particularly reluctant to lower money wages. This is a last-resort action. Dunlop early on

had observed that "much more attention must be directed toward speeds of reaction" (1944: 6). These lags can now be much better sustained, as recent European and American experiences have shown, as a result of the welfare state than in its absence. The welfare state has become the one indispensable support for policies that rely on market adjustments (often induced) instead of direct governmental action to "cure" depression, and also, inflation. The newer liberalism makes possible the older conservatism.

Equilibrium at full employment is not the normal state of affairs. It is a tendency, but long-lasting disequilibrium situations deserve careful examination. Labor markets move toward equilibrium but usually slowly and incompletely. This requires greater emphasis on studies of disequilibria, as so often argued by Nicolas Kaldor and by Janos Kornoi, among others.

8. Unions are complex organizations. They are not unitary. In particular, there usually is a separation of interest between the goals of the members and of the leaders—the former interested in what they get out of the contract and the latter additionally interested in the welfare of the organization and of themselves as leaders, with consequent goals that sometimes differ from those of the members. This is now a central point in what has come to be called "public choice" theory in the realm of public policy decisions, where public officials have their own separate goals aside from serving the public. Unions are more political than economic organizations, with the leaders having their own concepts of maximization, and the strike is sometimes an internally political as well as an economic act.

Ross made the classic statement (1948) about the union as a political organization. The concept of a distinction between the interests of the leaders and of the members emerged from the discussions that Ross, Fisher, and I had (the "California school"—for a discussion of the California school, see Kerr, 1948, 1954b, 1977). The point was introduced by Fisher with reference to the "iron law of oligarchy" of Robert Michels (1915). But this separation was also implicit in E. Wight Bakke's *Mutual Survival: The Goal of Unions and Management* (1946: 13)—"A union is a political institution in its internal structure and proceedings"—and might just as well have been taken over from Berle and Means (1932) on the separation of management from ownership in the corporation—or even from Machiavelli. It was for political as well as economic reasons that Ross's "orbits of coercive comparisons" were so important in some situations.

Unions do not just "sell" labor. The battle beween Ross and Dunlop (1944) was never really joined. No one in the world knew better than Dunlop already knew and came to know even better that unions are political organizations. What he was doing in 1944 was carrying out a brilliant analysis of what unions might be trying to maximize if they were viewed as "selling labor." It turned out that it was not all that easy to answer this apparently simple question, and Dunlop developed several alternatives.

It should be noted that employers' associations are also complex organizations, as Fisher and I once described (1948).

There are few clear two-person games in actual practice in industrial relations. What often looks like a two-person game is really a multiperson game because of the divisions within as well as between opposing sides. These divisions make it impossible clearly to define *welfare,* in purely economic terms.

9. Organized power in opposition to market forces becomes a more significant factor as industrial society advances, thus the importance of studying the conduct of unions and of union impacts on wages. The theme of organized employer power in the labor market was raised by Adam Smith. It became central to the analysis of exploitation by Marx and, in more refined form, by Robinson. And Wootton (1955: 65) concluded, in a much broader way, that the "hierarchy of pay should correspond with the hierarchy of authority."

But power is a very complex force, and it is not limited to employers, and it has its limits. I once concluded (1954c) that union power had largely been limited, among the several forms of wage differentials, to reducing only personal differentials within the firm and firm differentials within the organized industry, and had not extended to interoccupational or interindustry or interregional differentials. Reynolds and Cynthia Taft later (1956) said they concurred with these conclusions. I also concluded that unions had little influence on labor's income share (1957) but had highly variable influences on the general level of money wages, depending on circumstances and policies (1959). Power is not the only determining factor in the labor market, and particularly not class power, as it was for Marx and still is for his current followers. It must be, instead, examined in detail as one force at work within specific situations. One of the contributions of the Marxists and neo-Marxists, however, has been to keep the impact of organized power on the agenda.

Not only the role of power, and also of the broader "mosaic of domination" (Bowles and Gintis 1986), but many other aspects of institutional arrangements that confine and direct economic activity are in constant process of change. The historical context deserves careful attention.

10. Bilateral monopoly is much more common than is the perfect market. Broadly defined, it may even be the most common case. It exists between employers and unions covering about 20 percent of external labor markets in the United States. Both informally, as well as formally, it covers 100 percent of structured internal markets where managers and workers carry on their bargains on how much will be produced and of what quality and under what conditions. Negotiations in internal markets are very complex and very important but are seldom seen, like the struggles in the walls and attics and

basements of the brown rats against the black rats in one of Selma Lagerlof's stories for children. In the very short run, bilateral relations are almost universal.

The importance of one form or another of bilateral monopoly has led Dunlop (1984a: chapter 1) to emphasize the study of negotiations as a more important method of decision making even than markets or even than the law in the modern economy. Competitive markets may be the easiest but not necessarily the only place to start a study of economic activity.

Changing the Emphases

To the extent that all the above is true, it suggests that economists, or at least labor economists, should be less concerned with studying solutions exactly determined (and thus subject to being known in advance) and more concerned with ranges of possible solutions, as Edgeworth and Pigou and Lester (1952) have argued: with the outer limits of such ranges, with the forces that set such limits, with the tendencies within these ranges, and with the strength of these tendencies. Both anticipation before the event and explanation after the event would be more realistic if this were the case, and economics would be less like a mechanical science and more like a biological science—dealing less with what are represented to be essentially inanimate subjects responding uniformly to external forces and more with animate subjects responding to variable internal considerations within complex external contexts.

What the neoclassical revisionists tried to do in labor economics was not so much to bring in new considerations as to change the emphases. The neoclassical labor economists, as represented by Marshall, Pigou, and the early Hicks, knew about monopolies and monopsonies and bilateral monopolies, about unions, about lags, about indeterminacy, about disequilibria, about imperfections, and about separations of types of labor markets, but they played them down. This partly reflects the times in which they lived but also their attachment to the ideal of perfect markets. They also concentrated too much on economic considerations alone and on situations where economic considerations led to determinate or nearly determinate results, as in perfect competition and in monopoly and in monopsony. They neglected, too much, noneconomic aspects and nondeterminate situations. What the revisionists did was to look more at the imperfections and at their consequences in an effort to understand the realities as they saw them.

Looking at reality required a more interdisciplinary orientation aided by advances in sociology, political science, and psychology. The Carnegie–Mellon "behavioral" school, concentrating on the theory of the firm, later on also employed such an interdisciplinary approach and supplied ideas about "satisficing" activity rather than maximizing, about "bounded rationality," about the importance and also the costs of good information, about the difficulties of calculating the welfare of any diverse and changing association of people, and about the tendency to make decisions by a process of trial and error, among other concepts. (For a summary, see March and Sevón 1984.) Herbert Simon, James March, and Richard Cyert, among others, concentrated on the firm, but their observations might also be applied to unions. They added support to, rather than inspired, the approach of the revisionist labor economists. (For an interesting contrast, however, in the broader field of market behavior, of the "employment contract" in labor markets and the "sales contract" in product markets, see Simon 1951.) They not only came later and worked in a different field, but also their methodology was different—more mathematical. They were, however, the most nearly similar effort to that of the labor economist revisionists within the whole body of economics. Both schools wanted to make an impact on understanding the real world within confines expanded beyond those of the neoclassical framework.

What the labor economist revisionists did not say is very important to understand, or it has often been misrepresented. They did not say that economic actors were irrational; and they did not even say that they had "bounded rationality." They did not say that economic actors were not utility maximizing individuals; and they did not even say that satisficing was the rule of economic behavior. In these respects they were more traditional than the Carnegie–Mellon school working on the theory of the firm, and did less to challenge basic tenets of neoclassical theory.

What the revisionists did say was that, in trying to be rational and in trying to maximize welfare, there were many considerations to be taken into account aside from easily calculable economic costs and economic rewards, including: (1) the quality and availability of information, (2) the valued attachment to social customs and to standards of fairness, (3) the role of inertia in human affairs as in the laws of physics, (4) the time it takes to adjust, (5) the attachment to symbols, (6) the restraints of contracts, (7) the bonds of mutual loyalty and conjoined interests between employers and workers, (8) the noneconomic costs of transference, (9) the lack of appropriate skills, (10) the impacts of discrimination for reasons of race and sex, (11) the role of mixed motives—some of them noneconomic, and much else. They saw the economic actors as trying to do their best under extremely complex conditions. They did not commit treason, as is sometimes suggested, against the doctrines of rationality and maximization. The decisive issues for them were not rationality and maximization, but what to be rational about and what to maximize. They were saying that there are more things on earth than are dreamt of in simplistic models.

The Revisionist Contribution

The historical situation may be summarized as follows:

Before the revisionists, satisfactory explanations had been developed for the operations of perfect, monopsonistic, and monopolistic markets, and the case of bilateral monopoly in labor markets had been explored. This was a world of certainty and of equilibria (except for bilateral monopoly).

The revisionists added knowledge (1) of external "natural" markets, (2) of internal markets, and (3) of trade union behavior on one side of bilateral monopolies. They also helped (4) to explain different types of wage differentials, (5) the dispersion of wage rates for similar workers in the same labor market, (6) the downward inflexibility of wage rates under conditions of unemployment, and (7) the upward bias of the wage-setting process even in the presence of unemployment. They portrayed a world of less certainty, of greater lags, of more disequilibria.

The Restorationists: Neoclassical and Marxist— 1960–1980

The influence of the revisionists declined sharply in the sixties, and the restoration efforts of the neoclassicists and the neo-Marxists took over the field of labor economics.

The Neoclassicists

Neoclassical labor economics experienced a great revival in the sixties, via the Chicago school led by H. Gregg Lewis with his influential study, *Unions and Relative Wages* (1963), but, more importantly, with his teaching. Lewis introduced more rigor than the revisionists had demonstrated, and this led to "a new wave of scientific research in labor economics." He became the "father of modern labor economics." (*American Economic Review*, September 1982, frontispiece; see also Rees 1976). He carried on the quantitative approach of Douglas, whose student and research assistant he had been. Armed with better statistical data, with the computer and econometrics, and aided by a conservative upsurge in the intellectual world, the neoclassical restorationists made great progress. One of the many contributions of the Chicago school has been to explain many "imperfections" in terms of rational economic behavior and in the modern language of technical economics. Also, participants have illuminated the intricacies of labor supply, especially as affected by individual and household decision making, while the revisionists had been more interested in demand impacts. Theodore Schultz and Gary Becker were the great leaders in the development of the enormously important field of human capital theory. But, the work of Lewis aside, the restorationists have generally neglected collective actions, and they also have avoided the impact of customary standards of behavior, although the role of "custom" has a tradition in economic literature that goes back to John Stuart Mill. A strong theme has been that institutions do not count much except in special and/or short-run situations, as Marshall and Milton Friedman had earlier argued (for a discussion of their views and a rebuttal, see Ulman 1955). Institutional behavior is, of course, difficult for them to handle. It does not lend itself so easily to statistical understanding as does mass individual behavior. Nevertheless, the restorationists have added very greatly to the richness of the literature.

Some of the restorationists have had another impact, and a rather unusual and quite unintended one: that is, to validate the observations of the revisionists. This has come often in the form of, for them, new discoveries. They have rediscovered internal markets and have even compared them to "marriage markets" once again—many years after Boulding; they rediscovered the inclination of some employers to pay above-market wages within the context of efficiency wages or transaction costs or implicit contracts—many years after Reynolds; and much else. Three additional examples: The importance of what are now called "incomplete labor contracts: where workers may or may not "give their best day's work" was described, in these terms, by Stanley Mathewson long ago—1931. The importance of "efficiency wages" (not as defined by Marshall but as wage levels that serve to raise productivity) was written about by Bakke: What the worker "does and what he is worth depends a lot on whether he feels he is fairly treated" (1946: 69). The importance of long-term staggered contracts, with their "built-in inflation" implications, was earlier explained by Joseph Garbarino (1962: 64).

Martin Segal, in his broad survey of labor economics, has found that the recent work of the restorationists requires no significant "modification" of the views of the revisionists: "The model is largely in accord with what is known today about the functioning of the labor market" (1986: 398). And Richard Freeman (1984), in his review of Reynolds' work on labor markets, has said it was "on target," and ended by saying: "May our own work look as good thirty years hence."

The difference, thus, turns out to be not so much in content, which is being validated, but in method, presentation, and terminology. The methods are more modern. The presentation is more in keeping with the dominant forms of economic literature today. The terminology is fresh; the labels are sometimes new. The restorationists also evolved out of the mainstream but are more defensive of it than were the revisionists, and are more easily read and accepted by the mainstream economists of today. Thus, some of the ideas of the revisionists are being endorsed, however unknowingly, by the neoclassical restorationists, and, with their endorsement, making more contact with the corpus of economic theory than the revisionists ever did. The restorationists are expanding the boundaries of what theoretical economists will consider and can explain, beyond the accomplishments of the revisionists.

The neoclassical restorationists, nevertheless, have their limitations. They do less well in explaining the new pluralistic world of negotiations than the older atomistic world of the market. The social forces that constrain the economic ones are, for them, largely terra incognita. Too often some of them try to explain away uncomfortable facts, so that "what looks to the naked eye like involuntary unemployment is really a massive investment in leisure or search" (Solow 1979: 348). This is ludicrous for some types of unemployment. Some of their attempted explanations of reality may be consistent with their theories, but they do not meet the tests of common sense.

The new generation of neo-neoclassical labor economists has not yet met the hopes of Rees (1971: 3) that they would "combine a knowledge of institutions with skill in theory and in econometrics." Rather, "the academic quest for rigor and for quantification in labor economics has perhaps gone too far, at the expense of a proper grounding in history and institutions" (Rees 1977: 4).

The Neo-Marxists

The Marxist restorationists entered significantly into labor economics in the United States for the first time in the sixties, at a time of great intellectual unrest. (They were not restoring an American tradition but a British and Continental one.) Some were trained technically; they were not all just the propagandists, scholastics, and pedants of old. They brought continued attention to important areas neglected by the neoclassicists: to the role of power in economic life, to the changing course of history, to the tightly woven web of cause and effect beyond the boundaries of economics, and to the role and the moral importance of values in human actions. They have served to broaden the definitions of the field, to make it more dynamic, to bring new insights.

The neo-Marxists, and they come in many flavors, also have limitations, however. They seem to look for sharper class lines than may actually exist (they have not adjusted to the shift from a more vertical to a more horizontal society); for rising levels of industrial conflict whether or not they occur; for conspiracies to perpetuate political class power, as well as economic monopoly, which may or may not exist; for proof that the state really is the executive committee of the bourgeoisie whether it is or not; for evidence that exploitation is deepening despite evidence to the contrary. These are all very important matters, but the neo-Marxists seem always to succeed in finding proof of their *a priori* convictions where others do not. Economists on the Marxist side have lived in a fairyland where, by use of a "magic mirror with a special power" (following Hans Christian Andersen in the *Snow Queen*), they can turn even"the loveliest of landscapes" into what looks "just like boiled spinach." (Some of the neoclassical restorationists also have their own magic mirrors that turn unemployment into a champagne party.)

It must also be noted that the neo-Marxists seem reluctant to apply their analyses and criticisms equally to socialist as to capitalist societies. Their credibility would rise if they did. They also see socialism and capitalism as more separate than does the view of them as two alternative forms of industrialism—each with its own advantages and disadvantages;and they view socialism not as a "substitute" for capitalism at a certain stage of history but as a successor to it (Robinson 1980: 15). Marxist analysis, as it turns out, is more helpful in explaining political power and economic conduct in developing countries, whether under colonial, dynastic, or Communist rule, than in advanced capitalist societies.

A Redivided World

As a result of these two restorationist schools, and of a growing group of adherents to the newer revisionism, labor economics has become once again a house divided against itself. There is no longer so single a core effort as after World War II, and particularly in the 1950s when the Wisconsin school had faded. The doctrinal quarrels of earlier times have resurfaced, even though neither markets nor class struggles are as central to economic life as they were in the nineteenth century. In the field of economics, as in the country at large, the moderates have come under increasing attack from both the left and the right. The New Left, and later, the Neoconservatives, have seized the initiative. It has not been shown conclusively that the center cannot hold, but the liberal center, including the labor economist revisionists, has certainly been under attack. It has been a time for antitheses, not for synthesis. The revisionists at the center, at least for a time, have lost their dominance.

The restorationists of both persuasions have illuminated many areas and, unquestionably, will continue to do so. Yet the field should not be left to them alone. The neoclassicists see too small a part of the world, while the neo-Marxists see the world as a whole but from a distorted angle. And their respective revivals may already seem a bit outdated as the neoclassical world fades into history and as the Marxist utopia disappears farther into the unlikely future.

The two restorationist schools share some common limitations. Both have a strong bias, a commitment: among the neoclassicists, to showing that rationality marks all behavior and that markets always work best; and among the neo-Marxists, that Marx was always right, or that where he was not may best be overlooked. The neoclassicists generally support capitalism (more as it once was than as it now is), and the neo-Marxists keep looking for signs that capitalism is (and should be) failing. These biases make restorationist recommendations lamentably predictable: Restore the free market, on the one side, or advance radical change, on the other. These are always their bottom line positions.

Moreover, when neo-neoclassicists and neo-Marxists study the same subject (for example, human capital formation or racial discrimination), they reach opposite conclusions about the factual situation. Does education create social returns or only enforce class lines and raise private returns? Is racial discrimination decreasing in terms of payment of compensation or not? Pick your school and you get your answer. Neither group seems to learn from the other; each only refutes the other when it can.

Labor economics is a small piece of "a science in crisis"—the attempted science of economics. There are competing theories, intense methodological discussions, and many unsolved puzzles. "One is tempted to sloganize: neoclassical economics is beginning to look like a case of techniques without relevance, Marxism of relevance without techniques." "We have institutionalized the distancing of the economist from the economies, through professional careerism, through various kinds of gaming, through the exaltation of cleverness, even through politicizing" (Ward 1972: 33, 91, 246).

"The purpose of studying economics," Joan Robinson (1980: 17) tells us, is "to avoid being deceived by economists."

Challenges Ahead and the Second Wave of Neoclassical Revisionists

The highest goal for labor economics is to help to provide a series of bridges to reality: between theory and practice, between economics and other disciplines, and between econometric and expository techniques. It is to pursue "realistic knowledge," as Pigou (1922) once wrote, and to fill well-chosen "boxes"—or even make new ones—with this knowledge. This is what the labor economics revisionists tried to do. They did bring in new realistic knowledge, as about the operations of external labor markets, and did create some new boxes, for example, the box of internal markets. Labor economics can contribute little, if anything, to abstract models—these are better left to applied mathematicians with an interest in economic problems. Labor economics will contribute more by helping to make sense of reality than by building more castles in the air. The field's future, at its best, lies more with the "analytical school," as defined by Ian Stewart (1979: 122), which includes Keynes, "who relied on his own knowledge and judgment" and who placed his emphasis on what he identified as "vigilant observation," than with creating abstract models; more with finding out and analyzing what is externally true than with analyzing only what is internally logical.

A central theme of Kant was that it is always a mistake to subordinate the real to the logical. And Amartya K. Sen (1970: 200) has noted that while "purity is an uncomplicated virtue for . . . heroines of folk tales, it is not so for systems of collective choice." Here impurities become important, and here is where the revisionists tried to be helpful. But the other side of the coin, as Donald N. McCloskey (1983: 485) notes, is that "fact without theory" is no more useful than "theory without fact." Information without analysis is unintelligible, and analysis without information is empty. As I interpret the analytical school, as defined by Stewart but not always by others, it seeks to work with both information and analysis, as did the labor economist revisionists.

At the empirical level, labor economics should draw on both quantitative and qualitative observations, with preference given to the former where it is useful. The latter, however, will be necessary in describing most historical changes, in undertaking most comparative studies among nations, in looking at small numbers of cases, in examining exceptions to the rule, in analyzing the one big event, in looking inside complex decision-making processes, and, more generally, in studying internal considerations and processes in relation to outside forces.

This brings me to the great importance of the new generation of labor economists arising since about 1975, and establishing dominance in the 1980s—the second wave of neoclassical revisionists. They go beyond both the neoclassical restorationists and the revisionists. This generation I define as those trained in econometric as well as in other techniques, and centered on what might be called the "Brookings school," the "Harvard–MIT axis," and the "Chicago revisionists." The members of this new generation seek to work between analysis and full range of facts, bringing more reality into theoretical considerations. They also approach problems in a less restricted ideological fashion than did the restorationist neoclassicists and neo-Marxists. They hold much less rigidly to what Wachter (174: 642) has called the "competitive model." The new revisionists with their superior econometric methodology, but not relying on it alone, are on their way to being the best ever as they seek a judicious blending of econometrics with realistic observation. Thus the older revisionists can more nearly rest in peace than they could in the 1960s.

In his presidential address to the Royal Economic Society, R.C.O. Matthews (1986: 903) said that "In the last few decades . . . the economics of institutions has become one of the liveliest areas in our discipline," and adds that "a body of thinking has evolved based on two propositions: (1) institutions do matter, (2) the determinants of institutions are susceptible to analysis by tools of economic theory."

Hirsch and Addison, in their recent survey (1986: 2,7,8) of the economics of institutions in the subarea of industrial relations, cite over six hundred references. Half of them are since 1980, and these references constitute a Who's Who of the new scholars in the combined fields of labor economics–industrial relations. Their central theme is "the emerging synthesis of an institutional and descriptive-based industrial relations literature with neoclassical microeconomic theory and modern econometric techniques." They find that the "new synthesis" has already "contributed enormously to our understanding," specifically to the "role of unions."

Another recent survey, this time of the labor market studies, by Marsden (1986), from a more British and Continental orientation, demonstrates how fully a consideration of institutional factors is now being integrated into older theory based on competitive models of labor markets. A central theme is the need to integrate the study of labor economics, and of industrial relations and of industrial sociology. Marsden's references, as another Who's Who, list some of the more important of both the new and the older labor economics revisionists. (For an earlier effort to integrate the work of first- and second-wave labor market revisionists, see also Annable 1984.)

My overall impression of developments in labor economics since 1960 is that some new knowledge has been added, particularly in analysis of human capital formation and its consequences and of supply-side aspects more generally, and that much prior knowledge has been verified and put into more precise form; also, that little prior knowledge has been falsified but has been given, instead, new and better explanations more consistent with neoclassical theory, including with utility maximization, with supply–demand analysis, and with cost-benefit analysis. Additionally, much more still needs to be done, in particular to make contact with public knowledge and public policy. The current renaissance in labor economics has aleady resulted in substantial advances, and the future for the field can now be viewed with the greatest of expectations. Table 1–1 shows the general location of the first- and second-wave revisionists within the broader historical scope of labor economics.

There is a broad range of intellectual challenges awaiting innovative analysis that includes both econometric and more qualitative observation. Among the tasks for labor economics (and for industrial relations—the two should never be separated too far from each other) are:

1. Better analysis of the different types of structured internal labor markets and of their impacts, including on productivity and on stagflation; and greater appreciation of the "pathology" of the labor market which "matters more directly for most people than . . . any other market" (Solow 1980: 2).

2. Deeper detailed examination of the X-Efficiency and X-Inefficiency factors as identified by Harvey Leibenstein (1978) and of productivity more generally. This will involve better appreciation of the comparative "capacity of

Table 1–1
Simplistic View of Alternative Approaches to Labor Economics

Emphasis	*Adherents*
1. Market forces (almost alone) in the competitive model	Hayek and other "Austrians" Hicks I Chicago restorationists
2. Market (and other) forces in competitive and semicompetitive models	Main line of labor economics (Smith, Mill, Marshall, Pigou) Reder, Rees
3. Market and *other* forces in competitive, semicompetitive, and noncompetitive models	Edgeworth Neoclassical revisionists Hicks II Okun and others Second-wave revisionists
4. Nonmarket forces	a. Institutionalists and structuralists (rules and laws) b. Marxists and neo-Marxists (class structures) c. Dual-market ("primary" and "secondary") theorists (discrimination)

workers and managers . . . to organize themselves for production" (Takezawa and Whitehill 1981: 3); and of the differing means to extract work willingly from hours of work.

3. Better understanding of the causes of stagflation and deeper analysis of possible policy toward it, including incomes policy (see Ulman 1982, for a good summary of the status of the debate over incomes policy).

4. The development of better models of the union. This will involve several models to fit several situations, including political, economic, and bureaucratic models; and an explanation of where and when and to what extent each model applies.

5. More detailed studies of negotiation processes seeking to combine the insights of game theory with the experience of actual practice. Howard Raiffa (1982: 2) argues for the necessity of a "marriage" between those who seek "mathematical elegance" (as he once did) and those who enter the "morass" of "real people in real situations" and try to understand what really goes on (which he later undertook to do).

6. Better elucidation of the evolution, operation, and consequences of the corporative state based on negotiations among industry, labor, and government agencies. This will require, once again, more attention to comparative industrial relations, especially to codetermination at the level of the economy and of the plant, as well as to the role of collective bargaining.

7. Greater understanding of the impacts of slower growth, no growth, and negative growth on labor economics and industrial relations within industries and within nations, and of the contrasting reactions to changing growth rates between and among industries and nations.

8. Reexamination of the "laws of motion" of industrial societies which were of such interest to Marx and to Schumpeter, and also to some of the revisionists.

These last three, in particular, require more attention to comparative international studies and not to ethnocentric ones alone.

The near-term success of labor economics, however, is more likely to turn on its analysis of stagflation and its potential cures than on any other topic, and of the closely related issue of the slowdown in the growth rate of productivity. These are currently the two areas of greatest public policy concern, but other large issues also merit consideration.

To accomplish the above, the study of labor economics and of industrial relations needs again to be combined, as it was by the revisionists. Much has been lost in their subsequent separation. Labor economics is best studied within the broader context of industrial relations, not by itself all alone. This was the early central theme when the Industrial Relations Research Association was started after World War II, particularly as a result of the initial efforts of Lester. Dunlop (1984b: 23) has recently argued for a renewed "conceptual blend" of these two related fields: "A sensitivity to industrial relations remains essential to an understanding and to any sensible policy prescription for labor markets and wage determination." Labor economics should look both to microeconomics and to industrial relations to fulfill its potential in understanding reality.

Some Ways of Seeing Reality

The experience of the revisionist labor economists of 1940–1960 suggests some general rules for the realistic study of labor economics as an applied field in its own right and as a source of service to general theory. It also emphasizes that to be all they should be, labor economists must make an enormous investment in reading and in experience, in gaining knowledge and in developing methodological competence.

1. The basic goal should be that set forth by R.A. Gordon: "Relevance with as much rigor as possible" (1976: 12); and thus to be as concerned with external truth as with internal logic. Labor economics makes its greatest contributions when it is reality oriented. Only then can it be, or become, a science. "It is a characteristic of scientific generalizations that they refer to

reality . . . . In this respect, it is clear, the propositions of Economics are on all fours with the propositions of all other sciences." "Economic laws have their limits and . . . it is important that we should realize wherein these limitations consist" (Robbins 1935: 104, 126). Science is the study of reality. It is not concerned with constructing imaginary worlds—that is better left to science fiction.

2. Use all good evidence, not only statistical. It is almost farcical to suggest that only statistical evidence should be accepted. It would be ludicrous for a court of law to so rule, for a political leader to so act, for an entrepreneur or a labor leader to so decide, for a scientist to so determine. Both primary and secondary evidence are important, but what is really important is the quality of each.

In the intellectual world, there are several ways to truth: through firsthand observation, as a participant, including as a physical scientist working with experiments, or as a nonparticipant observer, including as an astronomer working with a telescope; through secondhand observation, as through statistics and documents; through contemplation, as in models based upon assumptions and in game playing; and, of course, through combinations of two or more of these. It is intellectually arrogant to argue that only one road to truth is permissible. Truth, as William James (1914: 198) argued, is agreement with reality, and there is more than one way to contact reality. To get truth, we need both the descriptive truth of who, what, when, and where, and the explanatory truth of why. Some people, of course, find their "truth" in an ideology or a religion or both, based on speculation or revelation, but their endeavors lie outside the realm of science.

3. Experience something of reality firsthand as well as secondhand through statistics. "In this generation the loss of practical knowledge might be permanent and irreversible" (Samuelson 1984: 8). Only firsthand contact can lead to an understanding of the internal processes that turn quantifiable inputs into quantifiable outputs.

4. Employ all useful methodologies. This was one of the basic rules of Descartes—to use the best methodology as related to the specific problem. Econometrics is not the only methodology. Sometimes it even seems that, for some econometricians, the means by themselves justify the end—another publication or another data set that may not add to knowledge.

5. Stay in contact with general theory in economics. Try to "contemplate the particular in terms of the general, and touch abstract and concrete in the same flight of thought" (Keynes 1933: 170).

6. Draw good ideas from all useful sources. Make contact with related social science disciplines where useful. Avoid being what Robbins once called "one-eyed monsters" (Robbins 1981). Boulding (1985: 7) has said that "my study of the labor movement . . . convinced me that I had to try to become a general social scientist;" and Hayek (1956: 463) warned that "the economist

who is only an economist is likely to become a nuisance if not a positive danger." There may even be a place for "economic sociology," which was one of Schumpeter's (1954) four branches of economics. Blaug (1978: 712) has defined economic sociology as a study of "social institutions that are relevant to economic behavior." There are several such institutions and they are very relevant.

7.   Do not neglect history. It was a strong theme of Spinoza that you cannot understand the present without reference to the past; also that you cannot understand an event without reference to its context; and, in addition, that removing theory from history and context is to falsify. This is the worst falsification of all. A labor economist out of context deserves the same fate as a fish out of water.

8.   Be reticent to recommend directly on policy. "The besetting methodological vice of neoclassical economics was the illegitimate use of macrostatic theorems, derived from 'timeless' models . . . to predict the historical sequence of events in the real world" (Blaug 1978: 701).

9.   Be satisfied with adding to understanding—understanding of the range of possibilities in advance and of the causes at work in retrospect; with developing concepts that have "repeated usefulness" (Machlup 1978) in aiding understanding. Social science research, as Carol H. Weiss and Michael J. Bucuvalas (1980: 271) have concluded, is most useful as it "produces conclusions that add to understanding." To be concerned only with situations which allow precise prediction is to be concerned mostly with what does not exist.

It is important to understand not only what is clearly true and clearly false, and why, but also what is probable and what is possible and, thus, what is provisionally true—which is where advances in knowledge arise. For these purposes, there are some advantages to a loose framework, as the labor economist revisionists had, as compared with a more rigid one, because it is more open to new developments: to the pressures of reality demanding explanation, to acceptance of concepts from other frameworks, and to a search for totally new concepts. Too many economists have been prisoners of too tight analytical formulas. It has been very hard for some of them to break out of these frameworks, as it was for the neoclassical economists when Keynes came along with his *General Theory*. It was a traumatic experience, even for graduate students of the time, as I well know. Daring to advance the provisionally true that is new makes a potentially greater ultimate contribution to economic understanding than alone to defend the old orthodoxy.

References

Akerlof, George A. 1984. *An Economic Theorist's Book of Tales: Essays that Entertain the Consequences of New Assumptions in Economic Theory*. Cambridge and New York: Cambridge University Press.

American Economic Review. 1982. Vol. 72, no. 4, frontispiece.

Annable, James E., Jr. 1984. *The Price of Industrial Labor.* Lexington, Mass.: Lexington Books.

Bakke, E. Wight. 1940. *The Unemployed Worker: A Study of the Task of Making a Living without a Job.* New Haven: Yale University Press.

———. 1946. *Mutual Survival.* New York: Harper.

Berle, Adolph A., Jr., and Gardiner C. Means. 1932. *The Modern Corporation and Private Property.* New York: Macmillan.

Berlin, Isaiah. 1953. *The Hedgehog and the Fox.* New York: Simon and Schuster.

Blaug, Mark. 1978. *Economic Theory in Retrospect,* 3d ed. Homewood, Ill.: Irwin.

Boulding, Kenneth E. 1951. "Selections from the Discussion of Friedman's Paper." In David McCord Wright, ed., *The Impact of the Union.* New York: Harcourt, Brace.

———. 1985. *Human Betterment.* Beverly Hills, Calif.: Sage.

Bowles, Samuel, and Herbert Gintis. 1986. *Democracy and Capitalism.* New York: Basic Books.

Bronfenbrenner, Martin. 1966. "A Middlebrow Introduction to Economic Methodology." In Sherman Ray Krupp, ed., *The Structure of Economic Science.* Englewood Cliffs, N.J.: Prentice–Hall.

Burton, John, and John Addison. 1977. "The Institutionalist Analysis of Wage Inflation: A Critical Appraisal." In Ronald G. Ehrenberg, ed., *Research in Labor Economics.* Greenwich, Conn.: JAI Press.

Cain, Glen G. 1976. "The Challenge of Segmented Labor Market Theories to Orthodox Theory." *Journal of Economic Literature* 14: 1215–1257.

Chamberlin, Edward. 1933. *The Theory of Monopolistic Competition.* Cambridge: Harvard University Press.

Commons, John R. 1950. *The Economics of Collective Action.* New York: Macmillan.

Doeringer, Peter B., and Michael J. Piore. 1971. *Internal Labor Markets and Manpower Analysis.* Lexington, Mass.: Lexington Books.

Douglas, Paul H. 1930. *Real Wages in the United States, 1890–1926.* Boston and New York: Houghton Mifflin.

———. 1931. *Problem of Unemployment.* New York: Macmillan.

———. 1934. *Theory of Wages.* New York: Macmillan.

Dunlop, John T. 1938. "The Movement of Real and Money Wage Rates." *Economic Journal* 48: 413–434.

———. 1944. *Wage Determination Under Trade Unions.* New York: Macmillan.

———. 1966. "Job Vacancy Measures and Economic Analysis." In *The Measurement and Interpretation of Job Vacancies.* New York: National Bureau of Economic Research.

———. 1984a. *Dispute Resolution: Negotiation and Consensus Building.* Dover, Mass.: Auburn House.

———. 1984b. "Industrial Relations and Economics: The Common Frontier of Wage Determination." Distinguished Speaker Address, *Proceedings of the Thirty-Seventh Annual Meeting,* Industrial Relations Research Association, December 1984.

Edgeworth, Francis Y. 1881. *Mathematical Physics.* London: Kegan Paul.

————. 1889. Presidential Address to Section F of the Royal Society. In John Creedy, *Edgeworth and the Development of Neoclassical Economics.* Oxford: Basil Blackwell, 1986.

————. 1891. "The Objects and Methods of Political Economy," Inaugural lecture, Professor of Political Economy, University of Oxford. In F.Y. Edgeworth, *Papers Relating to Political Economy,* Vol. 1. London: Macmillan, 1925.

Fearn, Robert M. 1981. *Labor Economics: The Emerging Synthesis.* Cambridge, Mass.: Winthrop.

Fisher, Lloyd H. 1953. *The Harvest Labor Market in California.* Cambridge, Mass.: Harvard University Press.

Freeman, Richard. 1984. "The Structure of Labor Markets: A Book Review Three Decades Later." In Gustav Ranis, et al., eds., *Comparative Development Perspectives.* Boulder: Westview.

Garbarino, Joseph W. 1962. *Wage Policy and Long-Term Contracts.* Washington, D.C.: Brookings Institution.

Golden, Clinton S., and Virginia D. Parker, eds. 1955. *Causes of Industrial Peace Under Collective Bargaining.* New York: Harper, esp. pp. 1–54.

Goldthorpe, John H. 1984. *Order and Conflict in Contemporary Capitalism.* Oxford: Oxford University Press.

Gordon, Robert Aaron. 1945. *Business Leadership in the Large Corporation.* Washington, D.C.: Brookings Institution.

————. 1948. "Short-period Price Determination in Theory and Practice." *American Economic Review* 38: 265–288.

————. 1963. "Institutional Elements in Contemporary Economics." In Joseph Dorfman et al., *Institutional Economics.* Berkeley, Calif.: University of California Press.

————. 1976. "Rigor and Relevance in a Changing Institutional Setting." *American Economic Review* 66: 1–14.

Hall, Robert Lowe, and C.J. Hitch. 1939. "Price Theory and Business Behaviour." *Oxford Economic Papers,* Vol. 2 (May), 12–45.

Harbison, Frederick H. 1939. *The Seniority Principle in Union–Management Relations.* Princeton: Industrial Relations Section, Princeton University.

Hayek, Frederich A. 1956. "The Dilemma of Specialization." In Leonard D. White, ed., *The State of the Social Sciences.* Chicago: University of Chicago Press.

Hicks, John R. 1930. "Edgeworth, Marshall, and the Indeterminateness of Wages." *Economic Journal* 40: 215–31.

————. 1932; 1963. *The Theory of Wages,* 1st and 2d eds. London: Macmillan.

————. 1955. "The Economic Foundations of Wage Policy." *Economic Journal* 65: 389–404.

————. 1974. *The Crisis in Keynesian Economics.* Oxford: Blackwell.

————. 1985. *Methods of Dynamic Economics.* New York: Oxford University Press.

Hirsch, Barry, and John T. Addison. 1986. *The Economic Analysis of Unions.* Boston, Mass.: Allen and Unwin.

Hirschman, A.O. 1970. *Exit, Voice and Loyalty.* Cambridge, Mass.: Harvard University Press.

James, William. 1914. *Pragmatism.* New York: Longmans, Green.

Kerr, Clark. 1933. *Self-Help: A Study of the Cooperative Barter Movement of the Unemployed in California, 1932–33.* Unpublished master's thesis (Economics). Stanford University.

———. 1939. *Productive Enterprises of the Unemployed, 1931–1938.* Unpublished Ph.D. dissertation (Economics). University of California, Berkeley.

———. 1941. "Industrial Relations in Large-Scale Cotton Farming." *Proceedings of the Nineteenth Annual Meeting*, Pacific Coast Economic Association.

———. 1942. *Migration to the Seattle Labor Market Area, 1940–42.* Seattle: University of Washington Press. Reprinted by Greenwood Press, Westport, Conn.: 1970.

———. 1948. "Economic Analysis and the Study of Industrial Relations." Institute of Industrial Relations Reprint 3. Berkeley, Calif.: Institute of Industrial Relations, University of California. Reprinted from *Proceedings*, Third Annual Conference on Research and Training in Industrial Relations, University of Minnesota, 1947.

———. 1950. "Labor Markets: Their Character and Consequences." *American Economic Review* 40: 278–291.

———. 1954a. "Balkanization of Labor Markets." In Social Science Research Council, *Labor Mobility and Economic Opportunity*. Cambridge, Mass.: Technology Press.

———. 1954b. Discussion at Conference sponsored by the International Economic Association (1954). Summarized in John T. Dunlop, ed., *The Theory of Wage Determination*. New York: Macmillan, 1957, p. 387.

———. 1954c. Paper given at conference sponsored by the International Economic Association (1954). Published as "Wage Relationships—The Comparative Impact of Market and Power Forces." In John T. Dunlop, ed., *The Theory of Wage Determination*. New York: Macmillan, 1957.

———. 1957. "Labor's Income Share and the Labor Movement." In George W. Taylor and Frank Pierson, eds., *New Concepts in Wage Determination*. New York: McGraw–Hill.

———. 1958. "The Prospect for Wages and Hours in 1975." In Jack Stieber, ed., *U.S. Industrial Relations: The Next Twenty Years.* East Lansing, Mich.: Michigan State University Press.

———. 1959. "The Impacts of Unions on the Levels of Wages." In Charles A. Myers, ed., *Wages, Prices, Profits and Productivity*. New York: The American Assembly, Columbia University.

———. 1969. *Marshall, Marx and Modern Times: The Multi-Dimensional Society.* London and New York: Cambridge University Press.

———. 1977. *Labor Markets and Wage Determination*. Berkeley: University of California Press. Introduction.

———. 1983. "The Intellectual Role of the Neorealists in Labor Economcs." *Industrial Relations* 22: 298–318.

Kerr, Clark, John T. Dunlop, Charles A. Myers, and Frederick H. Harbison. 1960. *Industrialism and Industrial Man*. Cambridge, Mass.: Harvard University Press.

Kerr, Clark, and Lloyd H. Fisher. 1948. "Multiple Employer Bargaining." In J. Shister and Richard A. Lester, eds., *Insights into Labor Issues*. New York: Macmillan.

———. 1950. "Effects of Environment and Administration on Job Evaluation." *Harvard Business Review* 28: 77–96.

————. 1957. "Plant Sociology: The Elite and the Aborigines." In Mirra Komarovsky and Paul Lazarsfeld, eds., *Common Frontiers of the Social Sciences*. Glencoe, Ill.: Free Press.

Keynes, John Maynard. 1933. *Essays in Biography*. New York: Harcourt, Brace.

————. 1936. *The General Theory of Employment, Interest, and Money*. New York: Harcourt, Brace and World.

Labor Study Group. 1961. *The Public Interest in National Labor Policy*, by an independent study group (Clark Kerr, Chairman; George P. Shultz, Study Director). New York: Committee for Economic Development.

Leibenstein, Harvey. 1978. *General X-Efficiency Theory and Economic Development*. New York: Oxford University Press.

Lester, Richard A. 1941. *Economics of Labor*. New York: Macmillan.

————. 1946. "Shortcomings of Marginal Analysis for Wage-Employment Problems." *American Economic Review* 36: 63–82.

————. 1947. "Marginalism, Minimum Wages, and Labor Markets." *American Economic Review* 37: 135–148.

————. 1952. "A Range Theory of Wage Differentials." *Industrial and Labor Relations Review* 5: 483–500.

Lewis, H. Gregg. 1963. *Unions and Relative Wages*. Chicago, Ill.: University of Chicago Press.

Machlup, Fritz. 1946. "Marginal Analysis and Empirical Research." *American Economic Review* 36: 519–554.

————. 1978. *Methodology of Economics and Other Social Sciences*. New York: Academic Press.

March, James G., and Guje Sevón. 1984. "Behavioral Perspectives on Theories of the Firm." Unpublished research paper.

Marsden, David. 1986. *The End of Economic Man? Custom and Competition in Labor Markets*. New York: St. Martin's Press.

Marshall, Alfred. 1873. "The Future of the Working Classes." In A.C. Pigou, ed., *Memorials of Alfred Marshall*. New York: Kelley and Millman, 1956.

————. 1890; 1920. *Principles of Economics*, 1st and 8th eds. London: Macmillan.

————. 1919. *Industry and Trade*. London: Macmillan.

Mathewson, Stanley B. 1931. *Restriction of Output Among Unorganized Workers*. New York: Viking.

Matthews, R.C.O. 1986. "The Economics of Institutions and the Sources of Growth." *Economic Journal* 96: 903–18.

McCloskey, Donald N. 1983. "The Rhetoric of Economics." *Journal of Economic Literature* 21: 481–517.

Michels, Robert. 1915. *Political Parties; a Sociological Study of the Oligarchical Tendencies of Modern Democracy*. London: Jarrold.

Myers, Charles A., and W. Rupert Maclaurin. 1943. *The Movement of Factory Workers*. New York: John Wiley.

Myers, Charles A., and George P. Shultz. 1951. *Dynamics of a Labor Market*. New York: Prentice–Hall.

Okun, Arthur M. 1981. *Prices and Quanities*. Washington, D.C.: Brookings Institution.

Perlman, Mark. 1972. "Some Reflections on Theorizing About Industrial Relations." In Norval Morris and Mark Perlman, eds., *Law and Crime*. New York: Gordon and Breach.

———. 1981. "Review of Paul J. McNulty, *The Origins and Development of Labor Economics*." *Journal of Economic Literature* 19: 1083–1085.

Perlman, Selig. 1928. *A Theory of the Labor Movement*. New York: Macmillan.

Phelps, E.S. 1979. *Employment and Inflation*. New York: Academic Press.

Phelps Brown, E.H. 1972. "The Underdevelopment of Economics." *Economic Journal* 82: 1–10.

Pigou, A.C. 1905. *Principles and Methods of Industrial Peace*. London: Macmillan.

———. 1912. *Wealth and Welfare*. London: Macmillan.

———. 1922. "Empty Economic Boxes: A Reply." *The Economic Journal* 32: 458–465.

———. 1945. *Lapses from Full Employment*. Edinburgh: R. and R. Clark.

Raiffa, Howard. 1982. *The Art and Science of Negotiation*. Cambridge, Mass.: The Belknap Press of Harvard University.

Reder, Melvin. 1952. "The Theory of Union Wage Policy." *The Review of Economics and Statistics*. 34: 34–45.

———. 1955. "The Theory of Occupational Wage Differentials." *American Economic Review* 45: 833–52.

———. 1957. *Labor in a Growing Economy*. New York: John Wiley.

———. 1958. "Wage Determination in Theory and Practice." In Neil W. Chamberlain, Frank C. Pierson, and Theresa Wolfson, eds., *A Decade of Industrial Relations Research, 1946–1956*. New York: Harper.

———. 1960. "Job Scarcity and the Nature of Union Power." *Industrial and Labor Relations Review* 13: 349–362.

———. 1963. "Wage Structure: Theory and Measurement." In *Aspects of Labor Economics*. New York: Arno Press (for the National Bureau of Economic Research).

———. 1964. "Wage Structures and Structural Unemployment." *Review of Economic Studies* 31: 309–322.

Rees, Albert. 1952. "Union Wage Policy." In George Brooks et al., eds., *Interpreting the Labor Movement*. Madison, Wis.: Industrial Relations Research Association.

———. 1962. *The Economics of Trade Unions*. Chicago: University of Chicago Press.

———. 1971. *The Current State of Labor Economics*. Reprint Series No. 16. Kingston, Ontario: Industrial Relations Center, Queen's University.

———. 1973. *The Economics of Work and Pay*. New York: Harper and Row.

———. 1976. "H. Gregg Lewis and the Development of Analytical Labor Economics." *Journal of Political Economy* 84: 53–58.

———. 1977. "Policy Decisions and Research in Economics and Industrial Relations: An Exchange of Views. *Industrial and Labor Relations Review* 31: 3–4.

———. 1979. "Douglas on Wages and the Supply of Labor." *The Journal of Political Economy* 87: 915–922.

Rees, Albert, and George P. Shultz. 1970. *Workers and Wages in an Urban Labor Market*. Chicago: University of Chicago Press.

Reynolds, Lloyd G. 1946. "Wage Differences in Local Labor Markets." *American Economic Review* 36: 366–375.

———. 1948 "Toward a Short-Run Theory of Wages." *American Economic Review* 38: 289–308.

———. 1949. *Labor Economics and Labor Relations*. New York: Prentice–Hall.

———. 1951. *The Structure of Labor Markets*. New York: Harper.

Reynolds, Lloyd G., and Cynthia H. Taft. 1956. *The Evolution of Wage Structure*. New Haven: Yale University Press.

Robbins, Lionel Charles. 1935. *An Essay on the Nature and Significance of Economic Science*, 2d ed. London: Macmillan. (1st edition, 1932.)

———. 1971. *Autobiography of an Economist*. London and Basingstoke: Macmillan.

———. 1981. "Economics and Political Economy," Richard T. Ely Lecture. *American Economic Review* 71: 1–10.

Robertson, Dennis H. 1931. "Wage Grumbles [1930]." In *Economic Fragments*. London: P.S. King.

Robinson, Joan. 1933. *The Economics of Imperfect Competition*. London: Macmillan.

———. 1980. *Collected Economic Papers, Vol. Two*. Cambridge, Mass.: MIT Press.

Ross, Arthur M. 1948. *Trade Union Wage Policy*. Berkeley, Calif.: University of California Press.

Samuelson, Paul A. 1951. "Economic Theory and Wages." In David McCord Wright, ed., *The Impact of the Union*. New York: Harcourt, Brace.

———. 1981. "Schumpeter's Capitalism, Socialism and Democracy." In Arnold Heertje, ed., *Schumpeter's Vision*. New York: Praeger.

———. 1984. "Evaluating Reaganomics." *Challenge* 27: 4–11.

Schumpeter, Joseph A. 1954. *History of Economic Analysis*. New York: Oxford University Press.

Segal, Martin. 1986. "Post-Institutionalism in Labor Economics: The Forties and Fifties Revisited." *Industrial and Labor Relations Review* 39: 388–403.

Sen, Amartya K. 1970. *Collective Choice and Social Welfare*. San Francisco: Holden–Day.

Simon, Herbert A. 1951. "A Formal Theory of the Employment Relationship." *Econometrica* 19: 293–305.

Slichter, Sumner H. 1941. *Union Policies and Industrial Management*. Washington, D.C.: Brookings Institution.

Solow, Robert A. 1979. "Alternative Approaches to Macroeconomic Theory." *Canadian Journal of Economics* 12: 339–354.

———. 1980. "Theories of Unemployment." *American Economic Review 70: 1–11.*

Stewart, Ian M.T. 1979. *Reasoning and Method in Economics*. London: McGraw–Hill.

Stigler, George J. 1947. "Professor Lester and the Marginalists," in "Communications." *American Economic Review* 37: 154–157.

Takezawa, S., and A.M. Whitehill. 1981. *Work Ways: Japan and America*. Tokyo: Japan Institute of Labor.

Taylor, Paul S., and Clark Kerr. 1940. *Documentary History of the Strike of Cotton Pickers in California of 1933*. U.S. Senate Committee on Education and Labor. Washington, D.C.: U.S. Government Printing Office.

Ulman, Lloyd. 1955. "Marshall and Friedman on Union Strength." *Review of Economics and Statistics* 37: 384–401.

————. 1982. "Unions, Economists, Politicians, and Incomes Policy." In Joseph Pechman and N.J. Simler, eds., *Economics in the Public Service*. New York: W.W. Norton.

Wachter, Michael L. 1974. "Primary and Secondary Labor Markets: A Critique of the Dual Approach." *Brookings Papers on Economic Activity* 3: 637–680.

Walzer, Michael. 1986. "Introduction." In Isaiah Berlin, ed., *The Hedgehog and the Fox*. New York: Simon and Schuster.

Ward, Benjamin. 1972. *What's Wrong with Economics*. New York: Basic Books.

Webb, Sidney and Beatrice. 1897. *Industrial Democracy*. London: Longmans, Green.

Weiss, Carol H., and Michael J. Bucuvalas. 1980. *Social Science Research and Decision Making*. New York: Columbia University Press.

Williamson, Oliver E. 1975. *Markets and Hierarchies*. New York: Free Press.

Wootton, Barbara. 1955. *The Social Foundations of Wage Policy*. New York: W.W. Norton.

2
Labor Markets and Wage Determination: Then and Now

John T. Dunlop

Fundamentals of Compensation and Labor Markets

There are a limited number of fundamental propositions that need to be discussed at the outset to provide a basis for reflection on compensation and labor markets. These points were widely recognized in the operational activity or articulated in the writings of labor economists of an earlier era (1930–60).

A Complex of Rules

Every workplace of size that persists over time develops and in turn is governed by a complex of rules created by its industrial relations system (Dunlop 1958: 13–16, 33–123; Kerr and Siegel 1955: 163–64). Such a "web of rules" emerges irrespective of labor organization or collective bargaining; no continuing workplace is ever truly unorganized (Dunlop 1948a: 177–79).

While there are literally scores of these rules in any workplace, the following headings provide some indication of their principal features:

1. Wage level and job classification structure and method of wage payment;
2. Fringe benefits: holidays, vacations with pay, health and welfare, pensions, et cetera;
3. Internal labor market movements: hiring, transfers, promotions, temporary layoffs, leaves, permanent layoffs, retirement;
4. Hours and shifts, overtime and premiums;
5. Manning rules;
6. Safety and health;
7. Discharge and discipline;
8. Dispute resolution procedures;
9. Status of worker and management (and government) organizations and representatives;

10. Special rules shaped by the particular technology or markets.

Many of these rules, aside from wages and fringe benefits, have significant effects upon labor costs to management and income to the work force. But many terms of employment are not reducible to money, or a trade-off in money, as a practical matter. The tendency to treat wages and benefits (or their change) as if they were equivalent to the terms and conditions of employment (or their change) is often a serious error. There are important substitutes among these terms and conditions of employment; there is no constant relationship or stable rate of substitution, however, among the complex of rules, and even in the course of the same negotiations the internal organization and shifting priorities of each side will affect the trade-offs (Dunlop and Healy 1953: 53–68; Dunlop 1984a).

Any measure of wages, such as average hourly earnings, is only an indicator of one dimension of a shifting complex of rules with many a pitfall for the simple number-cruncher in search of the price of labor.

Compensation Schedules and Administration

A distinction needs to be drawn between the periodic (yearly) specification or change in the *wage and benefit schedule* of a unit and the *administration* of the internal labor market of the unit on a day-to-day basis under the rules of the workplace (Dunlop 1966: 33–38; Kerr 1954: 101–03; Doeringer and Piore 1971). These are quite different activities made in quite different time frames, often by very different members of management, and usually with quite different objectives. All the manpower decisions in the internal labor market are likely to affect average hourly earnings of the unit, as are changes in output under incentive systems.

It is a gross misunderstanding of the wage-determination process to lump these two processes together or to fail to recognize that all wage and benefit data, save for that relating to wage, salary, and benefits schedules (which are not generally available to or used by economists), are the undistinguished product of both types of decisions.[1] Average hourly earnings data for many problems need to be reviewed to judge the relative influence of day-to-day administrative actions involving rate ranges, shifts among occupations and units, premium hours, incentive effects, et cetera, as compared to the influence of wage and benefits schedules.

Institutional Forms of Markets

There are no disembodied markets. The institutional organization, the rules, procedures, and circumstances under which buyers and sellers are brought together, affect the performance of the market, its prices, and quantities transferred. These institutional forms and rules are shaped by the participants and external organizations, including government. Thus, the margin requirement rules affect the performance of stock exchanges. Labor markets, exterior to establishments, are similarly affected by their institutional forms and rules of operation.

The hiring fairs for agricultural labor in seventeenth-century England were an organized and even ritualistic way to bring together workers and their families and prospective employers each autumn to establish employment arrangements and compensation for the next year (Mund 1948: 98–102). In the unstructured harvest labor market in California, the labor contractor developed a structure relating to employment, compensation, and other rules, an activity now regulated by government agencies and in some instances by labor organizations (Fisher 1953).

Take any labor market—for nurses in northern New Jersey, pipeline construction workers in Alaska, professional firefighters in Boston, able-bodied sailors on U. S. flag vessels on the Pacific Ocean, X-ray technicians in metropolitan hospitals, MBA graduates seeking starting positions with business—and it is possible to specify the institutional forms within which these buyers and sellers generally operate.

These forms are particularly influenced by a casual or more steady employment relation, the technical and professional qualifications required, the degree of specialization and division of labor utilized, and the range of job classifications encompassed by the particular operations or activities. The rules and procedures of labor markets influence the flow of information on job and worker availability, who has access to such information, the qualifications for such jobs and potential employees, the frequency of hiring opportunities, and the duration of employment.

Forty years ago I concluded that "labor markets do not resemble bourses, auctions, nor closed bid arrangements"; they are "found to be structurally different from a bourse; wage rates are typically quoted prices" (Dunlop 1944: 11, 118).[2]

It is significant that it is leading macroeconomists, rather than microeconomists, who currently agree with the assessments of the 1930–60s. For instance, James Tobin stated (1972: 3, 9):

> Keynes emphasized the institutional fact that wages are bargained and set in the monetary unit of account. Money wage rates are to use an un-Keynesian term, "administered prices." That is, they are not set and reset in daily auctions, but posted and priced for finite periods of time.

Robert M. Solow has written (1986: S23–S34):

> Someone once defined an economist as a parrot trained to repeat "Supply and Demand, Supply and Demand." There are many worse things you could teach

a parrot to say—and we hear them every day—but I want to suggest that, in the case of the labor market, our preoccupation with price-mediated market-clearing as the "natural" equilibrium condition may be a serious error.

The labor market is not to be envisaged as a bourse with wage movements clearing the market or with unemployment an indicator that wage rates are necessarily excessive. This conclusion leaves much of microeconomic wage theory in jeopardy. No wonder the recent rush to patch up the theory and to provide theoretical explanations for wage differentials and for unemployment.

Social Aspects of Labor Markets

The labor market is a very special kind of market, with both social and economic aspects. Sir John Hicks in the commentary to his own *Theory of Wages* states (1963: 317, 319):

> The labor market is—by nature, and quite independent of Trade Union Organization—a very special kind of market which is likely to develop "social" as well as purely economic aspects. . . . For the purely economic correspondence between the wage paid to a particular worker and his value to the employer is not a sufficient condition of efficiency; it is also necessary that there should not be strong feelings of injustice about the relative treatment of employees (since these would diminish the efficiency of the team). . . . Wage rates are more uniform between workers, and over time, than they would be if the labor market worked like a commodity market. . . . There are important social (and expectational) elements even in the "free market" part of wage determination. Even these wages are not simply determined by supply and demand.

An understanding of labor markets and compensation requires a recognition that the workplace is a social organization, at least informally, and that labor markets take on significant social characteristics that do not characterize commodity and financial markets and that are not readily encapsuled in ordinary demand and supply analysis (Dunlop 1948a: 177; Mayo 1945). Formal economic analysis is too narrowly conceived to preempt the study of labor markets and wage determination. The authors of the 1930–60 period all clearly understood this observation and incorporated its perspective in analysis and in policy prescriptions.

The social aspects of labor markets, to use Hicks's term, are particularly significant to the operation of internal labor markets and to the grouping of enterprises used for compensation comparisons in the external labor market. (The discussion of internal labor markets from an earlier presentation is incorporated by reference. See Dunlop 1984b: 15–18.) These social aspects help to provide particular labor markets with their institutional forms.

Noncompeting Groups

A main theme in the literature on wages and labor markets over the past century has been the necessity to disaggregate the universe into a limited number of "non-competing" categories. J.E. Cairnes used these words (1874: 72–3):

> What we find, in effect, is, not a whole population competing indiscriminately for all occupations, but a series of industrial layers, superimposed on one another, within each of which the various candidates for employment possess a real and effective power of selection, while those occupying the several strata are, for all purposes of effective competition, practically isolated from each other. We may perhaps venture to arrange them in some such order as this: first, at the bottom of the scale unskilled laborers . . . second, the artisan . . . third, producers and dealers of a higher order such as engineers and opticians . . . fourth, the learned professions and the higher branches of mercantile business.
>
> We are thus compelled to recognize the existence of non-competing industrial groups as a feature of our social economy.

Cairnes meant no hard lines of demarcation, but competition was limited for practical purposes to a certain range of occupations.

The principle of noncompeting groups in wage determination applies today, but specialists in labor markets and compensation would present a somewhat different set of broad categories. The lines of demarcation again are not hard, and they are drawn in somewhat different sectors and industries. Suggested categories of noncompeting groups are shown in table 2–1. The percentages of the total civilian labor force indicated for each group are

Table 2–1
Suggested Categories of Noncompeting Groups

Category	Percentage of Total Civilian Labor Force
1. Production and maintenance in larger enterprises (nonexempt employees)	20
2. Supervisory, technical, and professional (exempt employees)	12
3. Clerical occupations in larger enterprises	10
4. Top management grades in larger enterprises	2
5. Self-employment	8
6. Voluntary associations	3
7. Public sector (federal, state, and local)	15
8. Small enterprises, all grades	30

intended to provide a rough approximation of the size of each category in the total labor force in the United States.

There are no doubt subdivisions in each category, and there is some overlap and movement among these groups. In the main, compensation data are collected and made available and comparisons are made internal to each of these groups. In the public sector, however, and particularly with respect to federal government employees, the principle of comparability with the private sector has been adopted in statutes, and annual surveys are made of private sector compensation for certain key occupations in the federal civil service.[3]

In the private sector, in categories 1 through 4, specialized enterprises have arisen to compile and market comparative compensation data, often by locality and sector, within each category. Wage control agencies in World War II and in the Korean War period also separated their regulations among similar categories. Compensation determination, and the operaton of labor markets, tends to be quite different among these contemporaneous noncompeting groups.

There are specialized factors operative in many of these separate categories: supervisors' compensation is often pegged to differentials over the top classifications they supervise; top management grades in compensation are typically related to executives in a grouping of firms thought to be comparable, a different grouping than used for production and maintenance or clerical employees; moreover, styles and levels of executive compensation are related to changes in the tax code and longer-term movements of the stock market. Self-employment compensation combines salary, benefits, and profits in different mixtures depending on tax considerations that make comparisons difficult with other categories. Voluntary associations have often had traditions and standards that result in lower compensation than in the for-profit sectors. Small enterprises tend to have lower compensation, and they often have less formal and more personalized compensation arrangements that are much more responsive to short-term labor market pressures than in large enterprises.

A generalized formulation of compensation determination does not fit well these separate noncompeting groups. Too often, wage discussions presume the production and maintenance group. But the full range of compensation groups needs to be appreciated. While there are some linkages in the responses to changes in the economy and society among these noncompeting groups, and there is general leadership from the large enterprises in most labor markets, the levels of compensation for comparable work, the extent and types of fringe benefits, the extent of internal labor markets and their administration, and the external labor market institutional arrangements in these categories are substantially different. An analytical framework that seeks to encompass all these separate noncompeting categories is likely either to be highly remote or inapplicable to the behavior of a number of these groups.

Compensation Decisions

A series of basic issues relating internal to external markets confront those charged with making wage, salary, or fringe benefit decisions—decisions made by managers, by the parties in collective bargaining, by arbitrators, or in government wage control or restraint programs. The perspective of microeconomists needs to be better informed by a recognition of these choices and decisions.

Internal and External Congruence.   Every compensation unit with more than one job classification faces the issue of internal consistency, fairness, or congruence among different job classifications and individuals, as compared to the wage and benefit relationships established in the relevant exterior market or contour (Dunlop 1957: 17). An internal job evaluation or job ranking plan, for instance, provides a relative ranking of job classifications that is almost certain to be different from wage and salary relationships among similar job classifications established outside the control of the internal decision makers. Are the differences tolerable? Do the differences apply to vital key jobs, such as hiring-in rates and some maintenance job classifications, that are often the subject of careful comparison by employees and managers? Or do the differences apply only to more specialized job classifications? Should the internal wage line between low- and high-paid job classifications be tilted up or down, or should *ad hoc* adjustments in the internal wage line be made in isolated classifications or job families? Will such adjustments destroy the integrity of the internal system?

While these issues are continuously under review, changes tend to be made only periodically in compensation schedules. The General Electric–IUE Agreement of 1982, for instance, provided a 2¢ per hour increment for every 15¢ in the step rates above $8.35 per hour, reflecting a concern that the internal ordering of wage rates yielded too low rates in some markets at the higher end of the wage scale. As another illustration of the issue, Harvard deans face tensions in seeking to pursue a salary policy of comparative equality internally among all tenured faculty members of a given age, irrespective of fields, against the tendency of many institutions in the outside market to compensate professors differentially by fields and by individual distinction. Wage and salary determination always involves a delicate balancing of internal and external considerations for the job classification schedule as a whole. This decision is not readily encompassed by ordinary microeconomics.

Level of Wage Schedule.   Every compensation unit of any appreciable size faces the issue of the relative level it seeks to maintain compared to the exterior market or contour that it regards as relevant as a matter of policy. This concern accounts for the extensive use of compensation surveys for varying groupings of establishments and enterprises, localities, and elements of compensation. Some deliberately prefer to be at the top, others at the midpoint, some at the 75th percentile, and still others on the low side. It also needs to be recognized that there are some cyclical variations in relative positions, and that in general the higher the relative level, the greater the degree of freedom in pursuing internal ordering policies.

Wage Schedules Across Different Product Markets.   An enterprise or wage decision unit that spans a number of exterior product markets often faces quite different competitive conditions in labor markets. For this reason it may have considerable difficulty in achieving uniformity of treatment and providing for the arrangements that facilitate mobility at managerial and other levels within the enterprise with economic viability in lower wage markets. The problems are illustrated in the experience of the major rubber companies in combining under the same master agreement, or related agreements, the production and maintenance classifications in rubber tire plants and those in rubber shoe or other rubber product plants. The wage and benefit levels in rubber tire plants could not be maintained in other rubber product plants, and considerable conflict was engendered over several decades in separating these compensation decisions. There have been similar problems in heavy and highway construction, as compared to commercial and industrial construction; fabricating plants and warehouse operations in steel plants in the basic steel industry; drug department job classifications as compared to those in meat, grocery, and produce departments of retail food stores, and so on. These problems arise both under collective agreements and without organization.

Standardization of Earnings and Labor Cost Under Piece Rates.   Under piece rate, incentive, or mileage methods of wage payment, special problems arise in grouping enterprises under a single compensation-making decision. Uniformity of such piece rates has the virtue of standardizing labor costs per unit of output, as was historically the objective in clothing, operating crafts of Class 1 railroads, and master freight trucking. But earnings per hour to employees will then tend to be higher, or hours of work shorter, among highly efficient, as compared to less productive, enterprises. Beyond some limits, these differences in earnings generate pressures among workers to raise piece rates in low earnings enterprises. But unequal piece rates will result in quite different labor costs and relative competitive positions. The periodic review of these tensions is a persistent issue of wage policy.

Defined Benefits or Defined Contributions.   In the benefits area, a basic question concerns whether pensions and health care are to constitute defined benefits, as a pension of so much after thirty years of service or at age sixty-five, or so much per day for hospitalization, with management purchasing these services or self-insuring, or whether a defined contribution of a specified dollar amount per hour is to be set aside to purchase pension and health care benefits, in whatever amounts the funds will purchase, as determined by trustees of the funds. The first method guarantees to employees specific benefits, and the second method guarantees to employers specific expenditures. The issues of unfunded liabilities and the consequences of inflation for pension plans are quite different in the two situations. The management of investment funds and the possibility of varying charges according to profits and tax liabilities, not to mention differential government regulations under ERISA, also present different opportunities and problems in the two types of plans.

Compensation decision makers and administrators in larger enterprises grapple with these and other fundamentals that vitally influence costs and earnings, morale and productivity, and the economic viability of the enterprise. It should be apparent that compensation decisions are not readily compressed into current formal microeconomic analysis that abstracts and distorts so greatly essential features of "the ordinary business of life", to use Alfred Marshall's phrase in defining economics (Marshall, 1920: 1).

Wage Structure and Labor Markets

The structure of wage and salary differentials—by job classification, industry, locality and region, size of establishment, sex, over the long term or through the cycle, under union and nonunion circumstances, and in the course of economic development—was studied intently in the period 1930–60.[4] The government wage control and manpower programs of that period provided access to mountains of compensation data by establishment and job classification, and many young labor economists and industrial relations specialists were educated through its use to the realities of the labor market and the details of compensation. Wage structure studies were reinforced by a large number of local labor market studies. Comparisons of wage structures among countries were part of the concern with European recovery and with economic development in the Third World.

The largest volume of wage structure studies of the period 1930–60 were designed to describe and generalize about major dimensions of differentials in the wage structure and their changes over time. The objective was to account for the cyclical and long-term changes in differentials that were identified. Thus, the magnitude of the changes in skill differentials in particular industries and in regional differentials in wages since the beginning of the century or from the start of wage data time series were carefully reported with ideas as to the active agents (see Lester 1945; Ober 1948; Lebergott 1947: 274–285; Douty 1984). On the whole, the work was of high quality and set the stage for considerable reflection on the reasons for these substantial and continuing differences and their implications for economic theory. The labor market was surprisingly different from the simplifications of the standard textbook, and those models surprisingly useless in confronting real problems. There is little reason to summarize the work here except to refer to some of the major studies in an endnote.[5]

The discussion that follows in this section considers a number of the features of the wage structure and labor markets that were the focal point of inquiry in the period 1930–60 and their implications for analytical work in economics and industrial relations.

Persistent Large Wage Differences Among Comparable Jobs. A conference on Research on Wages, sponsored by the Social Science Research Council, April 4–5, 1947, reflected the concern with various dimensions of the wage structure and their changes, reasons for these differentials, and the effects of unions on the structure of compensation.[6] At the conference, my summary of the behavior of wage rates (Reynolds 1947: 11) included: "At any time in any labor market one finds a great diversity of rates for identically defined jobs. . . . there are vast differences in the rates paid for comparable work in a given industry in a given labor market area. Cross-sectionally, one finds that large firms tend to pay higher wages than smaller firms." On the same theme, the conference considered the possibility that differentials only reflected differences in ability of workers. It was concluded (Reynolds 1947: 27): "Most of those present, however, were of the opinion that real wage differentials for comparable work can and do continue indefinitely in particular communities."

The same theme was developed in a conference held by the International Economic Association in 1954. My paper presented the wage rates for motor-truck drivers in Boston, showing that twenty-three different groups of employers paid rates ranging from $1.20 for wholesale laundry and $1.38 for wastepaper to $2.25 an hour for magazines and $2.16 for newspaper drivers. In the paper I said (1957: 20):

> In a significant sense, the case constitutes a kind of critical experiment. One type of labor performing almost identical work, organized by the same union, is paid markedly different rates by different associations of employers in the truck transportation industry. Why the wide range in wage rates? Are the disparities temporary? Do they arise from "friction" or "immobilities" in labor market? Are they primarily the consequence of a monopolistic seller of labor discriminating among types of employers? I believe the answer to these questions is in the negative.

I then asked (1957: 20–21):

> Why do not teamsters all move to the higher paying contours? Or, why do not the employers in the higher paying contours set a lower wage rate since similar

labor seems to be available in other contours at lower rates? In a perfect labor market (a bourse) such changes toward uniformity would tend to take place.

I argued that the explanation did not lie primarily with the existence of a union because "the type of wage spread is so general." Neither did the explanation depend importantly on any differences in job content or quality of workers or compensating differentials among job classifications. Some of the explanation was to be found in the historical sequence of growth of the separate contours. In order to attract labor, job classifications related to newer products often enter the wage structure toward the top end of the array of wage differentials, as in the case of petroleum truck drivers. Fundamentally, the structure of the product markets and their competitiveness tended to be reflected into relative wage rates in the labor market.[7] I developed the concepts of job clusters and wage contours to help explain these differentials (Dunlop 1957).

One consequence of this view is to make clear that the concept of "industry" and its measurement with SIC numbers for wage data is fundamentally flawed for an understanding of wage setting, since wage-making forces or wage contours almost never correspond to SIC-defined industries. In teaching, I always cited SIC code 32, "Stone, Clay and Glass Products," as a grouping that encompasses a large number of separate wage contours. Some are national, regional, and local in scope, respectively, as illustrated by flat glass with a national bargain, glass bottle with several regional scales, flint glass with a traditional piece-rate scale for various branches, and brick and tile manufacturing with a large number of separate locality-oriented wage scales. These sectors have almost nothing in common in their interaction or interdependencies for understanding wage decisions or changes. To average these numbers or relate an average to any variable such as profits, productivity, or unionization is to risk economic hash.

General Wage Regulation 17 of the Wage Stabilization Board (Korean War) stated that in processing an application on grounds of interplant inequities, "the Board will first determine the appropriate group of establishments in an appropriate industry or area with whose wage and salary rates the petitioner's rates are to be compared." Wage structures and wage differentials cannot perceptively or reliably be studied with SIC code categories.

The notion that wage differentials for carefully defined job classifications persist among establishments in the same labor market, and that they are not to be explained away as compensating differentials for working conditions or the quality of the work force, are propositions that would have been almost universally accepted as fact by students of the labor market and wage determination of the period 1930–60.

Internal Wage Structures. The scope of job classifications and their duties, the internal alignment of wage rates, and their relationships to external establishments were a central focus of attention in wage control programs and in academic writings in the period 1930–60. The National War Labor Board and specialized committees created for this purpose developed major reforms in the internal wage structures of a number of major industries: West Coast airframe, meat packing (in both of which Clark Kerr played a major role), shipbuilding, tool and die jobs (particularly in the Detroit area), and the basic steel and cotton textile industries. In the latter two industries I played a staff role in the process of decision making and implementation by the War Labor Board. These committees or commissions required complete wage data for each job classification in each establishment, and often for each worker. No one who did not see these data can fully appreciate the messy wage structures that prevailed in many industries exaggerated by wartime manpower pressures[8]. It needs to be emphasized that internal wage relationships often explicitly required attention to interfirm, interindustry, and interlocality relations for given job classifications, as in airframe and shipbuilding in Seattle and tool and die workers in captive and contract shops in Detroit. General standards for intraplant wage changes were a major feature of the wage stabilization programs of the period.

These experiences and the data they generated, firsthand or further removed, found their way into academic work or affected the interests of the research community. One illustration is provided by Jack Stieber's volume (1959) on the emergence of the Cooperative Wage Survey (CWS) in the basic steel industry. E. Robert Livernash's work (1957) on internal wages reflected the wisdom of a rich experience. A wide variety of industry studies concerned with collective bargaining dealt with the internal wage structure (see Macdonald 1963; Gomberg 1955; Meij 1963).

Reference is also appropriate to the intensive work on the wage structure and work rules of the railroad industry undertaken by the Presidential Railroad Commission.[9] I had proposed the formation of the commission in an earlier Emergency Board Report (Board 109, 1955) and served on the commission where we examined all features of the compensation system and rules for operating crafts.

The interest in internal wage structures and the considerations affecting the alignment and relationships among job families contributed to the development of the more formal concept of internal labor markets (Dunlop 1984b: 15–18). Since relative wages are vital to internal patterns of movements of workers—transfers, promotions, temporary assignments, hiring-in points, the measurement of seniority—the larger concept provides a setting for internal wage relationships and job clusters.

Wage Structure as the Focus of Wage Controls. The stabilization of wage structures was the centerpiece of wage controls in World War II and the Korean War period. While issues concerning the general wage level or the relationship of wages to the CPI cannot be avoided, the management of wage differentials among enterprises in the same industry and locality and internal wage structures is the heart of wage stabilization, in my experience. Contrary to many impressions, the Little Steel formula in World War II and Regulation No. 6 in the Korean War period did not tie wages to living costs, but rather severed any relationship between further increases in the CPI and increases in the general wage level, while at the same time allowing units that had lagged behind in general increases to catch up to the stabilized level. The action was thus concentrated on wage structures, that is, on relative wages.

The underlying problem in compensation confronting a stabilization program is that some wages have jumped out in front of others as a consequence of the accidents of expiration dates of collective agreements, or annual review dates, or adjustments made out of time by the pressures of wage determining factors. These new wage relationships create further changes in other wages, and the dynamics of relativities generate continuing wage inflation. The fundamental task of stabilization is to develop a forum and a process to restore the old wage relationships and to establish new relativities regarded as appropriate to the economic environment of the period ahead.[10]

The single wage guidepost standard of the Kennedy-Johnson Council of Economic Advisers or the Carter anti-inflation program, whether the number be 3.2, 5.5, or 7 percent, is an ineffectual tool ill-adapted to stabilize the wage structure deformities of an inflationary period (Dunlop 1966: 81–96). D. Quinn Mills has well said that "An incomes policy is an exercise in microeconomics, at a time that macroeconomics gets most attention. An incomes policy is an exercise in the economics of particular industries, occupations and geographical areas, at a time when industrial, occupational and geographical studies are not widely pursued" (Mills 1981).

The construction industry stabilization program of 1971–74, which I organized and chaired for most of the period, was entirely geared to the stabilization of intercraft and adjacent area wage relationships, measured by the hourly wage rate plus contributions to fringe benefit funds. (D. Quinn Mills and Albert Rees also served on the commission.) Data on these wage relationships, for the period back to 1960, were used as a benchmark to establish wage-package relationships on which to plan the stabilization of a locality and to act on individual agreements by labor organizations and contractors or to settle disputes over the terms of collective agreements. The actions of CISC were almost always unanimous. The data base was critical. The CISC reduced, without work stoppages, between 1,500 and 1,800 step increases in collective agreements that had already been negotiated, contained wage settlements for the industry well within the general standards, largely eliminated distortions in the wage structure of the industry that had developed to serious proportions in the period 1966–71, and provided a dispute settlement function for open collective agreements (see Goodwin 1975)."[11]

Any future wage stabilization program needs to understand the central role of wage structure differentials and distortions in constraining wage inflation.

Impact of Unions on Wage Structures. A significant volume of academic work of the 1930–60 period undoubtedly was concerned, at one point or another, with the question of the effects of collective bargaining on wages. The issue is very old, and statistical work on the matter likewise goes back many years. Thus, Paul H. Douglas in 1930 concluded (1930: 562): "The evidence seems to indicate that when labor organization becomes effective, it yields very appreciable results in its early stages, but that thereafter the rate of gain enjoyed by its members tends to slow down to a speed which does not appreciably exceed that of non-union industries."

The period 1930-60 saw a proliferation of studies that attempted to measure the wage consequences of unionization. Among such efforts were the work of two of my students, Joseph Garbarino and John E. Maher.[12] There is no point here in seeking to comment in any detail on this mountain of investigation, particularly since there are many summaries and commentaries.[13] George Hilderbrand (1958: 137–8) concluded, "Part of the economic power attributed to American unionism is more illusory than it is real. To the extent that it is real, it carries more promise than it does menace." Freeman and Medoff concluded (1981: 49): "Unions and collective bargaining have substantial real effects on diverse economic outcomes; and many of the real union effects are the result of institutional factors, which many economists have neglected in recent years." Sumner H. Slichter (1954) concluded that wage fixing under collective bargaining had a small inflationary bias. In periods of expansion, strong unions increase wages in some occupations or industries sooner or faster than elsewhere, bringing about other adjustments. In periods of contraction, he believed the influence of unions on wages was less. Slichter also identified in other writings (1961) the major positive effects he believed labor unions had on management.

I have always suggested that the problem of the impact of unions is complicated by the wide variety of avenues of influence—the resource allocation or monopoly effect, concern with joint collusion (Henry Simons), influence on training, morale, productivity, industrial jurisprudence and industrial democracy, the quality and organization of management, influences through the product market, national and local public policies, intensity of industrial conflict or orderly resolution of disputes, et cetera. These influences vary from one workplace to another. The simple fact is that workplaces operating under collective agreements are different from those without formal organization, and they operate differently and are typically managed in quite different ways. No simple comparison or generalization or statistical estimate is likely to be very fruitful.

Comparative Labor Markets and Wage Structures in Advanced Countries.
Special mention is appropriate concerning the widespread interest in the
1945-60 period in the reconstruction of Western Europe and Japan and their
labor markets, wage structures, and industrial relations. These topics had
received relatively little attention in pre-World War II years, save for comparisons with Great Britain, Sweden, and a few other studies. Lloyd G. Reynolds
(1956) compared wage structure developments in France, Great Britain,
Sweden, and Canada with those in the United States. A number of the studies
of industrial relations of countries in the Wertheim series dealt with wage
structure and labor market issues.[14] The OECD study (1965) under the
chairmanship of Peter deWolff examined changes in wage differentials and the
patterns of employment with the implications for incomes policies. We were all
indebted to the work of Henry Phelps Brown (1968) of England and his
treatment of wages in five countries over the hundred years 1860-1960, and to
a large number of younger British specialists for their work on wages and
industrial relations.[15]

Developing Countries. The concern with the emergence and growth of labor
markets, wage structures, and industrial relations institutions in the course of
economic development was central to the Inter-University Study of Labor
Problems in Economic Development. These matters are treated in chapters 8
and 9 of my *Industrial Relations Systems* (1958) and in more detail in
Industrialism and Industrial Man (1960).[16] Among the summary propositions
as to the effects of the course of development on labor markets and industrial
relations are the following (Kerr, Dunlop, Harbison, and Myers 1960: 256):

The proportion of total compensation paid in kind generally declines.

The number of components of compensation tends to expand.

The explicit wage-rate structure of job classifications or occupations arises in
the enterprise.

Wage-rate differentials that arise at the outset of economic development and
which reflect differentiation (for example, by sex, tribe, nationality, or race)
among workers significant to pre-industrial society tend to narrow or to be
eliminated.

A greater degree of interdependence in the inter-enterprise wage structure is
likely to emerge first among enterprises in the same or closely allied product
markets in a locality. . . .

The geographical differentials in the wage-rate structure tend to narrow only
at a later phase in economic development.

The inter-industry wage-rate structure among countries tends to be somewhat
similar, and new industries emerge often at the higher end of the wage-rate
structure.

The studies considered in detail the development of an industrial labor force, its recruitment, discipline, and maintenance, including the establishment of labor markets.

Perspective on the Contemporary Scene. In a review of Lloyd Reynolds' *Structure of Labor Markets* (1951), in the volume that constitutes a tribute to his work, Richard Freeman (1984) compared the findings of the New Haven labor market study with contemporary results of research on labor supply and wage determination. He finds (1984: 219) "most specific findings have been corroborated in succeeding work."

Reynolds (1951: 248, 260) had concluded that supply sets "surprisingly wide" limits to wage differentials, with the result that "the wage structure is shaped mainly by variations in companies' ability to pay and variations in the degree to which management chooses, or is forced by union pressure, to pay as much as it can rather than by a strong tendency to set wages barely sufficient to attract a labor supply." Freeman (1984: 219) concludes that recent work supports this earlier view as to "the essential passivity of supply in wage determination."

Despite the enormous amount of effort devoted to labor supply decisions in the past twenty years in the the form of the influence of education and training, the conclusion is that whatever their influence on labor force participation or human capital investment, the effects of supply on wage structure determination are small or long term in their consequences, as with changing age cohorts or professional manpower. Freeman suggests that it is this different view on the role of labor supply that accounts for the current divergences between the competitive model of labor markets and reality (also see Segal, 1986).

The New Haven labor market study was one of a large number of such studies made in the period 1930–50 with varying interests and reasons for the research. One of the early ones was Clark Kerr's (1942) inquiry into the Seattle labor market in wartime and the pattern of migration and adaptation. Charles A. Myers and W. Rupert Maclaurin (1943) reviewed the depressed community of Fitchburg, Massachusetts, in 1937–40. Further detailed work such as E. Wight Bakke's *The Unemployed Worker: A Study of the Task of Making a Living Without a Job* (1940) and Richard A. Lester's *Company Wage Policies* (1948) rounded out the same view of the labor market.[17]

The legacy of these early labor market studies and the subsequent work on displaced workers and technological and market changes were also to provide ideas for the governmental manpower programs that arose in the 1960s (see Shultz and Weber 1966; Hill and Harbison 1959).

In my own teaching I developed a framework of different ideal types of labor markets and the characteristics that distinguish each. Labor market types were labeled as casual, craft, industrial, and professional, and they differ with regard to job content, extent of investment in training, the amount of associated capital, the attachment to a single enterprise, and the extent to which labor adopts a career perspective. These characteristics frame the operation of very different types of labor markets.[18]

In recent years many microtheorists, and some macroeconomists, have turned to the labor market (and wage setting) and have tried to impose a single model of economic rationality. This effort lacks a recognition that wage setting and labor markets do not well fit within the conventional view. Robert M. Solow (1986) comments that "there is a valid and important question why workers who are involuntarily unemployed do not actively bid for jobs by nominal wage cutting. It is an equally interesting observation that employers do not usually encourage such behavior." Economic theorists have recently sought explanations in such ingenious ideas as asymmetric-information theories, efficiency-wage theories, relative-wage theories, bargaining theories, fairness theories, insider-outsider theories, implicit contracts, and so on. There is no coherent view of how any of this would work to explain what we know of labor market and wage determination behavior. Solow concludes that economic theory has not done justice to the institutional affective complexity of the labor market.[19]

A paper by Alan B. Krueger and Lawrence H. Summers (1986: 30-31) concludes that "the inter-industry wage structure cannot possibly be interpreted as a competitive outcome." This has significance for both micro- and macro-economic issues. It undermines the classical assumption that markets allocate output in an optimal fashion, renders plausible claims that economies are subject to chronic involuntary unemployment, and casts doubt on the equilibrating properties of the free market.

Thus, the conclusion seems to me to be warranted that within a wide range the individual supply calculus has little effect on the determination of wage and benefit schedules, that microeconomic models (including recent styles and fads) do not well explain the failure of the wage-rate to clear the market, and that wage differentials for essentially the same job classifications tend to persist in the same labor market area. The history of discussions of labor markets and wage setting over a hundred years surely would have led to no other view.

The General Level of Wages

The determination of the general level of wages has had a checkered intellectual history. There are, of course, two histories, one for money wages and the other for real wages, an index of money wages divided by some index of prices. And money wage levels have one story in a closed economy and another in an open economy.

If we leave behind the era of the wage fund, the level of money prices has been thought historically to be related to or determined by the quantity theory of money, and the money wage level could then be derived from the price level, at each level of output and employment, by the aggregate supply of labor forthcoming. An open economy and the gold standard complicated adjustments of wage and price levels in this framework.

In the late 1920s and the 1930s there was extended debate on the issue of whether Great Britain had returned to the gold standard in 1925 at too high a price for the pound relative to the dollar and other currencies, thereby requiring a reduction in British prices and wages to be competitive in world export markets (see Clay 1930: 58-80, 202-03). Unemployment increased. Wages were rigid downward. The resistance to wage cuts fomented widespread industrial strife and contributed to the 1926 general strike in Britain.

In the *General Theory* (1936), by measuring values in wage units, Keynes made it unnecessary to have an explanation for the general level of money wage rates; it was determined outside the system and given by collective bargaining or government fiat.[20] Many economists have protested the use of wage-units as a *numeraire*, but no general statement of determinants of the general level of money wages or their consequences is commonly accepted.

The Money Wage Level

I have always preferred to begin the discussion of the general level of wages with the recognition that the concept is a substantial abstraction, and a vast complex of wage, salary, and benefit structures is the reality. These complexes are one important instance of the rules, that may take a variety of institutional forms, created by a national industrial relations system (see Dunlop and Rothbaum 1955). Moreover, the forms and elements of compensation, and the methods of pay, vary appreciably among many countries. The thirteenth-month pay in Italy, the annual bonus in Japan, the family allowance system in France, and the private pension and health programs in this country are illustrative. The calculation of comparative compensation in two countries is a most difficult research exercise, even for a single type of activity, as anyone has discovered, for instance, who has put his mind seriously to calculating the compensation of Japanese and United States autoworkers.[21]

It is no doubt easier, conceptually, to envisage an index of change in the level of wages, salaries, and benefits than by seeking change in the complex of these rules from one period to another. But when these changes take place in the separate components of compensation in a highly decentralized mode, it is not easy.

In only a few countries is it possible to approximate a general change in the wage level, for only a few countries have had a mechanism to change all or most compensation at the same time. The Australian Court of Conciliation and Arbitration and its general wage cut of 10 percent in January 1931 is one illustration. At times, key national wage bargains in Sweden have spread widely throughout the economy, although the wage ripples or wage drift was not uniform. In the Soviet Union, wage mechanisms are available to decree change of all wages at one time (Kirsch 1972). In a number of developing countries, government employment has been a substantial proportion of total employment subject to government wage decision. But in the United States and most Western countries, a general wage change is only a change in some average measure, such as average hourly earnings, spread over a period with various interactions among sectors to the forces initiating the change. In these circumstances there is no genuine or pure form of a general wage or compensation change. Many factors affect a change in an average hourly earnings index aside from a general change in wage or salary schedules.

Macroeconomists who wish to consider "general wage changes" need to recognize that in this country, and in most countries, there is no way to make such a change, and the interaction and interlocking nature of wage changes among sectors in the total wage surface is rather a matter for an industrial relations specialist. Further, the long duration (three years) of many collective bargaining agreements in the United States often frustrates the macroeconomist seeking to use his tools to influence the wage level or its rate of change.

If one accepts the severe limitations of treating (gross) average hourly earnings in current dollars for production or nonsupervisory workers in the private nonagricultural economy of the United States as a rough proxy for the general wage level, or at least an index of change in the level, then the general wage level since the Great Depression should be regarded as a continuing inclined plane in the upward direction. That index has never fallen from year to year in that period. Average hourly earnings increased over 21 times since 1933 and almost 8 times since 1947. (The CPI increased approximately 8.5 and 5.5 times in the same time periods.)

Even in the widely publicized "concession years" of the 1980s, average hourly earnings continued to rise. One has to go back to the years 1930-32 to find a reduction in aggregate measures, and the reductions were large, 15 percent on an average year-to-year basis and 23 percent if the low point in the spring of 1933 is used. Such figures reflect how far the 1980s are from the experience of the 1930s with regard to wages. There is no price of a producer or consumer good and no price in the financial markets, of which I am aware, that behaved over the past fifty years as average hourly earnings have behaved. The first law of the general level of money wages in our times is that it goes up sometimes rapidly and sometimes more modestly.[22]

Analytical View of the General Level of Money Wages

I have thought that the appropriate general paradigm with which to examine the movement of the level of money wages was to relate the change in gross product (X-axis) or activity (to use Keynes's phrase) to changes in the general level of money wages (Y-axis).[23] At negative rates of increase in gross product, as in a depression, money wages will either increase slightly or may even decline, depending on a mechanism set forth below. At intermediate rates of growth of product or activity, money wages will advance at moderate rates. And at very rapid rates of growth of product, money wages will advance at rapid rates through the mechanisms set forth below. It is not employment and unemployment, as in the Phillips curve, that is decisive to wages, although unemployment may be expected to be appreciable in periods of declining activity. Similarly, employment may be expected to rise with moderate rates of increase in activity, depending on labor force and immigration growth, and unemployment may be expected to be low after periods of rapid growth in activity. (Money wage movements in major sectors of the economy may be looked at through the same schema.)

Only one set of forces ever are effective to *reduce* money wage levels: In some periods of depression, declines in product prices may be of such a magnitude and competition in these product markets of such a character as to compel a reduction in wages. Marginal labor costs exceed price, and the enterprise has no option but to reduce wages or go out of business. This experience is widespread and not confined to marginal enterprises. A general recognition of the reality of these price declines and competition in these product markets eases some of the conflict and pain that accompanies any reduction in wages. Unemployment itself has little if any role in influencing wage reduction behavior except in relatively small establishments. This is a view developed in my *Wage Determination Under Trade Unions* (1944), chapters VI and VII. The same perspective assists in understanding the major sectoral declines in wages and relative readjustments of the 1980s in internationally competitive industries such as basic steel and automobiles, in deregulated sectors such as airlines and trucking, and in some sectors of construction in some localities.

As to increases in the general level of money wages, or increases in major sectors, it is increases in prices, both living costs and those associated with increased business activity (and, most particularly, increased profit margins), that are effective in leading to money wage level increases. At times an increase in margins may be facilitated by contemporaneous or expected increases in labor productivity. It is not the reduction in unemployment that is the active ingredient for wage increases. It is no accident that the criteria of cost-of-living, profits, and productivity are most frequently advanced in negotiations and dispute resolution proceedings for compensation increases, apart from the reference in individual sectors to relativities in "comparable" enterprises.

The Natural Rate of Unemployment

One of the concepts that macroeconomists have developed in the past twenty five years is the "natural rate of unemployment." While various definitions have been developed, for this brief discussion Martin Bailey's (1982: 1) phrasing is suitable: "A unique rate of unemployment exists that is neither too high or too low, and if this rate is maintained, wage inflation will not accelerate." Moreover, this rate can be estimated or found by trial and error, and a clear policy target is available.

But everything we know about labor markets and wage determination explicitly precludes any simple or direct or stable relationship between the general level of wage, salary, or benefit schedules and aggregate unemployment, as in a Phillips curve, or that changes in the age and sex composition of the labor supply are likely to have any systematic effect through a change in the "natural rate of unemployment" on the general level of wage schedules. Inflationary pressures on the price and wage structure of the economy are never uniformly distributed throughout all sectors. It makes a lot of difference to wage changes whether the pressures originate in the heavy industry sector, in construction, in state and local government, in a rise in food prices from agricultural sector developments, or the price changes from exchange rates or import prices. Inflation does not conform to one model. The duration of collective bargaining agreements, the presence of escalator clauses, the regional distribution and relativities involved all will materially influence in any year or two the response within the wage structure and the average hourly earnings level.[24] As argued earlier, just such differential changes in wage structures and benefits are the centerpiece of the problem to be dealt with in wage and price controls. The single, macro wage standard is a conceptual and practical mistake.

Because of the very nature of labor markets and the process of wage determination in Western countries, there can be no single, stable unemployment rate at which wage inflation begins or accelerates.

General Level of Wages and Unemployment

General economics has had two quite different streams of thought over the past fifty years as to the relations between the level of money wages and employment or unemployment, although both views have antecedents to the earliest days of the discipline. Edwin Cannan (1932) in his presidential address to the Royal Economic Society succinctly stated one conclusion: "But general unemployment is in reality to be explained almost in the same way as particular unemployment. . . . General unemployment appears when asking too much is a general phenomenon." The other stream is reflected in the *General Theory* (1936) of John Maynard Keynes. We are all familiar with the intellectual framework, but permit several brief quotations:

> But if the classical theory is not allowed to extend by analogy its conclusion in respect to a particular industry to industry as a whole, it is wholly unable to answer the question what effect on employment a reduction in money wages will have. (p. 260)

We can, therefore, theoretically at least produce precisely the same effects on the rate of interest by reducing wages, whilst leaving the quantity of money unchanged, that we can produce by increasing the quantity of money whilst leaving the level of wages unchanged. (p. 266)

I am now of the opinion that the maintenance of a stable general level of money-wages is, on balance of considerations, the most advisable policy for a closed system; whilst the same conclusion will hold for an open system, provided that equilibrium with the rest of the world can be secured by means of fluctuating exchanges. (p. 270)

An enormous literature developed around the issues of analysis and the practical considerations of private and public policy that are involved in these contending views. For two or three decades it appeared that the intellectual controversy had been largely resolved on the Keynesian side, in part by the absence of deep and continuing recessions, but in recent years the dispute has been revived in both macroeconomics and in academic policy debates. The old arguments reappear with some new terminology.

One instance of the revolt against the Keynesian conclusion is represented by Mancur Olson (1982: 201). He emphasizes:

> *The main group that can have an interest in preventing the mutually profitable transactions between the involuntarily unemployed and employers is the workers with the same or competitive skills. They have a substantial interest in preventing such transactions, for their own wages must be lowered as extra labor pushes the marginal revenue product of labor down. The only way that the existing workers can prevent the mutually advantageous transactions is if they are in one way or another informally able to exert collusive pressure.*

Olson attributes the failure to achieve full employment to imperfections and monopoly power in labor and product markets, and he finds the "ultimate source" of the problem with Keynes's analysis to be that it did not explain "the inflexibility of many wages or prices" (1982: 230). This brings us back to the notion that the labor market is, or should behave as, a bourse. Labor markets have never behaved and are inherently incapable of behaving as Mancur Olson would like.

The European Experience in the 1980s

The persistence of high unemployment in the 1980s in Europe, in particular, has spawned a resurgence of views that high wage rates and "rigid" labor markets are uniquely responsible for the unemployment. The argument takes various forms with various new terms. According to Blanchard and Summers, hysteresis and the European unemployment problem are generated by the behavior of "insiders" as compared to "outsiders" in employment. "If wage bargaining is a prevalent feature of the labor market, the dynamic interactions between employment and the size of the group of insiders may generate substantial employment and unemployment persistence" (1986: 16). Aside from the fact that the distinction between insiders and outsiders in wage discussions is as old as the hills (Dunlop 1944: chapter III), it is a long way to relate the idea to European unemployment when there are a wide range of countries and quite different bargaining structures. According to J. Sachs (1983), the unemployment in European countries, sometimes labeled Euro-sclerosis, is directly derived from the lack of competitive adaptability in its labor markets.

A restatement of the Keynesian conclusion is provided in a paper by Robert M. Solow (1986) that reviews theoretical issues suggested by the debate over European unemployment. He emphasizes that "groups of workers and employers cannot bargain over the real wage," only the money wage. Further, the view that the money wage is too high is no more analytically valid than the statement that the money supply is too low.

As might be expected, the resurgence of opinion attributing unemployment to lack of labor market competition has had considerable political expression, as in the London statement of heads of government of Western countries that called for much greater flexibility in labor markets.

A more detailed and balanced presentation on the subject is found in three statements developed by the OECD. The first is a joint statement by the Business and Industry Advisory Committee and the Trade Union Advisory Committee to the OECD; the second is a report of a high-level group of experts to the secretary-general that stresses the enormous differences among countries and the wide range of measures that may be appropriate; the third is a technical report by the Secretariat.[25] The views of these current OECD reports stand in stark contrast to the simplicity and imperialism of macroeconomic prescriptions in the pattern of treating problems as common among countries.

Summary Statement: Structure and Level of Wages

The following is a summary statement of how I have sought to understand the behavior of wage and benefit schedules, wage differentials, and the wage level outside the limits of competitive theory.

1. It is product market differentiations of enterprises, profit or non-profit, that are fundamental for wage differentials by enterprise as reflected into the labor market. It is seldom if ever true that an enterprise, or even an establishment, produces a single output, product or service. The segmentation of market products in an enterprise under different competitive market

pressures creates differentiation in wages, or pressures for such differentiation, even though job classifications are indistinguishable. Thus, tire plants have more inelastic demand than most industrial rubber or rubber shoe plants of the same company, regardless of location. Drug departments of a food chain store have different markets than meat, produce, or grocery. A plastics plant making optical glasses is competitively quite different from one manufacturing plastic kitchenware. Heavy and highway construction is competitively different from central city commercial construction, and branches of the local trucking industry face very different markets.

The tendency of competitive pressures in the product market to compartmentalize the labor market always confronts administrators of enterprises, companies, and multi-employer groups in a community or nationally. This is true with collective bargaining or without. In defining the scope of wage uniformity, there is always tension between these competitive product market forces and the administrative pressures from managements acting alone or in collective bargaining. The simplest illustration is the tension between the administrative internal job evaluation plan of an enterprise and the hierarchy of wages for job classifications reflected in the market. The uniformity of wages for a job classification for multi-establishments of an enterprise or multi-employer groups reflect the same sort of tensions.

At times, market forces reduce and constrain the scope of the wage contour, or subdivide it into several wage levels, overcoming contrary administrative pressures. At times, market forces permit areas of expanded uniformity, yielding to administrative interests. In times of most intense product market competition, as in deep and continuing recession, these differentiations are multiplied and extended. Very tight and prolonged high employment, with associated enterprise and product market conditions, tends to make for a larger scope of uniformity and lesser differentiation.

The statistical organization of wage data, (that is, average hourly earnings) into SIC codes to conform to very broad product classifications thus misses the extent of product market differentiation and is reflected in a wide spread and diffusion of earnings in the labor market for the reported industry groupings. The differences between wages in large and small enterprises in part reflects genuinely different product markets. Localities comprised of a number of industrial groupings accordingly tend to reflect even wider dispersion for a given job classification.

Labor market influences are not to be excluded entirely in their influences on differentials by enterprise, although in the main their influence is relatively passive. Methods of wage payment may vary; locations in a locality or region may play a role; work operations and job requirements may have subtle differences; product market influence on wages may result in management or collective bargaining policy to adapt to the wage established; and so on.

2.   In a dynamic sense, with the passage of time, new industries, enterprises, or occupations may be expected to come into a locality at somewhat higher rates in order to recruit or attract labor. A rapid expansion of a smaller existing enterprise may have some impact, but generally of a smaller nature. The consequence is more differentiation in the locality and industry. The spread is likely to be preserved as future general increases are made, save in the event of significant adverse product market developments.

3.   It is important to specify the ways in which "social and expectational" elements, to use Hicks's phrase, operate to affect wage determination and wage differentials even in the "free market," beyond "supply and demand." Social elements are not entirely unyielding, but it may take very powerful market forces to violate them. It is not appropriate simply to treat deviations from the free market as unexplained residuals, frictions, or imperfections and label them "social elements."

In the inter-enterprise wage relationship, particularly among closely related product markets, social factors in the form of relativities and approved norms, often reflected in historical wage relationships, play a role in setting and providing legitimacy to wage differentials.

In intra-enterprise wage relationships, the internal labor market, with its detailed administrative rules, arranges the hierarchy of wage rates and relates them explicitly to the movement among job classifications—hiring-in points, transfers, promotion ladders, et cetera.

In earlier writing (Dunlop 1957), my concepts of wage contours and job clusters were designed to reflect the way "social and expectational elements" enter systematically into wage structure determination. They have had explicit correspondence in wage stabilization programs and their detailed regulations; in that sense the concepts have proved to be administrable, even though they may not conform to concepts of microeconomists.

4.   As to the money wage level, the record of the past fifty years is unequivocal; the money wage level only goes up; the rate of increase in a given economic setting may be in doubt.

Only major changes in the competitive position of the economy, or in a major sector, that force down product prices can be expected to reduce the wage level either at the aggregate level or in a major sector. Unemployment, even massive unemployment, is not likely by itself to be effective to reduce wages. This result is not contingent on formal labor organization, but is derived from the costs in morale, productivity, replacements, workplace relations, and in social approbrium. Prolonged unemployment, measured in years, is likely to have more effect than shorter-term periods out of work.

Increases in the money wage level are likely to be related within relatively narrow limits to increases in prices, particularly as measured by the CPI. Increases in labor productivity and increases in profits are likely to have some effect in a far less focused way.

In part, the wage structure and level march to the drummer of the economy, but in part they march to a separate beat, that of the industrial relations drummer.

Old and New Methods: "The Medium is the Message"

The method of approach to a problem often predisposes analysis, results, and also prescription. The methods used to explore the behavior of labor markets and wage structures of the 1930–50s were very different from those in fashion in the 1970–80s.

The earlier period produced a large number of individual case studies of labor markets that involved gathering of statistical cross-section and time series data; extensive interviews with large numbers of managers, labor union officers, workers and their families, and some government representatives, in an attempt to relate migration, hiring, turnover, and separation data in establishments to other characteristics; and in the end, teasing from this material generalizations concerning the operation of particular and various types of labor markets. The studies of Lloyd Reynolds of New Haven, Clark Kerr of the wartime Seattle, and Richard Lester of Trenton and of company-wide wage policies all illustrate this method. Some coordination and exchange of views over the method of such studies and their results was provided by the Labor Market Committee of the Social Science Research Council and the leadership of Paul Webbink.

The study of wages was conducted with very much the same methods, except that substantial data were available from the Bureau of Labor Statistics, labor unions and trade associations, and local employer organizations with periodic wage and benefit surveys. Extensive field work within a sector or area was requisite.

Some consequences of this approach to labor markets and wage determination were that the researcher, and students, came into firsthand contact with various levels of management, community institutions, labor organizations, and workers. Aside from gathering data from records or questionnaires, they were able to ask questions and appraise responses. They heard about scores of factors and considerations they had never envisaged. At an early stage in their careers, graduate students came to appreciate the complexity of behavior of labor market institutions. They came to have impressions about how management and labor organizations operate. The history of ideas in the literature over the long past was also a required part of an education in labor market related behavior. The students were more broadly and more generally trained. Experience became an enforcer of intellectual humility.

In contrast, the almost invariant method of the contemporary era seems to be to take some fact or casual observation that happens to strike the microeconomist, create an analytical explanation that might be regarded as plausible, draw data from the CPS surveys (or occasionally from the establishment survey), run various regressions, and publish. The fact that Henry Ford decided to pay five dollars a day, a rate apparently above the market, stimulates the notion of an efficiency wage explanation for wage differences; the fact that the unemployed take different time periods in finding jobs creates a complex of constructs of search theory; the observation that some employees, like certain ones in Japan, stay with a single employer for very long periods generates the implicit contract boom. The classic problem of compensating differentials in jobs generated by health and safety risks, working conditions, and so on generates efforts to measure these differentials as a major component of wage differentials; the suggestion that wages may be used as a substitute for supervision and that unemployment serves as a device to generate worker discipline leads to other constructs.

This process almost never confronts a real labor market, a real workplace, or real participants in the market. The crucial test is statistical congruence or compatibility with the general corpus of microeconomic theory, not its capacity to illuminate the full range of labor market behavior or to provide an explanation for wage decisions. If the pursuit of understanding of labor markets and wages proceeds in this way, the inevitable results are those that are achieved.

The fact is that these recently advertised ideas usually have a long history in the literature. Thus the "efficiency wage" concept is a very old idea in various forms that appears widely in wage determination literature. J.W.F. Rowe's *Wages in Practice and Theory* (1928: 212–25) has an extended discussion.[26] The notion that wages may be used as a substitute for the costs of supervision is an idea that may have some validity through the substitution of piecework for day work, as in cotton textiles or in the early stages of economic development, but as a general basis for wage setting the idea is scarcely worthy of consideration.

A special word needs to be said concerning the limitations of recent investigations with the CPS surveys that emerged in the 1970s. It is no accident that the formalization of human capital theory after 1960 and the social concerns with discrimination and equal employment opportunities found the CPS longitudinal and cross-section data reinforcing. Data in one place on age, sex, race, union affiliation, educational level, broad occupational category, and a measure of ordinary earnings proved to be irresistible. While these categories are significant to some issues, such as discrimination, as developed in the previous section the judgment must be that they are not very instructive in understanding wage schedule determination.

Information reported by household interviews when compared with employer records reveal substantial variation on a number of matters. The occupational and industry classifications that are pivotal for understanding wage setting have been found to be particularly unreliable.[27] Household respondents reported hourly earnings within 10 percent of the employer's records only 60 percent of the time, and the employee was within that limit only 72 percent of the time. Not a basis to construct much of a wage theory! I am no less concerned that interview data in no way secures wage or salary schedule data but rather averages that reflect administration of wage schedules, even if the reports are an accurate representation of employer records.

The quest in labor market and wage structure research is to identify the factors influencing results, the direction of effect, and a general sense of large or small under various circumstances. There are no quantitative constants or universal coefficients in labor market or wage structure operations such as the speed of light or pi. Within one period, or over the course of economic fluctuations, the magnitude of these influences and determinants is likely to show considerable variation. Interindustry, interregion, and intercountry comparison can be stimulating, but there are no constants. While econometric methods may be helpful even in this setting, the comparative advantage over the older methods is likely to be doubtful and small, and the exclusive preoccupation with the restricted and focused current method is at considerable disadvantage as compared to the wide-ranging methods of the earlier period in discovering how labor markets and wage determination operate.

It is tragic that contemporary microeconomists show no familiarity with the vast wealth of wage data beyond a few CPS or special tapes prepared by the Bureau of Labor Statistics. In the study of wage differentials and wage structures there are vast opportunities in the compensation surveys that are maintained by groups of businesses and nonprofit employers, and occasionally by parties to collective bargaining, in almost every major metropolitan area or state or industry, showing ranges and averages for large numbers of defined job classifications and specified establishments.[28] The Boston Wage Survey has been conducted for over thirty years with more than thirty enterprises and more than one-hundred-eighty job classifications. There are similar data bases in Central Massachusetts and Springfield, Massachusetts, and so on. A number of national or regional trade associations, professional associations, and consulting firms have maintained compensation surveys for years. Among these are the American Compensation Survey, the Hewitt Associates Compensation Exchange, American Society for Personnel Administration and A.S. Hansen Survey of Personnel and Industrial Relations Positions, the work of Hay Associates, and so on. Seldom, if ever, have I seen reference to these sources or to their use by academics. The methods of research have severely restricted even statistical sources in the universe of data.

My most serious concern is with the development of young scholars, many of whom have considerable ability. The path of the youth of each generation is influenced significantly by sources of funding, research methods, and the hurdles for academic standing and tenure. These influences are creating a generation largely devoid of contact with labor market institutions and the setting of wages. In a few instances they may come into contact with research personnel, not line officers. The reliance upon econometric methods and related techniques, admittedly essential as one phase of training, is creating a generation of labor economists inappropriately suited to address the problems that investigations are always confronted with by labor market institutions. The current generation is being trained so that they have so much to unlearn. The modern medium is not the message.

Contrasts in Approach to Policy

Pat Choate (1986: 134) has well said, "If your only tool is a hammer, everything else in the world tends to look like a nail. Accordingly, most economists narrowly view the manipulation of fiscal, monetary, trade, and exchange rate policies as the only economic tools available."

The earlier period thrust research into labor markets and wage structures into the center of policy debate and decisions on account of the urgent problems and issues requiring practical decisions, such as: (1) What should be the minimum wage of a sector, between thirty and forty cents an hour, and how do wages above the minimum adjust to an increase at the low end? (2) What compensation standards should be set in a wage and price control program in wartime? (3) What wage decisions should be made in major labor–management disputes as in basic steel, coal mining, railroads, maritime, and so on? (4) In an era of high and prolonged unemployment or in periods of very tight labor markets as in wartime, how do labor markets operate, and what policies can be developed to facilitate their functions? (5) With rapid migrations from farm to city and to the Sunbelt, and with shifting location of industry, what are appropriate private and public labor market policies? (6) What policies are appropriate to reducing discrimination on account of race, sex, or age?

It should be noted that the earlier period (1930–60) had the great advantage of seeing labor markets with the greatest and most prolonged unemployment and the tightest labor markets we have probably ever experienced, all in a span of ten to fifteen years. This had to be instructive. The current period has had no comparable range of variation.

Research into wage structures and labor markets in the more recent period appears to me to have no comparable actionable focus, and the significant policy questions under debate relate more to broad policy issues of inflation, trade, taxes, deficits, exchange rates, and macroeconomics. So microeconomics has been expanding into labor markets and wage structure determination, propelled not by the discipline and direction of practical problems but rather by a deep conservative, market-oriented bias, among many participants. Because research has not been compelled to concentrate on many real issues, and the researchers themselves have had no relation or responsibility for solutions, unlike an earlier day, they appear rather aimless and remote. Moreover, private and public policymakers of the present day have not found the view or advice of microeconomists generally to be helpful or influential (see Dunlop, 1977; Rees, 1977).

This contrast with an earlier era is reflected not merely in the specialist in labor markets, but in the general economist as well. I invite you to re-read J.M. Clark's guide (1949: 147–77) to labor and management as to appropriate wage policy. I remind you that Alvin H. Hansen advocated a set of guidelines for separate industries with productivity changes at different rates (see Dunlop 1948b). I am at a loss to find any comparable specific suggestions or advice to private parties, in collective bargaining or for management alone, among general economists today that deserves to command respect or attention.

Consider illustrative policy issues of our times that involve some attention to labor markets and wages: unemployment of minority youth, inflation in health charges and costs, high unemployment rates in Europe, and the state of the American economy. What do we get today out of micro- and macroeconomics to deal with these issues? Much of the time we read: reduce the minimum wage; introduce more deductibles and co-payments into health care and take away tax exemptions for insurance premium fringes; reduce real wages in Europe and make European labor markets more flexible (whatever that means), and in the United States rely on a monetarist policy and supply-side tax policy.

Fortunately there are academics and practitioners working on such problems who suggest more viable approaches growing out of a general familiarity with the institutions and how they work. The new students need to see more of them. Richard Freeman writes with respect to black youth unemployment: "Major progress will not be possible without a strengthening of public and private social institutions, ranging from schools, churches and community organizations, to the welfare and criminal justice systems." Institutional changes in health care brought about by HMOs, PPOs, new roles for management and labor, and even new regulatory arrangements (DRGs) are reducing rates of increase in charges. The OECD report of a high-level group of experts has a very different set of policy recommendations for European unemployment. As to our domestic economic problems, Paul Volcker has said, "A single, broad-brush policy instrument cannot, at one and the same time, restrain excessive debt creation and shift resources away from consumption and back into investment, manufacturing, and exports—as desirable and important as all those goals may be."

In sum, the research of the earlier period, and the training of young scholars, was directly derived from and related to policy issues of the era. The scholars of that period, by the methods of research, had to become acquainted with labor market institutions, enterprises, and labor organizations alike, and how they functioned generally. The immediate focus of research yielded a larger range of knowledge. The connections to policy issues were fairly direct and often involved the same people. In the current period, the focus of interest has been to seek to expand the main body of analytical microeconomics through econometric methods, irrespective of relevance or applicability. At no time in the research or training of younger scholars do they come into contact with labor market institutions, and they have little knowledge of the vast literature prior to the past decade or two.

Autobiographical Note

Professor Charles A. Gulick, Jr., taught my first semester course in labor economics at the University of California, Berkeley, in my junior year in 1933–34. Solomon Blum's textbook was the most general reading. A subsequent seminar required the reading and critical discussion of such classics as Sidney and Beatrice Webb, *Industrial Democracy*; Selig Perlman, *A Theory of the Labor Movement*; Thorstein Veblen, *The Theory of Business Enterprise*; selections from John R. Commons, and inevitably Gulick's interest in the Austrian labor movement.

In my first year of graduate work at Berkeley, 1935–36, in addition to teaching sections in a senior course in statistics, I was most interested in the course in economic theory taught by Leo Rogin and that on ethics taught by George P. Adams in the Philosophy department. In my second graduate year, 1936–37, I moved to Stanford and taught two quarters of my first labor economics course. I attended Jacob Viner's course on economic theory and returned on Wednesdays to Berkeley for Frank H. Knight on the new *General Theory* of John Maynard Keynes. After I completed the general examinations, a Social Science Research Council predoctoral fellowship permitted me to spend the academic year 1937–38 at Cambridge University, England, reading economics, arguing with Piero Sraffa and others at tea, and working on a thesis topic on wages. In September 1938, thanks to a suggestion from John Kenneth Galbraith, I arrived in Cambridge, Massachusetts, as a teaching fellow, and have been based there ever since.

My first visit to Washington, D.C., was in the summer of 1938. Working on a dollar-a-year basis in the Bureau of Labor Statistics, I examined additional wage data for the dissertation in more detail than permitted by published industry studies on an establishment and job classification basis. Work then followed with the BLS and the Temporary National Economic Committee, the Cost–Price Committee of the National Bureau of Economic Research, and then with the National War Labor Board.

The doctor's degree was awarded from Berkeley in 1939. Five chapters of the thesis were separately published, including my first article, "The Movement of Real and Money Wage Rates," *Economic Journal*, September 1938.

The preface to the dissertation begins with a theme that has been a constant in my work from those days:

> It has frequently been said that there is a tendency in the social sciences, particulary in Economics, towards the development of "a very deep hiatus between the more empirically and theoretically minded workers. The tendency of a complete divorce, a mutual repudiation of the legitimacy, of each other's work and interest . . . is disquieting" (Talcott Parsons). The following study of wage-rate movements in business fluctuations is intended as an illustration of the fruitfulness of the interaction of empirical material and analytical models.

In 1940 I began to teach in the undergraduate labor economics course at Harvard with Sumner H. Slichter, and the following year and thereafter until the 1970s, the instruction of Harvard undergraduates in the field was primarily my responsibility and enjoyment. The graduate course and the seminar to bring outside guests weekly to Harvard was a continuing academic assignment beginning after World War II. The supervision of approximately a hundred Ph.D. dissertations over these years, mainly in the field of labor economics and a few in health economics, has contributed importantly to my own insights. Teaching in the Harvard Trade Union Program since its establishment in 1942 has enriched my understanding of the labor movement, its strengths and limitations. Interfaculty responsibilities and executive programs helped me to appreciate the contributions of the mainstream of the Law School, Business School, School of Government, School of Public Health, and so on to the field of labor economics and industrial relations, and helped to attract a wider range of students to the issues.

A series of different patterns of experience outside the classroom, and reflection on these activities, were to stimulate and to shape my ideas respecting economics, labor and product markets, wages and prices, business organizations and their decision making, labor organizations, industrial relations, and government. Among the more important activities were the following:[29]

1.   My work with the War Labor Board started in 1943 as director of research and statistics. My responsibility was to work with the Bureau of Labor Statistics and generate wage data appropriate for the operation and

evaluation of the wage stabilization program. Soon my interests and opportunities shifted to dispute settlement, negotiations and mediation, national economic and stabilization policy for wartime and the postwar, the relations of wages and prices, governmental processes, and collective bargaining institutions and their consequences. The period with the War Labor Board (including vice-chairman of the New England regional board and public member of the construction agency) and the direct association with William H. Davis, George W. Taylor, David L. Cole, and Nathan P. Feinsinger was a rare opportunity. A lifetime of learning and acquisition of labor–management–government know-how was crowded into a few intensive years. The close association with George W. Taylor and David L. Cole was to continue for years in a variety of professional activities (the Korean War National Wage Stabilization Board, the Kaiser Steel Long Rage Committee, the New York Commission on Public Employees, et cetera). The War Labor Board experience led naturally to extensive arbitration, mediation, and dispute resolution in a very wide range of industries and types of arbitration, umpire posts, and interest arbitration, and to assignments on boards of inquiry and emergency boards, and to various governmental commissions.

2. The Inter-University Study of Labor Problems in Economic Development, with Clark Kerr, Frederick H. Harbison, and Charles A. Myers, and a large number of associates, provided an additional intellectual focus in the 1950s and 1960s building upon a long-term interest in developments overseas. Our *Industrialism and Industrial Man* (1960), and various revisions and commentaries, stressed at an early stage the importance of a comparative, developmental, and analytical approach to industrial relations and labor markets. The interuniversity projects involved considerable travel and direct comparisons of overseas experience. *Industrial Relations Systems* (1958), written in the International Labor Office in Geneva, sought to make one analytical world of a rich experience in the United States and the international and economic development perspective. The organization of an international conference on wages for the International Economic Association (1954) and a half-dozen conferences in the 1960s with the Soviets and Eastern Europeans and U.S. and Western European economists on labor productivity, wages, market, and planned economies had to be broadening experiences.

3. The aggregate impact was substantial from fourteen years, in whole or part, enmeshed in the formulation and administration of wage and price controls in four programs (World War II, Korean War, the 1971–74 construction program and Phases III and IV of the Cost of Living Council, 1973–74, and the Carter wage standards, 1979–81). One should learn a bit about wage and price decisions from responsibility in such programs.

4. The editorship of the Wertheim Series of volumes on industrial relations has provided an opportunity to encourage Ph.D. students, colleagues, and associates to develop themes in labor history and union governance,

comparative international studies, collective bargaining in various industries, wage structures, and the like. In the period from 1945 to 1985, the series added fifty volumes. Each study has been an opportunity to work closely with a research project and to learn more about labor market institutions and how they operate in various circumstances.

5. In the late 1960s and 1970s, inside and outside the university, executive and managerial responsibilities provided new levels of relationships in business, government, and labor, new understandings of the processes of public and private decision making, and new insight into a variety of issues vital to academic discourse and the interactions of these organizations in the American policy and economy. These experiences ranged from dean of the faculty in turbulent times, membership on the board of directors of companies and nonprofit organizations, director of wage and price controls, a cabinet-level position in the federal government, state government responsibilities, health care organization activity, and the mediation of a very wide range of disputes. Interaction with the press is a vital aspect of all of these positions.

The perspectives formed from this wide range of experience inevitably provide personal insights, as well as scars, concerning private and public organizations, their internal processes and values, and their interactions. The preceding account may make more understandable the judgment that the imperialism and rigor of much recent economics related to labor markets and wage determination is little relevant to the understanding of real decisions.

Postscript

After participating in the Conference on "How Labor Markets Work" and reflecting on the commentaries, the following summary judgments are offered.

The work of the 1930–60 period on labor markets and wage determination was in the mainstream of economics and an extension of still earlier mainstream work. It was not an institutional sideshow. The major figures in the discipline accepted the reported description of the operation of labor markets and the determination of wage structures and the wage level and the legitimacy of the analytical implications.

The more recent work with newer methods and data, largely on the supply side, does not detract from "the apparently small impact of supply on the wage structure and the importance of employer wage policy in wage determination" (Richard Freeman). Supply has a role, of course, affecting hours worked and mediating the long-term effects of population, age cohorts, and professional manpower changes. But it rarely has impact on wage and benefit schedules set in the shorter term.

I cannot accept the assertion of some economists that purely competitive models yield better predictions as to wage structures and the operation of labor markets than "more realistic" theories of an earlier day. Such competitive models are not useful in the analysis of practical problems confronting private or public decision makers, in my experience. They flunk the test of relevance to the compensation landscape. Moreover, contemporary mainstream economists (for example, Samuelson, Solow, and Tobin) have expressed the view that competitive models are inappropriate to labor markets.

Notes

1. It should be recognized that this distinction is vital to the formulation and administration of wage controls. Hundreds of economists and industrial relations specialists of an earlier era were trained in the importance of this distinction. The War Labor Board, and later wage control agencies, developed separate regulations to govern these types of wage decisions. See U.S. Department of Labor, *The Termination Report, National War Labor Board*, Washington, D.C., 1947, vol. 2. Compare General Orders No. 5 and No. 6 (pp. 169–71) and No. 31 (pp. 207–13) with increases in wages, salaries, and benefit schedules requiring pre-approval.

2. In 1980 Robert E. Hall (1980: 120) concluded that "There is no point any longer in pretending that the labor market is an auction market cleared by the observed hourly wage."

3. See *Staff Report of the President's Panel on Federal Compensation*, Washington, D.C., 1976. Vice-President Nelson A. Rockefeller was chairman of the panel and John T. Dunlop was a member.

4. For evidence on the cyclical behavior of the wage structure, see Dunlop (1939: 30–9; 1944: chapter VII).

5. Reynolds and Taft (1956), Lester (1946), Slichter (1950), Segal (1960), Hildebrand (1963), Rees and Shultz (1970), Kerr (1977).

6. See Reynolds (1947). The conference was initiated and arranged by a subcommittee consisting of John T. Dunlop, Richard A. Lester, Charles A. Myers, and Lloyd G. Reynolds. Clark Kerr was a member of the Committee on Labor Market Research that included in 1947 J. Douglas Brown, chairman, E. Wight Bakke, Phillip M. Hauser, Gladys L. Palmer, Carroll L. Shartle, Dale Yoder, and Paul Webbink, staff.

7. In 1979 the general freight and parcel delivery drivers were at the top at $10.15, rates for magazines were at $9.85, and rates for newspapers were at $8.84, while wastepaper was the bottom at $6.30. The general freight and parcel delivery driver rates since the 1960s are nationally, not locally, determined.

8. See U.S. Department of Labor, *The Termination Report, National War Labor Board*, Washington, D.C., 1948, vol. I, section II, p. 829–1213, and vol. III for a review of these specialized agencies.

9. *Report of the Presidential Railroad Commission*, Washington, D.C., February 1962. Charles A. Myers was also a public member.

10. For an elaboration of these views, see Dunlop (1975; 1981) and Dunlop and Fedor (1977).

11. Also see the *Economic Stabilization Program Quarterly Reports*, Cost of Living Council, 1971–74.

12. These studies are discussed in Lewis (1963).

13. See Hildebrand (1958), Lewis (1963), and Freeman and Medoff (1981).

14. See, for example, Walker (1956) and Leiserson (1959). There are fifteen volumes in the series on industrial relations systems in other countries.

15. See, for example, Robertson (1960) and Knowles and Hill (1956).

16. Also see Harbison and Myers (1959).

17. Also see Harbison (1954), Wilcock and Sobel (1958), Myers and Shultz (1951), and Bakke (1954).

18. For an elaboration of this approach to labor markets, see Freeman (1972: 4–7).

19. Similarly, I concluded (1944: 5) "One of the more dangerous habits of mind that economic theory may create is an imperialism that insists that all aspects of behavior, particularly any activity related to markets, can be explained by models with the usual economic variables. . . . A basic perspective of these pages, therefore, is that wider analytical models than economic theory must be constructed for successful explanation of even market-oriented behavior."

20. See Keynes (1936: 40–5) and a letter written to me by Keynes dated April 1938.

21. See Labor–Management Group, *The Competitiveness of the U.S. Automobile Industry*, July 31, 1984 (unpublished).

22. In earlier periods the wage level behaved quite differently. See Long (1960), and Rees (1961).

23. I have often discussed these issues with Professor James S. Duesenberry and have much profited from his comments.

24. For earlier statements of this view, see Dunlop (1957: 416–7; 1959: 149–60). I sought to identify the sectors with the highest diffusion rating, spreading cost and price increases through the system.

25. See, respectively, *Full Employment and Growth as the Social and Economic Goal, A Joint Statement by BIAC and TUAC*, (1986); OECD, *Labour Market Flexibility, Report of a High Level Group of Experts to the Secretary-General*, (1986); and OECD, Manpower and Social Affairs Committee, *Technical Report by the Secretariat of Labour Market Flexibility*, (July 29, 1986). The latter study is an excellent one.

26. Dunlop (1957: 13, footnote 1) traces the discussion of this idea back through Slichter, Rowe, H.L. Moore, Alfred Marshall, and Francis A. Walker. Slichter (1919: 277) observes, for example, "The employer does not wish a workman who is simply *willing* to work at the wages he receives. He wishes a workman who enters into his work with some degree of pleasure and enthusiasm, who is pleased with his job and his employer, who takes a genuine interest in his work and has a feeling of good will toward his employer. . . . The good will and loyalty of workmen cannot be obtained by paying them simply the bare amount they are willing to work for, the minimum which the market compels the employer to pay."

27. See Mellow and Sider (1983) and Bureau of Labor Statistics, *Weekly and Hourly Earnings Data from the CPS*, Special Labor Force Report 195 (1977).

28. For a historical reference, see Tolles and Raimon (1952). A more recent discussion is provided by the series of papers contained in the section "Sources of Labor Statistics in an Era of Budget Cutbacks: What are the Alternative Sources for IR Data?" Industrial Relations Research Association, *Proceedings of the Thirty-Eighth Annual Meeting* (Madison, Wis.: IRRA: 26–51).

29. See Publisher's Forward in Dunlop (1984a) for more detailed listing.

References

Bailey, Martin Neil. 1982. *Workers, Jobs, and Inflation*. Washington, D.C.: Brookings Institution.

Bakke, E. Wight. 1940. *The Unemployed Worker: A Study of the Task of Making a Living without a Job*. New Haven: Yale University Press.

———. 1954. *Labor Mobility and Economic Opportunity*. New York: John Wiley.

Blanchard, Oliver, and Lawrence Summers. 1986. "Hysteresis and the European Unemployment Problem." Harvard Institute of Economic Research, Discussion Paper 1240.

Brown, E.H. Phelps, and Margaret H. Browne. 1968. *A Century of Pay: The Course of Pay and Production in France, Germany, Sweden, the United Kingdom and the United States, 1860–1960*. London: Macmillan.

Cairnes, J.E. 1874. *Some Leading Principles of Political Economy, Newly Expounded*. London: Macmillan.

Cannan, Edwin. 1932. "The Demand for Labor." *Economic Journal*, September, 357–70.

Choate, Pat. 1986. *The High-Flex Society*. New York: Alfred Knopf.

Clark, John M. 1949. *Guideposts in Time of Change: Some Essentials for a Sound American Economy*. New York: Harper.

Clay, Henry. 1930. *The Post-War Unemployment Problem*. London: Macmillan.

Doeringer, Peter, and Michael Piore. 1971. *Internal Labor Markets and Manpower Analysis*. Lexington, Mass.: Lexington Books.

Douglas, Paul. 1930. *Real Wages in the United States 1890–1926*. Boston, Mass.: Houghton Mifflin.

Douty, H.M. 1984. "A Century of Wage Statistics: The BLS Contribution." *Monthly Labor Review*, November, 16–28.

Dunlop, John T. 1939. "Cyclical Variations in Wage Structure." *Review of Economics and Statistics*, February, 30–9.

———. 1944. *Wage Determination Under Trade Unions*. New York: Macmillan.

———. 1948a. "The Development of Labor Organization: A Theoretical Framework." In Richard Lester and Joseph Shister, eds. *Insights into Labor Issues*, 163–93. New York: Macmillan.

――――. 1948b. "Productivity and the Wage Structure." In *Income, Employment, and Public Policy, Essays in Honor of Alvin H. Hansen*, 341–62. New York: Norton.

――――. 1957. "The Task of Contemporary Wage Theory." In John T. Dunlop, ed., *The Theory of Wage Determination*, 3–27. London: Macmillan.

――――. 1958. *Industrial Relations Systems*. New York: Henry Holt.

――――. 1959. "Policy Problems: Choices and Proposals." In C.A. Myers, ed., *Wages, Prices, Profits, and Productivity*, 137–60. New York: The American Assembly.

――――. 1966. "Job Vacancy Measures and Economic Analysis." In *The Measurement and Interpretation of Job Vacancies*, 27–47. New York: National Bureau of Economic Research.

――――. 1975. "Inflation and Incomes Policy: The Political Economy of Recent U.S. Experience." *Public Policy*, Spring, 135–66.

――――. 1977. "Policy Decisions and Research in Economics and Industrial Relations." *Industrial and Labor Relations Review*, April, 275–82.

――――. 1981. "The Incomes-Policy Alternative: Some Comments." In *The Conference Board, Colloquium on Alternatives for Economic Policy*, 66–69. New York: Conference Board.

――――. 1984a. *Dispute Resolution: Negotiation and Consensus Building*. Dover, Mass.: Auburn House.

――――. 1984b. "Industrial Relations and Economics: The Common Frontier of Wage Determination." Industrial Relations Research Association, *Proceedings of the Thirty-Seventh Annual Meeting*, 9–23. Madison, Wis.: IRRA.

Dunlop, John T., and Kenneth J. Fedor. 1977. *The Lessons of Wage and Price Controls—The Food Sector*. Cambridge: Harvard University Press.

Dunlop, John T., and James J. Healy. 1953. *Collective Bargaining: Principles and Cases*. Revised edition. Homewood, Ill. Irwin.

Dunlop, John T., and Melvin Rothbaum. 1955. "International Comparisons of Wage Structures." *International Labour Review*, April, 347–63.

Fisher, Lloyd. 1953. *The Harvest Labor Market in California*. Cambridge: Harvard University Press.

Freeman, Richard. 1972. *Labor Economics*, 2d ed. Englewood Cliffs, N.J.: Prentice-Hall.

――――. 1984. "The Structure of Labor Markets: A Book Review Three Decades Later." In Gustav Ranis, et al., eds., *Comparative Development Perspectives*, 201–26. Boulder: Westview.

Freeman, Richard, and James Medoff. 1981. "The Impact of Collective Bargaining: Illusion or Reality?" In Jack Stieber, et al., eds., *U.S. Industrial Relations 1950–1980: A Critical Assessment*, 47–48. Madison, Wis.: IRRA.

Garbarino, Joseph. 1950. "A Theory of Inter-Industry Wage Structure Variation." *Quarterly Journal of Economics*, May, 233–305.

Gomberg, William. 1955. *A Trade Union Analysis of Time Study*, 2d ed. Englewood Cliffs, N.J.: Prentice–Hall.

Goodwin, Craufurd D. 1975. *Exploration and Control: The Search for a Wage–Price Policy, 1945–1971*. Washington, D.C.: The Brookings Institution.

Hall, Robert E. 1980. "Employment Fluctuations and Wage Rigidity." *Brookings Papers on Economic Activity*, vol. 1, 91–123.

Hicks, John R. 1963. *The Theory of Wages*. 2d ed. New York: St. Martin's Press.

Hildebrand, George. 1958. "The Economic Effects of Unions." In Neil Chamberlain, et al., eds., *A Decade of Industrial Relations Research 1946–56, An Appraisal of the Literature in the Field*, Madison, Wis.: IRRA. 98–145.

———. 1963. "External Influences and the Determination of the Internal Wage Structure." In J.L. Meij, ed., *Internal Wage Structure*, 260–99. Amsterdam: North Holland.

Hill, Samuel, and Frederick Harbison. 1959. *Manpower and Innovation in American Industry*. Princeton, N.J.: Industrial Relations Section.

Kerr, Clark. 1942. *Migration to the Seattle Labor Market Area*. Westport, Conn.: Greenwood Press.

———. 1954. "The Balkanization of Labor Markets." In E. Wight Bakke, ed., *Labor Mobility and Economic Opportunity*, 92–110. Cambridge, Mass.: The Technology Press of MIT.

———. 1977. *Labor Markets and Wage Determination*. Berkeley: University of California Press.

Kerr, Clark, John Dunlop, Frederick Harbison, and Charles Myers. 1960. *Industrialism and Industrial Man*. Cambridge: Harvard University Press.

Kerr, Clark, and Abraham Siegel. 1955. "The Structuring of the Labor Force in Industrial Society." *Industrial and Labor Relations Review* 8 (January): 151–68.

Keynes, John Maynard. 1936. *The General Theory of Employment, Interest, and Money*. New York: Harcourt, Brace.

Kirsch, Joel Leonard. 1972. *Soviet Wages: Charges in Structure and Administration Since 1956*. Cambridge: MIT Press.

Knowles, G.G.H.C., and T.P. Hill. 1956. "The Variability of Engineering Earnings." *Bulletin of Oxford University Institute of Statistics*, May, 97–140.

Krueger, Alan, and Lawrence Summers. 1986a. "Reflections on the Inter-Industry Wage Structure." Harvard Institute of Economic Research, Discussion Paper 1252.

———. 1986b. "Efficiency Wages and the Wage Structure." Harvard Institute of Economic Research, Discussion Paper 1247.

Lebergott, Stanley. 1947. "Wage Structure." *Review of Economics and Statistics*, November, 274–85.

Leiserson, Mark. 1959. *Wages and Economic Growth in Norway*. Cambridge: Harvard University Press.

Lester, Richard, 1945. "Trends in Southern Wage Differentials Since 1890." *Southern Economic Journal*, April, 317–44.

———. 1946. "Wage Diversity and Its Theoretical Implications." *Review of Economics and Statistics*, August, 152–59.

Lester, Richard. 1948. *Company Wage Policies, A Survey of Patterns and Experience*. Princeton University, Industrial Relations Section, Research Report Series No. 77.

Lewis, H. Gregg. 1963. *Unionism and Relative Wages in the United States*. Chicago: University of Chicago Press.

Livernash, E. Robert. 1957. "The Internal Wage Structure." In George Taylor and Frank Pierson, eds., *New Concepts in Wage Determination*. New York: McGraw–Hill.

Long, Clarence D. 1960. *Wages and Earnings in the United States 1860–1890*. Princeton: Princeton University Press.

Maher, John E. 1956. "Union, Nonunion Wage Differentials." *American Economic Review*, June, 336–52.

Marshall, Alfred. 1920. *Principles of Economics*, 8th ed. London: Macmillan.

Mayo, Elton, 1945. *The Social Problems of an Industrial Civilization*. Boston: Harvard University Press.

Macdonald, Robert M. 1963. *Collective Bargaining in the Automobile Industry: A Study of Wage Structure and Competitive Relations*. New Haven: Yale University Press.

Meij, J.L. 1963. *Internal Wage Structure*. Amsterdam: North Holland.

Mellow, Wesley, and Hal Sider. 1983. "Accuracy of Response in Labor Market Surveys: Evidence and Implications." *Journal of Labor Economics*, October, 331–44.

Mills, D. Quinn. 1981. "U.S. Incomes Policies in the 1970s—Underlying Assumptions, Objectives, Results." *American Economics Review*. May, 283–87.

Mund, Vernon A. 1948. *Open Markets*. New York: Harper.

Myers, Charles, and Rupert Maclaurin. 1943. *The Movement of Factory Workers: A Study of a New England Industrial Community*. New York: John Wiley.

Myers, Charles, and George Shultz. 1951. *The Dynamics of a Labor Market*. New York: Prentice–Hall.

Ober, Harry. 1948. "Occupational Wage Differentials, 1907–1947." *Monthly Labor Review*, August, 127–34.

Olson, Mancur. 1982. *The Rise and Decline of Nations, Economic Growth, Stagflation, and Social Rigidities*. New Haven: Yale University Press.

Palmer, Gladys. 1947. *Research Planning Memorandum on Labor Mobility*. New York: Social Science Research Council.

———. 1954. *Labor Mobility in Six Cities: A Report on the Survey of Patterns and Factors in Labor Mobility, 1940–1950*. New York: Social Science Research Council.

Rees, Albert. 1961. *Real Wages in Manufacturing 1890–1914*. Princeton: Princeton University Press.

———. 1977. "Comment." *Industrial and Labor Relations Review*, October, 3–4.

Rees, Albert, and George Shultz. 1970. *Workers and Wages in an Urban Labor Market*. Chicago: University of Chicago Press.

Reynolds, Lloyd. 1947. *Research on Wages: Report of a Conference Held on April 4–5, 1947, at the Yale Labor–Management Center*. New York: Social Science Research Council.

———. 1951. *The Structure of Labor Markets*. New York: Harper.

Reynolds, Lloyd, and Cynthia Taft. 1956. *The Evolution of Wage Structure*. New Haven: Yale University Press.

Robertson, D.J. 1960. *Factory Wage Structures and National Agreements*. Cambridge: Cambridge University Press.

Rowe, H.W.F. 1928. *Wages in Practice and Theory*. London: George Routledge.

Sachs, Jeffrey. 1983. "Real Wages and Unemployment in OECD Countries." *Brookings Papers on Economic Activity*, vol. 1, 255–89.

Segal, Martin. 1960. *Wages in the Metropolis, Their Influence on the Location of Industries in the New York Region.* Cambridge: Harvard University Press.

———. 1986. "The Post-Institutionalists in Labor Economics: The Forties and Fifties Revisited." *Industrial and Labor Relations Review.* April, 388–403.

Shultz, George P. 1951. *Pressures on Wage Decisions: A Case Study in the Shoe Industry.* London: Chapman and Hall.

Shultz, George, and Arnold R. Weber. 1966. *Strategies for the Displaced Worker, New York: Harper and Row.*

Slichter, Sumner. 1919. *The Turnover of Factory Labor.* New York: Appleton.

———. 1950. "Notes on the Structure of Wages." *Review of Economics and Statistics,* February, 80–91.

———. 1954. "Do the Wage Fixing Arrangements in the American Labor Market Have an Inflationary Bias?" *American Economic Review,* May, 322–46.

Slichter, Sumner, James J. Healy, and E. Robert Livernash. 1961. *The Impact of Collective Bargaining on Management.* Washington, D.C.: Brookings Institution.

Solow, Robert. 1986. "Unemployment: Getting the Questions Right." *Economica* (Supplement), S23–34.

Stieber, Jack. 1959. *The Steel Industry Wage Structure, A Study of the Joint Labor–Management Job Evaluation Program in the Basic Steel Industry.* Cambridge: Harvard University Press.

Tobin, James. 1972. "Inflation and Unemployment." *American Economic Review,* March, 1–18.

Tolles, N. Arnold, and Robert Raimon. 1952. *Sources of Wage Information: Employer Associations.* Ithaca, N.Y.: Cornell University Press.

Walker, Kenneth E. 1956. *Industrial Relations in Australia.* Cambridge: Harvard University Press.

Wilcock, Richard, and Irving Sobel. 1958. *Small City Job Markets: The Labor Market Behavior of Firms and Workers.* Urbana. Ill.: Institute of Labor and Industrial Relations.

3
Wages, Benefits, and Company Employment Systems

Richard A. Lester

This paper will focus mainly on four subject areas where most of my research was centered during the first two postwar decades. The areas are: wage differentials, especially in local markets; differentials in employee benefits; company goals and management decision making of importance for labor analysis; and the development of large-company internal employment systems. These four interrelated subjects are treated in that order in the body of the paper. In each subject area, the results of my research and that of others in the postwar period are discussed, and implications for theory are indicated. For the most part, the subject material is presented in chronological order.

An introductory section precedes the body of the paper. It deals with economists, economic developments, and professional experience early in my career that influenced my thinking and research.

Early Influences

As a senior majoring in economics at Yale, I persuaded Irving Fisher to let me enroll in his graduate course, which, in 1928, dealt especially with interest theory and monetary theory. My long paper for the course attempted to explain why, since colonial times, real wages have been higher in this country than in England. Stimulated by Fisher's course, I decided to become a Ph.D. candidate in economics at Princeton University. In my graduate study I was particularly impressed by Frank D. Graham's analytical skill applied to problems in money and banking and in international trade and finance. In 1930–31, I was an exchange student at the University of Bonn in Germany, where I had Joseph A. Schumpeter in a course on the history of economic thought.

This paper has benefited from helpful comments by Charles A. Myers.

The Great Depression. One can appreciate the disruption of employment relationships in the depression of the 1930s from the fact that by 1933 a quarter of the nation's labor force was totally unemployed, and many others were on short work weeks in order to spread the available employment. As a Ph.D. topic I chose "Unemployment Relief in New Jersey," remarking that I wanted to know all about the burgeoning relief program, as I might soon need to become a client. Classical economics in the textbooks was of little help in understanding the collapse of the economic system or for reasoning about a program for recovery. Many of us, therefore, became followers of J.M. Keynes when his book, *The General Theory of Employment, Interest and Money*, was published in 1936.

During the period 1933–38, I was an instructor at Princeton, teaching in Graham's course in money and banking and teaching with J. Douglas Brown in David A. McCabe's course in labor. During those years, I published articles on money and unemployment relief and worked with Brown on the New Jersey unemployment compensation law. Also I attended some of the five-day Fall Conferences in Industrial Relations which began in 1931 and were led by Brown, who was director of the Industrial Relations Section. The conference was designed for senior industrial relations executives in companies in the United States and Canada to exchange, off the record, their ideas and experiences.[1] Attendance at the conference gave me an opportunity to learn about the aims and effectiveness of the personnel and employee-benefit programs of companies in this country and Canada that were cooperating in the section's work.

The summer of 1936 I spent abroad, studying the postwar monetary experience of Sweden, Denmark, and Norway. In 1937–38, while a visiting assistant professor at Haverford College replacing faculty on leave, I studied colonial experience with paper money, publishing journal articles that supplied new and favorable light on that subject.

Realizing that no opening on the Princeton faculty would exist for a person with my interests, I sought an academic post elsewhere. I accepted the first offer I received, which was an appointment as assistant professor of labor at the University of Washington in Seattle, teaching undergraduate and graduate courses in that subject. At once I began to prepare a labor textbook, stressing economic analysis. The book, *The Economics of Labor*, was published in 1941. It contained eighteen references to Keynes, twenty to Sumner H. Slichter, and fifteen to Paul H. Douglas.

During the two years I was at the University of Washington, I studied the multicompany, two-union bargaining setup in the West Coast pulp and paper industry[2] and also learned about the West Coast operations of the Teamsters union under Dave Beck, a genuine advocate of business unionism. In the fall of 1940, I joined the Economics Department of Duke University and began to study wages and labor relations in the South.[3]

The War Period.   Academic economists gained a great deal of new knowledge about product pricing, wages, and business practices from working for the government in Washington and out of regional offices during the World War II period.

In May 1941, on leave from Duke, I joined J. Douglas Brown in setting up a branch of the Labor Division of the Office of Production Management, of which Sidney Hillman, longtime president of the Amalgamated Clothing Workers, was co-director. The assignment of our branch was to work with the chiefs of industry branches on labor supply problems and conversion of company work forces to military production, and to consult with pertinent unions in the industry on such matters. Among the labor economists recruited for our staff were Frederick H. Harbison, Charles A. Myers, and Sidney Sufrin.

In mid-1943 I returned to North Carolina to teach in the Army Finance Program at Duke. In addition I engaged in two labor-related programs. On several occasions I served as the neutral chairman on ad hoc tripartite panels appointed by the Atlanta regional board of the National War Labor Board to make recommendations for the resolution of interest disputes between labor and management of a company. Early in 1945 I became chairman of the tripartite Southern Textile Commission appointed by the National War Labor Board to complete the development of an occupational wage structure for the cotton textile industry in the South.[4]

Economists who participated in the War Labor Board's program of wage control generally were surprised to find the wide dispersion in wages between similar industrial plants in the same labor market area. As officially requested, the Bureau of Labor Statistics (BLS) in 1943 and 1944 made wage surveys in some sixty metropolitan areas around the country. The purpose was to find out whether there were "brackets of sound and tested going rates of pay" by occupations in particular labor market areas that could be used by the War Labor Board and the regional boards to judge whether plants in a labor market had wages that were substandard or clearly inequitable—out of line in a wage structure.

In 1945, I made an analysis of that BLS data for manufacturing industries in forty-eight labor market areas to determine the spread in hourly earnings between the average for the highest-paying plant and for the lowest-paying plant for each selected occupation.[5] For the 2,910 separate wage arrays by occupation included in my analysis, the average of the highest-paying plant exceeded that of the lowest-paying plant in the labor market area, on the average, by 50 percent. The wide dispersion of wage rates paid by firms in the same labor market for work in the same occupation seemed to show that firms often had significant latitude in wage determination, that demand and supply did not normally result in a single "competitive" rate or even a very narrow range of rates for an occupation among comparable firms in a labor market area in the absence of collective bargaining or company collusion.

In 1943, Charles A. Myers and W. Rupert Maclaurin presented an analysis of the Fitchburg, Massachusetts, area labor market. With respect to wages and the movement of factory workers among thirty-seven firms between 1937 and 1939, their study showed that: (1) a considerable spread existed between the wage level of high-paying firms and low-paying firms; (2) the high-wage firms generally had superior working conditions and much more ample benefit programs; (3) relatively little active competition for labor existed among the employing firms, due partly to compliance with an "anti-pirating" policy; and (4) movement of labor from low-wage to high-wage firms was largely ineffective in reducing wage-rate differences for comparable jobs (Myers and Maclaurin 1943: 59–60, 73, and 76). Such findings were hardly supportive of classical labor market theory.

In the fall of 1945, I returned to Princeton University as an associate professor of economics and a faculty associate in the Industrial Relations Section. That meant that part of my time was devoted to research in the section's program. I continued my research on wages, which benefited from discussions I had with industrial relations executives in the section's annual conference and from discussions with union research directors in the section's annual Seminar in Labor Relations for Union Research and Staff Personnel, held yearly from 1947 through 1958, for which I provided leadership in the section (Industrial Relations Section 1986: 12–13 and 19).

In 1948, the Industrial Relations Research Association (IRRA), which I helped to found, held its first annual meeting, having already acquired over a thousand members. The main purpose of the IRRA was to encourage research and discussion of research findings in the field of industrial relations, broadly defined. As indicated in the IRRA's constitution and in its first proceedings (Derber 1949: 2–4, 236), the association's aim was to include contributions from psychologists, sociologists, political scientists, and legal scholars as well as economists, and also to have the benefit of input from professional practitioners in management, labor, and government. In part, the IRRA represented a reaction to the narrowness and abstractness of classical economics as a basis for analyzing wages, labor markets, labor relations, and other labor matters.

Wage Differentials in Local Markets

Cotton Textiles. In 1945, I began a study of wages of companies in the South producing cotton thread and woven goods on standard machinery. In addition to the wage statistics collected on cotton textile companies in 1943 by BLS for the War Labor Board's use, I had the advantage of access to the 1945 wage data submitted by textile companies to the Atlanta regional office of the War Labor

Board in connection with the work of the Southern Textile Commission. As chairman, I had the opportunity to discuss the data with practitioners in the industry.

For communities or labor market areas where cotton textiles were the dominant industry, analysis of the data showed that: (1) mills tended to be high-paying or low-paying for each of the four standard machine-tending jobs[6] chosen for comparisons; (2) labor market areas varied somewhat in the range of company wage differentials, but the occupational wage of the highest-paying mill tended to exceed that of the lowest-paying mill by 25 percent or more in most cases; and (3) within the range of pay from the low-wage mill to the high-wage mill, there was often a scatter of pay rates without any definite central tendency (Lester 1946a: 254–60 and Lester 1946d: 154–57). Such findings showed a need for a body of theory to explain how a mill comes to have a certain position within the range of wage rates locally and why it tends to stay in that relative position when the whole range moves unevenly upward.

Company Wage Policies.   In 1946–47, I made a study of the wage policies of 107 companies cooperating with the section that had a total of around two million employees (Lester 1948). Mostly they were large firms: more than four-fifths of them were multiplant companies.

The policy of about half of the companies in the study was to orient their wages to the scales being paid by other companies in the local labor market area. A firm's management is likely to know wage scales of many other local firms, because it is a common practice for a management association or a large firm in the area periodically to make a wage survey for use by cooperating companies.[7] Companies also informally exchanged information and opinion with one another. Most of the companies with a local orientation said that they aimed to be in the upper half of the community array or range of company rates, and some said they sought to be at the top of the range.[8]

Some industries, such as oil, steel, and auto assembly, have a distinct wage pattern, to which major firms in the industry conform. One-quarter of the companies studied had an industry-wage orientation, nationwide. Some of them even had sought an assumed advantage from being somewhat above their industry level. The remaining quarter of the companies used some combination of community and industry rates in determining the level of their wages in a community.

Company executives gave such reasons or objectives as the following for pursuing a high-wage policy and for trying to be early in a round of wage increases: to avoid being unionized, to preserve employee attachment to the company, to maintain good employee morale, which can facilitate supervision and increase productivity, and to assure the desired quality of labor. The importance of particular wage objectives may vary with economic conditions and other circumstances.

Some companies reported that, after being unionized, they ceased trying to lead in general wage increases, partly because the union tended to use the company to set a pattern for wage increases (Lester 1948: 29–30).

In a 1980 study of twenty-six large nonunion companies, Fred Foulkes found that almost all of them sought to lead with respect to wages and employee benefits in their industry and in the communities where their plants were located.[9]

The New Haven Labor Market. Lloyd Reynold's comprehensive study of the New Haven, Connecticut, labor market covering the period 1940 to 1948 made a major contribution to the analysis of wages in a middle-sized metropolitan area (Reynolds 1951). His findings, based in part on the wage structure and change of twenty-eight manufacturing firms, included the following: (1) A quite wide band or range of individual company wage levels existed in the New Haven labor market area, with the band as wide in July 1948 in a tight labor market as it was earlier in July 1940 in a fairly loose labor market (Reynolds 1951: 190, 233–35); (2) the high-wage firms had good wage-paying ability due to such factors as unusual efficiency of plant design or management ability or a special position in their product markets, and the major factor that propelled the band upward was "difference in the companies' wage-paying ability," plus union pressure in some cases (Reynolds 1951: 190, 232); and (3) the difference in the average quality of the work force in individual plants was considerably less than the difference in their wage levels, so that labor was costing low-wage firms "less *per efficiency unit* than it [was] costing the high-wage firms."[10]

In their labor market study of Nashua, New Hampshire, Myers and Shultz also found, from ranking thirty-eight manufacturing firms, a wide range between the high-paying and the low-paying companies in 1948. The figures for the company with the highest minimum wage or the highest average hourly earnings were about double the figure for the lowest-paying companies. The authors indicate that allowance for differences in the quality of workers would reduce that spread to some extent (Myers and Shultz 1951: 159–62).

The Trenton Labor Market. During the Korean War period, I made a two-stage study of the Trenton labor market area which included in-depth interviews with executives in eighty-two manufacturing firms. The first stage, beginning in the fall of 1951, dealt with wages, company hiring practices, and the extent of competition for labor at that time when some labor shortages were first commencing to develop as a result of expansion in employment at four plants—the construction and then operation of the new Fairless Works of U.S. Steel, work on defense contracts at two aircraft companies, and the operation of a new shell casings plant.[11] The second stage, which involved reinterviewing, dealt with the adjustments that were made in wages and in company employment policies in some companies and not in others by the first half of 1953, when the labor supply stringency in male labor reached its peak.[12]

Among the significant results from both parts of the Trenton study are the following:

1. A considerable range or band of wage rates existed for the same job classification or occupation in groups of manufacturing plants or firms.[13] For example, in 1951, for the twelve rubber products firms, the male starting rate of the highest-paying firms was 38 percent above that of the lowest-paying firm, and for just four firms producing rubber hose, that figure was 15 percent. Many factors helped to explain such wage-level differences among firms in the Trenton labor market area (Lester 1954: 75–80).

   With the growing labor stringency up to mid-1953, a total of twelve companies, on labor supply grounds, gave special pay increases in some categories (starting rate, skilled maintenance rates) or hired in above the starting rate. None of the high-wage metal working companies did so, and their starting pay increases in that period were almost uniform—twelve to fourteen cents per hour. There was no close correlation between a firm's position in the community wage hierarchy and the magnitude of its labor supply problems during the period of increasing stringency for male labor and, later, for female labor.

2. Certain employment policies and practices of established firms attach their employees, with (say) two years or more of services, to the firm, so that they remained out of the labor market—were not attracted to the expanding new plants even though those employers were offering jobs up the occupational hierarchy, a good seniority position, and better pay. Practices that make intercompany transfer costly and risky and, thus, help to restrict competition in labor include the following: hiring in only at bottom-level jobs, on-the-job training for advancement, promotion only from within,[14] length of company service governing opportunity to qualify for promotion and determining the order of layoff and recall to work, employee benefits and vacation rights according to length of service, and companies' adherence to an anti-pirating code practiced widely, under which a company will not hire an employee of another company if the latter's management objects for work force reasons.

   Such practices explain why, in interviews, company managements were practically unanimous in claiming that they were not aware of being in competition with any particular firm for factory labor, and why intercompany differences in pay seemed to have little influence on management views that most of a company's work force was not a part of labor market competition (Lester 1954: 65–72).

3. In 1951, most of the seventy-eight firms were not experiencing much difficulty in recruiting the quality of labor they normally hired. Generally they did not expand much in employment in the next two years. The very low-wage firms were, however, not able to recruit the quality of labor that the high-wage firms were recruiting. Management officials of companies were questioned about the quality of their work force compared with the work force of companies in the area with higher or lower wage levels. They found it difficult to give an informed judgment; some thought the difference among firms, except at the extremes of the community's wage hierarchy, was not substantial (Lester 1954: 48–51, 73–75).

   The follow-up interviews in 1953 showed that (1) about half of the firms lowered their quality standards for new employees, and about a third made some change in their recruitment methods; (2) a majority of the firms were not significantly influenced in their policies or operations by the scarcity of labor that developed; and (3) most of the workers who transferred to other employers were short-service employees with less than two years' seniority; the longer-service employees generally remained tightly attached to their companies (Lester 1955: 50–54, 25–27, 44–45, 68–70).

The labor market studies discussed above indicate the existence locally of a continuing band of differentials in plant wage levels that cannot be accounted for by differences in the quality of plant work forces or by differences in benefit programs and working conditions in the plant. Indeed, high-wage establishments generally have more generous employee benefits and better working environments.

In part, the contributions of the postwar labor economists to the analysis of wage determination, wage differentials and patterns, and company adjustment to wage changes and the implications of their findings for wage theory are presented in *New Concepts in Wage Determination* (1957), edited by George W. Taylor and Frank C. Pierson. Included in the book are papers by Pierson, Dunlop, Kerr, Lester, Reynolds, and Arthur M. Ross.

Employee Benefits

The subject of private benefit plans for plant employees has lacked extended treatment in the economic literature. Few attempts have been made to integrate expenditures on nonwage forms of employee compensation into the main body of economic theory.

The treatment here will focus on the following topics: (1) the extent to which company benefit expenditures differ from cash wages as a form of employee compensation; (2) the factors responsible for the great growth in company expenditures on employee benefits; (3) the important role that unions and collective bargaining have played in the development and spread of employee benefit programs; and (4) the size-of-establishment differential in benefits and in wages.

Characteristics of Employee Benefits. In analyzing company benefit plans for blue-collar workers, certain distinctions need to be drawn. Some plans provide eligible employees with cash income during a period of unemployment, disability, sick leave, or retirement. Others, like hospital, medical, and dental benefit plans, provide uniform protection for some or all of the costs of specific services that the employee and his/her dependents receive, the value of which will vary with personal incidence and number of dependents. Such benefits are not related to the employee's pay or work status. Many group life plans also provide the same death benefit for all covered employees whatever their level of pay or performance.

Most company pension plans that have been negotiated with unions for blue-collar workers, especially by large firms in the mass-production industries, provide "flat benefits." Typically, the benefits are based on a single dollar figure multiplied by the employee's number of credited years of service. Benefits are uniform for each year of service; they are not related at all to the employee's past earnings or to individual productivity. Less common are negotiated plans that relate retirement benefits to both the employee's average monthly or annual earnings and his/her years of service. There are, of course, variations in the features of individual plans.[15]

Many large companies continue health benefit coverage for former employees during retirement, and in some cases the pension benefits of retired employees have been increased, either by collective bargaining or unilaterally, several years after the employee's retirement, when costs of living have increased significantly.

Thus, a significant part of company expenditures on employee benefits is not really compensation for work being currently performed and is not essentially a variable cost. Rather, those expenditures may, at least in part, be fixed costs. And some benefits, like pensions and hospital insurance, may not be fully employee-effective until far into the future. Single, youthful recruits may not find them very attractive.[16] Thus, various components of a company's program of employee benefits may have varying appeal and effects on different groups in a plant's work force. It is very difficult to try to apply marginal productivity analysis to employee compensation that includes company benefit programs.

Growth in Benefit Expenditures. A few progressive companies introduced pension plans, profit-sharing plans, and group life insurance for plant employees in the period 1901 to 1911. The plans were intended to promote employee loyalty to the company and, in some cases, to counter unions (Stewart 1931: 22–23).

Until 1940 there was not much enduring expansion in company benefit plans. During World War II, with federal control of wage increases, however, company dollar contributions to private benefit programs in the United States expanded greatly—about four times from 1940 to 1945 and then three times from 1950 to 1955. Thereafter the increase every five years was between 1.6 and 2.0 times.[17] For the year 1984, the total dollar figure for such insurance-type benefits was around $193 billion. That was the equivalent of 9 percent of total wages and salaries in this country.[18]

Growth in benefit expenditures has varied considerably by industry and individual company. For instance, the oil industry has been a leader in developing and expanding employee benefits. Standard Oil of New Jersey first instituted a pension plan for plant employees in 1903. In 1959 the average expenditures for private benefit plans in petroleum refining and related lines was 37¢ an hour, or 12.2 percent of gross payroll.[19] The next highest industry was primary metals (mainly steel), with 19.2¢ per hour, or 6.8 percent of payroll (U.S. Bureau of Labor Statistics 1962: 9). For the U.S. Steel Corporation, the cost of company insurance-type benefits rose from 0.3 percent of straight-time wages in 1947 to 15 percent in 1963, and for the General Motors Corporation the increase was from 0.5 percent in 1947 to 12 percent in 1963 (Lester 1967: 489).

Statistics show that the percentage of payroll and the cents per hour that companies spend on their benefit plans increase with (1) the level of wages they pay, (2) the size of the establishment measured by number of employees, and (3) the extent to which the plant's employees are covered by collective bargaining agreements (Lester 1964: 337, table 14).

The great growth in company benefit plans has been powered, in part, by tax advantages and union pressures. Unlike wages, company contributions to benefit plans are tax free for the employees and are deductible from the employer's gross income for tax purposes. Also, they have the price advantage of group purchase involving large numbers. The tax-free advantage is especially significant for high-wage employees subject to high income tax brackets.

The Role of Unions. Labor unions have played a major part in the shaping and growth of company benefit plans, especially since the Supreme Court ruled in 1949 that pensions and group health insurance are mandatory bargaining subjects under the National Labor Relations Act.[20] Richard Freeman has made an impressive study of the effects of unions and collective bargaining on company employee benefits, so that here I need only provide a summary statement of his findings (Freeman 1981: 492–509). Freeman concluded that unions, through collective bargaining: (1) raise the share of compensation allotted to employee benefits and also the total level of compensation; (2) raise employee benefits by a greater percentage amount than they raise straight-time pay; (3) have their greatest positive effect on pensions, on life, accident, and health insurance, and on vacation and holiday pay; and (4), especially in the case of pensions, provide a strong incentive to remain employed with the company and to keep out of the external labor market.

Negotiation of a benefit plan for production workers or a marked extension of an existing plan may enable a union to claim institutional credit more clearly than it could for an equivalent wage increase. Also, surveys show that union members, particularly senior workers who exert considerable influence on union demands, favor increased company expenditures on pensions, health insurance, and paid vacations over an equivalent increase in cash wages (Lester 1967a: 490–94 and Freeman 1981: 492–94).

Union leaders have sought to achieve a new or enlarged benefit plan at a leading company and then to spread the pattern. Fred Foulkes found from his study of twenty-six large nonunion companies that they were apt to be paying benefits equal to or higher than were being paid by comparable unionized companies, and that many nonunion companies sought to lead in the introduction and enlargement of benefit plans in their industry or in areas where their plants are located (Foulkes 1980: 60, 150, and 210).

The question has been raised whether some company managements, either voluntarily or under union pressure, have not been spending too much on employee benefits. One may ask how much a company needs to spend on different benefit programs in order to attract and keep employees attached to the company, and how much various benefit programs serve to increase employee productivity, especially if they provide flat benefits unrelated to the individual's earnings or performance. Even in normal times, it is argued, the equivalent sum spent on wages or other items than benefits might provide a better return.[21]

Benefit programs can become exceedingly expensive when an industry, for reasons such as low-cost foreign competition, suffers a severe secular decline. An example is the steel industry, which has been greatly curtailing employment and closing unprofitable plants. Employment in the industry declined 50 percent from 1949 to 1984. The consequence has been sharp increases in supplemental unemployment benefits and high pension and medical costs for employees who elect early retirement (Wayne 1986: D1 and D4). A study shows that U.S. Steel Corporation paid out over $550 million nationwide in pensions and medical benefits to retired employees in 1985, of which about $164 million went to recipients of early pensions and medical benefits. The cost of supplementary unemployment benefits the year before was almost $49 million (Davis and Montgomery 1986: D1 and D10). The functions that employee benefits perform as part of a company employment system are discussed below.

Size-of-Establishment Differentials in Benefits and Wages. A pattern of higher wages and bigger benefit expenditures as plant size increases has characterized manufacturing in this country at least since the late 1930s. The difference that size of industrial plants makes in company wages and company benefit expenditures can be illustrated by some figures. Calculations based on Census of Manufacturers data for 1947 and 1954 show that, for industries like chemicals, electrical equipment, petroleum, and rubber, the level of wages in "small" plants (100 to 249 employees) was 15 to 20 percent below the level for "large" plants—those with 1,000 or more employees.[22]

Company expenditure on private insurance-type benefit plans in 1962 was 4.0 percent of payroll for plants with less than 100 employees, 5.3 percent for plants with 100 to 499 employees, and 7.4 percent for plants with 500 or more employees. In cents per hour, the benefit expenditures of large plants were more than double those of small plants. Studies show that size-of-establishment differentials have been considerably greater for benefits than they have been for wages.[23]

The literature on the size-of-establishment (or firm) differential in wages is much more extensive than that dealing with the size–benefits differential. To some extent, benefits serve different functions than wages do. The discussion here will deal with both the wage–size effect and the benefits–size effect, but will deal somewhat more with the wage–size differential in discussing the results of studies.

Four broad factors have been offered to explain size-of-establishment (or firm) differentials in employee compensation (wages and benefits). They are: (1) large plants (firms) generally recruit and have higher quality employees than small plants—higher pay compensates for higher quality; (2) large plants have to pay higher wages to compensate for working conditions that are less desirable, on balance, than they are in small plants; (3) large plants (firms) are more likely to be unionized than small plants, and collective bargaining results in higher wages and higher benefit expenditures in the larger plants or companies; and (4) large and growing firms, for various reasons, are likely to have more ability to pay and more willingness to pay high wages and provide ample benefits.

Several studies have been made in an effort to determine the extent to which those four broad factors and others, either singly or in combination, can explain the size-of-establishment (firm) differential in wages or wages and benefits combined.[24] Generally speaking, the studies have not been able to uncover the factor or factors that can account for most of the size–wage effect and size–benefit effect. Partly the problem is that a factor like "quality of a plant's work force" or "conditions of work in a factory" is difficult to define and measure, and the proper data to use in the analysis are not readily available.[25]

Taking account of previous studies by others, Charles Brown and James Medoff have made statistical analyses of the explanatory power of several factors, especially the quality of factory work forces and the working conditions in manufacturing plants. They concluded that differences in the quality of company work forces might explain roughly one-half of the plant-size effects on wages in the case of skilled workers but less than that for workers at lower levels. They found no size–wage effect for blue-collar workers in unionized settings (Brown and Medoff 1986: 15 and 17). Their analysis indicates that the conditions of work explained very little of the size–wage effect. Indeed, they question whether there is persuasive evidence that working conditions are less favorable in larger workplaces (Brown and Medoff 1986: 22). From their extensive analysis, Brown and Medoff conclude that the size–wage differential needs a "credible" body of theory to explain its size and widespread existence (Brown and Medoff 1986: 45).

Walter Oi has also analyzed the persistent wage differential between large and small firms and concluded that neoclassical theory cannot adequately explain that systematic difference (Oi 1983a: 71 and 73). He stresses, as an explanatory factor, the differences in company managements' policies and ability to organize production and supervise workers. Stating that large firms are generally run by very able entrepreneurs, Oi hypothesizes that a comparatively small number of firms that grow to very large size are controlled by exceptionally able managers who desire well-paid, productive employees requiring less monitoring of their work performance.[26] From his research, Oi concludes that the neoclassical model of the labor market is being replaced by a more "loosely knit" body of "theory, in which the labor market is characterized" by such practices as lifetime tenured employment, deferred pay in the form of pensions and other benefits, seniority governing layoffs and promotions, and predetermined wages under long-term collective agreements (Oi 1983a: 104).

Labor Markets and the Manpower Program

Study of public employment exchanges in operation and employer use (or lack of use) of their nonfee services can be instructive for both program functioning and development of labor market theory.

My special interest in public employment exchanges began with service as chairman of the New Jersey Employment Security Council (1955–65). The council's assignment was to review and make recommendations with respect to the state unemployment compensation law and operation of the state employment service.

The innovative Federal Manpower Development and Training Act of 1962 did not mention the Federal–State Employment Service, composed of fifty state-administered, federally financed units. Obviously that instrumentality would need to play an important role in a comprehensive program to reduce unemployment by training and other means of fulfilling employers' manpower requirements. The act's inclusion of support for research to further its purposes was a unique feature in such legislation.

A Subcommittee on Research of the National Manpower Advisory Committee was established, of which I served as chairman (1963–68). During most of those years, I was also a member of the National Manpower Task Force,[27] a group of academicians that prepared papers and advised the secretary of labor on selected subjects. For instance, in 1968 the task force arranged with our Princeton section to hold a conference on means for facilitating the transition of youth from school to work (Maruhnic 1968).

In 1964 I began a study of the operations of the Federal–State Employment Service in the field and at headquarters in four eastern states. Then in 1965, in Europe, I studied the public manpower programs in Sweden, Germany, and Great Britain and the way the public employment service operated in each country.

As I explained in my book, *Manpower Planning in a Free Society* (Lester 1966), Sweden had an exemplary comprehensive labor market setup. A national labor market board, having both management and labor members, was established to direct and coordinate the different programs, with the employment service serving as the principal operating agency. Sweden's "active manpower policy" had the following aims and means of achieving them: (1) to have the active participation of management and organized labor in carrying out the program; (2) to provide the public with abundant, up-to-date information on job vacancies; (3) to train and support a corps of schoolteachers as vocational or career counselors and to have the study of jobs in industry as part of the school curriculum; (4) to provide well-designed training programs, with financial support for trainees; and (5) to subsidize the movement of selected jobless workers and their families from areas of declining employment to locations that promise to have continuing need for more workers. Also, with four weeks of paid vacation required by law and worker benefits provided largely by government and union programs, interfirm mobility in Sweden was less restricted by such factors than it was in this country. Conditions in Sweden were relatively favorable for the operation of market forces. In a number of respects, labor market conditions in West Germany were very similar to those in Sweden.

The situation in the United States was different. Instead of a single, national employment service with countrywide programs and standards, we have fifty state services, separately staffed and administered. By means of its financing of the state services, the federal government, through the Labor

Department, sought to bring about some coordination and compliance with operating standards. However, the Federal–State Service was not well suited to serve large companies with plants in a number of states.

Compared with Germany and Sweden, the Federal–State Service was spending more staff time and attention on filling job orders by making referrals that result in "placements" (hires) and was devoting less time on gaining a good understanding of employers' work-force needs and their employment policies. The time spent on different employment-service functions in the country as a whole in 1957 was estimated as follows: 75 percent on placement work, 6 percent on vocational counseling, 5 percent on demand and supply material, 4 percent on aptitude testing, and 10 percent on various other services or activities. Despite the stress on placement, an estimate made in the U.S. Department of Labor shows that state employment services accounted for only 16 percent of the total new hires in 1960, compared with estimates for Sweden and Germany of 33 and 40 percent of all new hires.

The jobs for which the Federal–State Employment Service is able to claim credit in providing a placement involve, to a large extent, employment with a short-term perspective. The jobs on the public agencies' lists are likely to have low education or skill requirements, little opportunity for promotion, and little in the way of private employee benefits. For example, the service has been extensively used for dealing with seasonal labor needs in agriculture and short-term employment in other industries.

The management of sizable, well-established companies tends to take a long-range, work-career perspective in hiring new employees. Where a company has on-the-job training and upper-level jobs filled by promotion from within, only low-level entry jobs are filled from outside supply. Even for appointment to entry jobs, such a company is likely to take into account the contribution that the individual would be likely to make during most or all of a work career in the company setting. That would involve assessing personal qualities such as dependability, ability to learn and adapt, and motivation, including genuine interest in making a long-time attachment to such a company.

A small but significant part of the large volume of research supported from federal funds under the Manpower Development and Training Act involved the operation and analysis of labor markets. Attention here is focused on that part dealing with what is called "the internal labor market," which may operate, to a considerable extent, independently of the "external labor market," which involves many firms and instrumentalities, including public employment services.

John Dunlop presented the concept of an internal labor market in 1966 at a conference on job vacancies, held by the National Bureau of Economic Research and financed by research funds under the Manpower Development and Training Act.[28]

The characteristics and operations of internal labor markets were set forth in detail in a 1971 study by Peter Doeringer and Michael Piore, drawing on interviews with management and union officials in some seventy-five companies. Financial support was provided for the project under the Manpower Development and Training Act.

Within a large manufacturing corporation, management, either unilaterally or in negotiation with union representatives, determines the company employment policies, work rules, wage structure, employee benefits, and other employment arrangements and conditions. Those items are not determined by market transaction within the company, although the external labor market may influence the determination by management or by collective bargaining. It may, therefore, be inappropriate and misleading to try to analyze by necoclassical labor market theory the combination of labor policies, programs, and practices that are consistent with the long-horizon, career concept of employment. This matter is discussed more fully following the next section.

Management Goals and Internal Decision Making

As previously explained, from my experience in the war agencies, from discussions with industrial relations executives, and from my then current research on company wage policies and the North–South wage differential, I realized how inadequate the classical theory of the firm and the marginal productivity theory of employment were for analyzing the policies and operations of corporations, especially in the labor field.

Drawing on my research and that of others, I published a paper in March 1946 that contained empirical results inconsistent with expectations based on the classical theory of the firm (Lester 1946c). Among the contrary findings were: (1) In questionnaire responses concerning the adjustments they would make to a wage-cost increase, executives of manufacturing firms stressed increased sales efforts and improvement in plant operating efficiency, which presumably would not be possible with enterprises operating at the point of maximum profits. (2) Sample plants or firms in manufacturing were found to have horizontal ("flat") or downward-sloping unit variable costs with operations expanding up to designed plant capacity;[29] the absence of an upward-sloping section of the variable cost curve short of plant capacity would mean that the cost curve would not meet the marginal revenue curve in the normal range of operations, a necessary condition for competitive equilibrium to be stable.[30] (3) Firms manufacturing the same products in the South as in the North were found not to adjust the use of labor and capital equipment to compensate for the marked differentials in wage levels in the two regions.

My paper and Fritz Machlup's critique (Machlup 1946) of it gave rise to considerable controversy concerning the neoclassical theory of the firm and the application of marginal analysis to sizable business enterprises.

Goals of Management. Much of the ensuing literature dealt with the question of the goal or goals that guide and determine decisions that management of well-established business companies make that affect such items as employee benefits and wage differentials.

Based on his study of leadership in large corporate enterprises, Robert A. Gordon wrote in 1948 that the criterion of "satisfactory profits" is likely to be the prime objective in mature, successful companies, and that product market share and financial security of the company may, in some circumstances, become the primary motive instead of profit maximization (Gordon 1948: 270–71). Later, Gordon emphasized the power and the discretion typically exercised by management of large corporations in the following statement:

> The development of the large corporation has obviously affected the goals of business decision-making . . . Almost certainly the personal and group goals of higher and lower executives are part of the total value system—the desires for security, power, prestige, advancement within the organization, and so on. One result, almost certainly, is that the maintenance of satisfactory profits is a more accurate statement of the profits objective than is complete profits-maximization. Perhaps it is not inaccurate to say that profits are viewed as the basic constraint subject to which other goals can be followed [by management]. Subject to this constraint, some profits will be sacrificed in pursuit of other goals. (Gordon 1961: xiv).

A significant contribution to the issue of the goals of business management was made by my colleague, William J. Baumol, who joined the Princeton Economics Department in 1949. From his extensive experience with a management consulting firm, involving analysis of the operations of many business firms and making and discussing recommendations for improvement with the company executives involved, Baumol became convinced that "in practice firms pursue objectives more diverse and complex than just maximization of profits."[31]

Based mainly on his consulting experience, Baumol developed two goal models, each with its own implications for business decisions. One model has maximum sales as the primary company goal, subject to the constraint of profits sufficiently high to finance the company's expansion plans and to keep stockholders satisfied. Baumol points out that maximum sales may compete with maximum profits, since sales can be increased by lower prices and by increased advertising costs and other marketing expenses.

Baumol's other goal model has maximum growth of the company's assets as the primary objective, subject to the same two constraints. He and other analysts of business firms have been impressed by the extent to which company managements are preoccupied with the growth of enterprises. Also, Baumol noted that executive salaries tend to be more closely correlated with the scale of the company's operations than with its profitability, and that growth in employment tends to increase promotion possibilities and to facilitate good labor relations.

The Process of Decision Making. In his comprehensive Nobel Prize address,[32] Herbert Simon not only explains why he favors tangible, measurable goals in place of just profit maximization, but he also shows the need for empirical studies to develop a body of theory concerning the decision-making process in organizations such as business corporations. That would involve systematic knowledge of corporations' internal structure and their mechanisms for making decisions and for adapting to change. With multiple goals for the firm, some goal conflict or divergence of interest may occur among groups such as stockholders, managers, employees, and executives of different functional departments or divisions. Data would be needed on the strength of different goals and the process by which various interests are accommodated in particular settings. Some pertinent studies have been made. Simon recognized that one cannot expect generalizations as simple and precise as those derived from the classical theory of the firm, which avoids the subject of decision-making processes (Simon 1979: 508).

From his research, including case studies, Oliver Williamson finds that the individual and collective objectives of managers have a systematic influence on the internal operations of the firm. Conditions in the firm's product market or markets determine the extent to which profits above an acceptable level (judged by historical standards or the performance of rivals) enable managers to increase expenditures in ways that enhance their prestige, power, security, professional standing, and reputation among employees and in the community. Such discretionary expenditures are used not so much to increase productivity as for the achievement of managerial satisfaction (Williamson 1964: 30, 165, 167). One is reminded of the pride that company executives have taken in being leaders in the establishment and enlargement of employee benefit programs.

In the analysis of wages, benefits, and other labor aspects of the operation of plants and companies, consideration needs to be given to the alternative goals, the processes of decision making, and the discretion or latitude that management has to pursue its individual and collective objectives. Such consideration is especially needed for application to large manufacturing companies in view of the internal employment systems they have developed.

Large-Company Employment Systems

Employment in large plants and companies has become a complex system, primarily administered by management. Only quite limited use is made of the market mechanism in a company's operation of its employment system.[33] The company is the only buyer of labor involved in its internal employment operations, and, as indicated above, it is a special kind of buyer. Its attached employees have no sense of being in a labor market within the company. A simple market framework is hardly appropriate for analyzing the employment systems in such large units, and it may be misleading to refer the employment complex of wages, benefits, procedures, rights, and relationships as a company's or plant's "internal labor market."

The extent to which the employment system of large companies does not directly involve the market mechanism and market forces is indicated by the following typical features of the system:

1. Production workers are only hired in at low-level entry jobs, with the expectation of promotion into higher-level jobs following in-plant training and company-related experience.[34] Upper-level jobs are reserved for regular employees who, as candidates, are usually considered one at a time in order of their seniority. Thus, the company creates the qualified supply, and openings are filled according to a nonmarket procedure. Where other companies in the locality follow the same policy of hiring at the bottom and filling upper levels from within the plant, much of the demand for workers' services never reaches the external market.

2. Other policies and programs that help to attach employees to the employer and promote career employment with the company include pensions, health benefits, and vacation rights by length of continuous service. With the great expansion of employee benefits and rights that are not transferable from company to company, workers have become even more reluctant to change employers. Understandably, managements of large companies do not visualize themselves as competing with each other for employees in their existing work forces.

3. The structure of pay differentials for plant workers in a large company is usually determined by a job evaluation procedure, so that the contents of the company's jobs, not individual workers' abilities or external market forces, determine the structure of time rates of pay for most plant jobs. Under collective bargaining, a general increase in the company's wage structure is predetermined by negotiation for a period of two or three years without regard to developments in the economy or the external labor market during that period.

In such ways, companies internalize their plant employment, and it takes on some of the characteristics of a long-term investment. Management tends to think of individuals in the plant work force in work-career or long-horizon terms.

The large-company employment system has advantages for both management and its employees. To mention some in general terms, this distinctly American system permits management to develop its own labor supply in its own way for the kinds of jobs that it has; it gives management an opportunity to counsel and evaluate employees over a sufficient period of time; it encourages cooperative work attitudes and loyalty to the company; and, by reducing labor turnover, it preserves and enhances the investment that the company makes in training and otherwise developing its employees.

For the employees, the system supplies training and learning opportunities practically free of charge;[35] provides them a considerable amount of employment security, including various benefits; saves them the costs and risks of changing employers; and encourages movement up promotion ladders.

This paper has focused on the compensation and employment arrangements for manual workers in manufacturing operations in sizable plants and companies. An attempt was made to show the need for both understanding and integration of company goals, managerial decision making, and company policies and programs with respect to wages, benefits, promotion, and other aspects of career employment.

Studies should be made of actual operation of the system under various sets of conditions, including an examination of the goal effectiveness of different components of the system. Also, it would be desirable to examine the extent to which this employment system or model is appropriate for analyzing company employment of white-collar, professional, and managerial personnel in manufacturing companies and for analyzing company employment of different categories of employees in public utilities, insurance companies, and large firms in other sectors of the economy.

The Japanese Large-Company Employment System. For four decades, Japan has had a large-company employment system that resembles in many respects the large-company employment systems in this country. After the mid-1950s, the *nenko* ("permanent employment") system spread from office workers and artisans to cover all "regular" production workers in most of the firms with a thousand or more employees and in some firms with less than a thousand employees, including small enterprises.

A brief statement indicating the main components of the Japanese large-company system will bring out the similarities and differences in the employment systems of the two countries.[36]

Most of a large company's new recruits each year are hired in a nationwide spring competition for male youths graduating from middle schools, high schools, and colleges and universities. What the company offers in recruiting, in addition to a good starting wage, is its career employment program, which includes extensive training, promotion opportunities, wages and benefits that increase with years of service, and steady employment until retirement.

An employee's entering wage is related to the level of his pre-employment education. Thereafter, pay increases have been based primarily on his age and length of service with the company. In the plants, much of the work is team or group work. Promotion to a higher level of responsibility and pay depends mainly on age, length of service, and extent of training, which is also related to years of service. Beginning in the 1970s, some companies used job evaluation and/or performance appraisal systems as a less important factor in wage determination.

Significant size-of-company differentials in wages and benefits have existed in their present form since the late 1940s (Tan 1982: 47). Large companies provide a complex system of benefits and welfare payments that also increase with the employee's length of service with the company. They include insurance plans, retirement allowances, housing support of various kinds, and recreation facilities, most of which are absent in small companies (Somers and Tsuda 1966: 206; Galenson and Odaka 1976: 659, 661).

In the 1950s, the wage differential between large and small firms in Japan was apparently somewhat greater than it was in this country (Tan 1982: 46; Taira 1961: 41, 47). By the 1970s, the size-of-firm wage differential seems to have been about the same magnitude in both countries (Oi and Raisian 1985: 2–3, appendix table 2).

The large firms engage heavily in training, especially on-the-job training but also internal classroom instruction in some cases. On-the-job training occurs especially with the frequent transfer from one kind of work to another, in the absence of occupational classifications with promotion ladders.

In Japan since World War II, most unions have been independent enterprise organizations, with the union covering both white-collar and blue-collar employees of the company. In large companies, membership is confined to "regular" or "permanent" employees. This union structure has implications for wages and other terms of employment.

Many studies have been made of wage determination in manufacturing, focused especially on firm-size differentials and the wage and employment practices of large enterprises. Various approaches and research methods have been used, and different sets of hypotheses have been subjected to testing. In a 1982 article, Hong Tan of the Rand Corporation reviews the extensive literature, pointing out the strengths and limitations of the various studies.

Although the Japanese large-company employment system differs from ours in many respects, study of it can add significantly to our knowledge by providing a basis for comparison.

Concluding Observations

The intellectual life of the labor economist would be simple and more serene if neoclassical theory were generally useful for explaining and predicting developments in labor markets. Unfortunately, the theory has become less suitable for analytical purposes as the economy has become more complex and more dominated by large companies, which administer their employment, their wages, their benefit programs, their training programs, and other aspects of their internal operations, often with input from negotiations with one or more certified unions.[37]

As explained in this paper, neoclassical labor market theory (including the marginal productivity theory of employment) is not well designed for analyzing and explaining such developments as the following:

1. Genuine wage differentials among manufacturing plants in a labor market area, with the wage rates for a particular job classification distributed over a significant range without a central tendency, and with that condition persisting for a decade or more.

2. The rapid growth from 1945 to 1980 in company-financed employee benefits, a good part of which are unrelated to the pay or productivity of the individual employee.

3. The differential in wages and in employee benefits by size of plant (company) that is marked and widespread in this country and Japan.

4. The large-company employment systems, centered on career employment for factory workers as well as white-collar employees, that have developed and expanded during the past four decades.

What is needed is the development of a body of theory designed to analyze, as a whole, the employment systems of large companies that have career-employment aims and expectations. Constituent elements of the company's employment system (for example, hiring policies, wage policy, training programs, promotion policy) could then be analyzed as parts of an overall system. That task presents a real challenge to aspiring labor economists.

Notes

1. For a concise report on the section's annual conference in the years 1931 to 1964, see *The Industrial Relations Section of Princeton University, 1922 to 1985*, published by the section (1986: 4–5 and 11–12). Many of the top industrial relations executives of large companies regularly attended and led sessions of the conference.

2. I presented an analysis of wages in the West Coast pulp and paper industry in *Wages under National and Regional Collective Bargaining* (Lester 1946e: 79–88).

3. For a summary of the results of the author's studies of the South–North wage differential that support conclusions in this paper, see Lester 1947: 386–94.

4. See National War Labor Board decision in the Matter of 25 Southern Cotton Textile Companies and Textile Workers Union of America, dated February 20, 1945. *Daily Labor Report* No. 37 (1945: F1) and *Daily Labor Report* No. 89 (1945: A15). David L. Cole was chairman of the Northern Textile Commission.

5. See Lester 1946d: 152–54. Although the occupations were "standardized jobs," no allowance could be made for differences in the quality of workers occupying the jobs in individual plants included in the survey.

6. With cotton textile machinery fairly standard and job duties similar across companies, it was difficult to explain by classical theory the wide intercompany differences in wage rates for the same occupation in a locality.

7. See Lester 1948: 10–13 for company reliance on wage surveys.

8. Given the significant intercompany differences in company wage levels in a community, some firms, such as major chemical and oil companies, select only high-wage or "progressive" employers with whose wage scales they wish to maintain parity.

9. Foulkes 1980: 150, 190. Six of the companies in my study were entirely nonunion, and other companies were partially nonunion.

10. Reynolds (1951: 219) pointed out the difficulties of determining the relative efficiency of different workers in particular jobs and the quality of a plant's work force for the functions it performs. As indicated subsequently, large companies, through on-the-job training and the quality of their supervision, can have considerable influence on the quality of their work forces.

11. The first-stage report is Lester 1954. Employment expanded by sixteen thousand at those four plants. There was very little net expansion in employment at the other manufacturing plants in the area.

12. The second-stage report is Lester 1955. By the first half of 1953, unemployment in the New Jersey part of the Trenton labor market area was down to 2.2 percent of the labor force.

13. The term *firm* will be used instead of *plant*. No company had more than one plant in the Trenton area.

14. In four-fifths of the companies interviewed, all or most of the jobs above the bottom grade were filled by promotions from within (Lester 1954: 32).

15. The pension plans of most nonunion companies are of the defined-contribution type, with the employer paying a stated percentage of the employee's earnings in his name into an invested fund to provide benefits, or the employer makes contributions necessary to pay a stated or defined benefit at retirement. The text is based on Freeman 1983: 25–29 and Gersh 1970: 53–76.

16. In recent years, companies have been adopting new, flexible benefit programs under which the employee can pick the mix of medical, dental, life, and retirement benefits that currently best suits his or her individual needs. Under such flexible plans, the company provides a specific sum of money for the employee, perhaps varying with his pay, to allocate as he wishes among the available benefit programs. The company may gain savings through the introduction of employee contributions and larger deductibles, but flexibility is likely to increase the administrative costs. In 1986 there were 432 large companies, with four million employees, that permitted choice among different levels of health, life, and retirement benefits. See *Business Week* 1986: 63–66.

17. Calculated from the Chamber of Commerce of the United States data in *Employee Benefits 1984* (1985: 31, table 21).

18. Chamber of Commerce of the United States 1985: 30, table 20. Paid vacations, holidays, and sick leave accounted for about 10 percent of wages and salaries, according to estimates by the Chamber of Commerce.

19. As wage surveys show, oil companies are also among the highest-wage employers in labor market areas.

20. The percentage of all workers under collective agreements who were covered by health and other insurances except pensions increased from 4 percent in 1945 to 78 percent in 1960. See Lester 1964: 343, table 16.

21. See, for example, Lawler 1986: 266.

22. Lester 1967b: 59, table 2; and 61, table 4. The textile and clothing industries showed very little establishment-size wage effects, for reasons stated in Lester 1967b: 60 and 62–63.

23. Lester 1967b: 61–62. The nationwide data included only establishments that had expenditures in 1962 for insurance-type benefits and pay for released time such as vacation, holiday, and sick pay.

24. A listing of pertinent studies is to be found in Brown and Medoff 1986: 52–55.

25. Such difficulties are discussed by Orley Ashenfelter in his comments on three papers dealing with the relation of plant and firm size and wages and employee satisfaction (Ashenfelter 1980: 380–82). A 1945 study I made comparing the effectiveness of factory labor in plants in the North and the South found that the quality of management can have a significant effect on the productivity of labor (Lester 1946b: 71–72).

26. Oi 1983a: 63 and 76. Additional papers by Oi in this subject area are: Oi 1983b and Oi and Raisian 1985.

27. Among the task force membership at various times were: John T. Dunlop, Eli Ginzberg, Frederick H. Harbison, Charles C. Killingsworth, Juanita Kreps, Sar A. Levitan, Garth L. Mangum, Ray Marshall, Charles A. Myers, Albert Rees, Gerald G. Somers, and George P. Shultz.

28. National Bureau of Econimic Research 1966. Earlier in 1958 I had explained that new dimensions had been added to factory employment, involving the elongation of the horizon of company managements and necessitating an enlargement of theoretical concepts and frameworks (Lester 1958: 439–46).

29. A colleague at Duke University, Wilford J. Eiteman, made contributions to the question of the determination of marginal cost and the shape of the cost curve. See Eiteman 1945 and Eiteman and Guthrie 1952. The flat or slightly declining cost curve in manufacturing plants seems to have become fairly well accepted.

30. Therefore, for management to adjust to a labor cost increase by reductions in factory employment and output may not be a rational decision.

31. This statement of Baumol's contributions is drawn from his books, Baumol 1967 and Baumol 1983: 319–21.

32. Simon (1979) deals with a wide range of relevant studies.

33. See Lester 1958 for an early discussion of the transformation in blue-collar employment in sizable companies.

34. A plant needs to be of sufficient size for extensive and regular use of on-the-job training to be economical. Also, large plants are likely to have a greater variety of jobs to be filled by promotion or transfer of employees within the plant or firm.

35. Under job evaluation, an individual's wage is not adjusted for the amount or level of education and training he receives as an employee.

36. For more detailed descriptions of the Japanese large-firm employment system at different times, see Somers and Tsuda 1966, Cole 1972, Galenson and Odaka 1976, and Jacoby 1979. For a comparative study of each system's operations in a large city, see Cole 1979. Recent size-of-firm comparisons between Japan and the United States with respect to long-term employment and the slope of earnings profiles are made in Hashimoto and Raisian 1985.

37. In 1985, twenty-five corporations in manufacturing had from one hundred thousand to eight hundred thousand employees, totalling almost five million.

References

Ashenfelter, Orley. 1980. "Commentary on Firm Size, Market Structure and Worker Satisfaction." In *The Economics of Firm Size, Market Structure and Social Performance*, ed. John J. Siegfried, 380–82. Washington, D.C.: Federal Trade Commission.

Baumol, William J. 1967. *Business Behavior, Value, and Growth*. Revised ed. New York: Harcourt, Brace and World.

———. 1983. "On the Career of a Microeconomist." *Banca Nationale del Lavoro Quarterly Review* 147 (December): 311–35.

Brown, Charles, and James L. Medoff. 1986. "The Employer Size-Wage Effect." Harvard Institute of Economic Research Discussion Paper No. 1202.

Bureau of National Affairs, Inc. 1945. *Daily Labor Report*, No. 37, p. Fl.; *Daily Labor Report, No. 89, p. A15*.

Business Week. 1986. "Benefits are Getting More Flexible But Caveat Emptor." No. 2963 (September 8): 64–66.

Chamber of Commerce of the United States. 1985. *Employee Benefits 1984*. Washington, D.C.: U.S. Government Printing Office.

Cole, Robert E. 1972. "Permanent Employment in Japan: Facts and Fantasies." *Industrial and Labor Relations Review* 26 (October): 615–30.

———. 1979. *Work, Mobility, and Participation: A Comparative Study of American and Japanese Industry*. Berkeley: University of California Press.

Davis, Otto A., and Edward Montgomery. 1986. "Study of Income Security in Basic Steel." *Daily Labor Report* No. 94 (May 16): D1–D10. Washington, D.C.: Bureau of National Affairs, Inc.

Derber, Milton. 1949. *Proceedings of the First Annual Meeting of the Industrial Relations Research Association*. Champaign, Ill.: Industrial Relations Research Association.

Eiteman, Wilford J. 1945. "The Equilibrium of the Firm in Multi-Process Industries." *Quarterly Journal of Economics* 59 (February): 280–86.

Eiteman, Wilford J., and Glen E. Guthrie. 1952. "The Shape of the Average Cost Curve." *American Economic Review* 42 (December): 832–38.

Freeman, Richard B. 1981. "The Effect of Trade Unionism on Fringe Benefits." *Industrial and Labor Relations Review* 34, No. 4 (July): 489–509.

———. 1983. *Unions, Pensions and Union Pension Funds*. Cambridge, Mass.: National Bureau of Economic Research, Working Paper No. 1226, November.

Foulkes, Fred K. 1980. *Personal Policies of Large Nonunion Companies*. Englewood Cliffs, N.J.: Prentice–Hall.

Galenson, Walter, and Konosuke Odaka. 1976. "The Japanese Labor Market." In *Asia's New Giant: How the Japanese Economy Works*, ed. Hugh Patrick and Henry Rosovsky, 589–671. Washington, D.C.: The Brookings Institution.

Gersh, Harry. 1970. *Employee Benefits Factbook*. New York: Segal.

Gordon, Robert A. 1948. "Short-Period Price Determination in Theory and Practice." *American Economic Review* 38 (June): 265–88.

———. 1961. *Business Leadership in the Large Corporation*. Berkeley: University of California Press.

Hashimoto, Masanori, and John Raisian. 1985. "Employment Tenure and Earnings Profiles in Japan and the United States," *American Economic Review* 75 (September 1985): 721–35.

Industrial Relations Section, Princeton University. 1986. *The Industrial Relations Section of Princeton University, 1922 to 1985*. Princeton, N.J.: Princeton University.

Jacoby, Sanford. 1979. "Origins of Internal Labor Markets in Japan." *Industrial Relations* 18 (Spring): 184–96.

Lawler, Edward E. 1986. "Determining Total Compensation: Strategic Issues." In *Strategic Human Resources Management: A Guide to Executive Practice*, ed. Fred K. Foulkes, 216–27. Englewood Cliffs, N.J.: Prentice–Hall.

Lester, Richard A. 1946a. "Diversity in North-South Wage Differentials and in Wage Rates Within the South." *Southern Economic Journal* 12 (January): 238–62.

———. 1946b. "Effectiveness of Factory Labor: South-North Comparisons." *Journal of Political Economy* 54 (February): 60–75.

———. 1946c. "Shortcomings of Marginal Analysis for Wage-Employment Problems." *American Economic Review* 36 (March): 63–82.

———. 1946d. "Wage Diversity and Its Theoretical Implications." *Review of Economics and Statistics* 28 (August): 152–59.

———. 1946e. *Wages under National and Regional Collective Bargaining*. Princeton, N.J.: Princeton University Industrial Relations Section.

———. 1947. "Southern Wage Differentials: Developments, Analysis, and Implications." *Southern Economic Journal* 13 (April): 386–94.

———. 1948. *Company Wage Policies: A Survey of Patterns and Experiences*. Princeton: Princton University Industrial Relations Section.

———. 1954. *Hiring Practices and Labor Competition*. Princeton: Princeton University Industrial Relations Section.

———. 1955. *Adjustments to Labor Shortages: Management Practices and Institutional Controls in an Area of Expanding Employment*. Princeton: Princeton University Industrial Relations Section.

———. 1958. "Revolution in Industrial Employment." *Labor Law Journal* (June): 439–46.

———. 1964. *Economics of Labor*, 2d ed. New York: Macmillan.

———. 1966. *Manpower Planning in a Free Society*. Princeton: Princeton University Industrial Relations Section.

———. 1967a. "Benefits as a Preferred Form of Compensation." *Southern Economic Journal* 33 (April): 488–95.

———. 1967b. "Pay Differentials by Size of Establishments." *Industrial Relations* 7 (October): 57–67.

Machlup, Fritz. 1946. "Marginal Analysis and Empirical Research." *American Economic Review* 36(September): 519–54.

Maruhnic, J. 1968. *The Transition from School to Work. A Report Based on the Princeton Manpower Symposium, May 9–10, 1968.* Princeton: Princeton University Industrial Relations Section Research Report No. 111.

Myers, Charles A., and W. Rupert Maclaurin. 1943. *The Movement of Factory Workers: A Study of a New England Industrial Community, 1937–1939 and 1942.* New York: John Wiley.

Myers, Charles A., and George P. Shultz. 1951. *The Dynamics of a Labor Market, A Study of the Impact of Employment Changes on Labor Mobility, Job Satisfaction and Company and Union Policies.* New York: Prentice–Hall.

National Bureau of Economic Research. 1966. *The Measurement and Interpretation of Job Vacancies.* New York: Columbia University Press.

Oi, Walter Y. 1983a. "The Fixed Employment Costs of Specialized Labor." In *The Measurement of Labor Cost*, ed. Jack E. Triplett, 63–116. National Bureau of Economic Research, Studies in Income and Wealth, Vol. 48. Chicago: University of Chicago Press.

———. 1983b. "Heterogeneous Firms and the Organization of Production." *Economic Inquiry* 21 (April): 147–71.

Oi, Walter, and John Raisian. 1985. "Impact of Firm Size on Wages and Work." Draft paper supplied to the author.

Reynolds, Lloyd G. 1951. *The Structure of Labor Markets.* New York: Harper.

Simon, Herbert A. 1979. "Theories of Decision-Making in Economics and Behavioral Science." *American Economic Review* 69 (June): 253–83.

Somers, Gerald G., and Masumi Tsuda. 1966. "Job Vacancies and Structural Change in Japanese Labor Markets." In *The Measurement and Interpretation of Job Vacancies: A Conference Report of the National Bureau of Economic Research*, 195–236. New York: Columbia University Press.

Stewart, Bryce M. 1931. *Development of Industrial Relations in the United States.* New York: Industrial Relations Counselors, Inc., mimeo.

Tachibanaki, Toshiaki. 1982. "Further Research on Japanese Wage Differentials: Nenko Wages, Hierarchical Position, Bonuses and Working Hours." *International Economic Review* 23 (June): 447–61.

Taira, Koji. 1961. "Japanese Enterprise Unionism and Inter-firm Wage Structure." *Industrial and Labor Relations Review* 15 (October): 33–51.

Tan, Hong W. 1982. "Wage Determination in Japanese Manufacturing: A Review of Recent Literature." *Economic Record* 52 (March): 46–60.

U.S. Department of Labor, Bureau of Labor Statistics. 1962. *Employer Expenditures of Selected Supplementary Remuneration Practices for Production Workers in Manufacturing Industries, 1959.* Bulletin No. 1308. Washington, D.C.: U.S. Government Printing Office.

Wayne, Leslie. 1986. "Steel's Pension-Funding Woes." *New York Times*, July 30, 1986, pp. D1 and D4.

Williamson, Oliver E. 1964. *The Economics of Discretionary Behavior: Managerial Objectives in a Theory of the Firm.* Englewood Cliffs, N.J.: Prentice–Hall.

4
Labor Economics Then and Now

Lloyd G. Reynolds

A Personal Preamble

I never decided to become a labor economist. Indeed, when I was an undergraduate at the University of Alberta, the subject had not yet been invented. I did take a course called "labor" taught by a young Rhodes scholar just back from Oxford and full of the British wisdom of that period. We began by reading a Disraeli novel, *Sybil; or the Two Nations* (1845), whose theme was the class divisions in British society. We read the Webbs' *History of Trade Unionism* (1894) and their *Industrial Democracy* (1897). Either in or out of class I read G.D.H. Cole, Bernard Shaw, Harold Laski, and other British Fabians. Over the course of four years I developed into a British labor party socialist. I took it for granted that government-owned enterprises were preferable to privately-owned enterprises and that trade unions were a necessary defense against exploitation of labor.

These beliefs were somewhat visionary, since I had never seen a factory or met an industrial worker. My only personal experience of labor was working every autumn in the wheat harvest, from sunrise to sunset, for the then substantial wage of five dollars a day.

In 1931 I went on to McGill for an M.A. and lived in Montreal through the worst years of the depression. This was my first exposure to unemployment, poverty, and urban slums. To earn my graduate fellowship of five hundred dollars a year, I worked on a research project run by a senior faculty member. As part of this project, I interviewed five hundred unemployed British immigrants to Canada. These poor fellows came every day to the public employment office and sat about waiting for jobs which never appeared. They were happy to relieve the tedium by recounting to me their early training, their migration history, their work record, and their job aspirations. One winter I lived in a settlement house in the worst Montreal slum, where I received free board and room in return for running a boys' club.

These extracurricular experiences had more impact on me than did graduate courses. The direct exposure to hardship confirmed my political beliefs. I served as leader of the Labor party in the McGill Debating Union, and founded and edited an incendiary campus magazine called *The Alarm Clock*.

All of my coterie at this point believed that the capitalist system was on its very last legs.

I proceeded to Harvard in 1934 as a Ph.D. student and later as an instructor in economics. The work there was hard enough to leave little time for political activism, though I remember carrying picket signs in an ILGWU strike in downtown Boston. At Harvard I worked mainly in industrial organization, as part of Edward Mason's expanding empire. I wrote articles on price theory and published a book on monopoly and competition in Canadian industry (Reynolds 1940). But I had some contact also with Harvard's labor economist, Sumner Slichter. While still in Montreal I had published a book on British immigration to Canada (Reynolds 1935), and it occurred to me that this might serve as a dissertation in labor economics. I took the book to Slichter, who found it suitable, and so I got my Harvard degree after two years without ever doing a thesis.

I was never anyone's disciple, but Slichter was the nearest thing to a mentor that I ever had. He came from a notable Wisconsin family—his father was dean of the graduate school at Madison and a brother became president of Northwestern Mutual Life—and he had the directness and basic friendliness that is commoner west of Chicago. In economics, he was an empiricist and a policy man rather than a model builder. His Brookings monograph (Slichter 1941) on the impact of trade unions on industrial management became a classic, sufficiently so that it was revised and reissued by younger colleagues twenty years later. In addition to providing ideas and much friendly counsel, Slichter served the most important function of a mentor—to write those authoritative letters of recommendation which launched me in the academic labor market.

In return, I did a few things for him. He was listed in the undergraduate course catalog for a one-term course in labor economics. At that time, however, teaching undergraduates was rather below the dignity of a senior professor. So the course was actually taught by Moses Abramovitz and myself. I imagine that Moe Abramovitz, who was and is a fine theorist, covered marginal productivity and wage theory. I suspect that my sessions were mainly institutional, even semisociological. I recall assigning John Dollard's 1937 *Caste and Classes in a Southern Town*. And I certainly covered trade union history and collective bargaining.

The event which led me deeper into labor economics was sheer accident. George Barnett, who taught labor economics at Johns Hopkins, died suddenly, and a replacement was needed. Slichter recommended me, and after the usual courtship rituals, I went to Hopkins in the fall of 1939. Having undertaken to teach labor economics, I was forced to think seriously about it, and to structure this still formless subject to my own satisfaction. But after two years of this academic activity, war preparations intensified and Washington beckoned. I worked for a while in the OPA with Kenneth Galbraith and spent a brief period with Bill Haber and Paul Webbink at the War Manpower Commission. But there was more excitement at the National War Labor Board, and I soon found my way over there. I chaired a tripartite Cotton Textile Commission, which handled a group of cases involving all unionized mills in New England, and another group covering all unionized mills in the South. Among other things, we established for the first time a uniform scale of occupational base rates for all the New England mills and a second, somewhat lower, schedule of rates for the Southern mills. Heady stuff for a thirty-year-old.

For most of the time at the board, however, I was a public member of the National Appeals Committee, handling cases appealed by one or both parties from decisions of the regional boards. Sitting with a management member on my right and a labor member on my left, I disposed of several such cases each day, involving a great variety of issues and with little time for reflection before issuing an award. This activity was enormously educational, more so than any amount of reading about collective bargaining. I also greatly enjoyed my panel colleagues, especially the labor members. Being primarily elected union officials, they had the light and amusing touch of politicians without the rigidity one often finds in management people.

To continue with the accidents which shaped my career: Lunching one day in the Labor Department cafeteria with a fellow Appeals Committee member, Wight Bakke, he told me of his plans for a new industrial relations center at Yale and asked whether I would be interested in joining the enterprise. I was interested, and so in the fall of 1945 I arrived in New Haven as a tenured member of the Economics Department and Associate Director of the Labor and Management Center. Oddly enough, I never taught labor economics at Yale. That was the terrain of my good friend Bakke, and I was not about to encroach on his jurisdiction. For some years I taught the required graduate course in economic theory, since in the then depleted state of the Yale Economics Department there was no one else available. Later on I taught graduate courses in comparative economic systems and in development economics. Intermittently I taught principles to undergraduates and also developed an honors seminar in the history of economic thought. Although many people still classify me as a labor economist, I would prefer the honorable title of general practitioner.

It is true that for about ten years my research activity focused on labor subjects. Wight Bakke ran our research center with a light hand, and each of us had to decide what we most wanted to do. Having grown up with price theory, and finding wage theory in a relatively undeveloped state, it occurred to me to see what I could do to put the study of wages on a firmer footing. This meant, to me, looking into the wage and hiring policies of employers, and the behavior of workers in choosing and changing jobs. So with help from Joe Willits at Rockefeller, who launched many of us on our research careers, I organized a substantial study of the market for industrial workers in New Haven. This involved using research assistants to collect work histories and attitudinal material from a sample of about a thousand workers, and interviewing all the industrial employers of any size in the city, a task which I did myself along with my colleague Joe Shister. The eventual outcome was a book, *The Structure of Labor Markets* (1951), about which I shall say more at a later point. The idea of local labor market studies was rather in the air at this time. I recall in particular the Myers and Maclaurin (1943) study of Fitchburg, Massachusetts, and the Myers–Shultz (1951) study of Nashua, New Hampshire. We formed a kind of club of new-style labor economists who got together frequently at small conferences to compare approaches and results.

A second research enterprise was an analysis of wage differentials, with special attention to occupational differentials and to interfirm differentials—an area in which Dick Lester, John Dunlop, and others were working at about the same time. I had voluminous files on the cotton textile industry from War Labor Board days. I assembled similar material on the pulp and paper industry from union and trade association sources. The wage structure of the basic steel industry was being rationalized at this time under union pressure, and accounts of that experience were available. One of my graduate students did a good thesis on the automobile industry (see Macdonald 1963). In addition to these U.S. case studies, I gathered material from several European countries, particularly Sweden, where wage studies were flourishing in the hands of Gosta Rehn and others, and France, with its distinctive SMIG (Salaire Minimum Interprofessionelle Garantie) system, which sets legal minima in considerable detail. The key question was how and why national wage structures change over the course of time. Does supply–demand analysis provide an adequate explanation, or do governmental and union pressures have substantial influence? This explains the title of a book which I did with Cynthia Taft, *The Evolution of Wage Structure* (1956).

My old and good friend Kenneth Galbraith has intervened in my career at a number of points, notably in 1952 when he recommended me to the government of Puerto Rico for a study of the labor aspects of their new industrialization program. They thought that they wanted a projection of future manpower requirements in the island. I convinced them that this was an unpromising enterprise and sold them on what amounted to a study of the market for industrial workers in Puerto Rico. A colleague recruited from Harvard, Peter Gregory, interviewed employers at length, squads of Spanish-speaking research assistants interviewed samples of workers, data were assembled on wage behavior, labor mobility and turnover, and labor flows between the island and the mainland. The fieldwork continued until the late fifties and, apart from its intellectual interest, had important policy implications, especially for minimum wage determination and the relation of Puerto Rican minima to those on the mainland. This was my first exposure to a "less developed economy" with surplus labor. Along with travel in Africa for the

Carnegie Foundation (in 1952) and travel in Asia for the Ford Foundation (1957), this stimulated me to found the Economic Growth Center at Yale in 1960 and to turn my research interests in that direction.

But in doing this, I was not entirely leaving labor economics. The less developed countries, after all, have problems of labor recruitment, training, and motivation, of wage determination and income distribution, as others on this panel can testify from the massive Kerr–Dunlop–Harbison–Myers (1960) study of labor in the industrialization process. In addition, an enterprising vice-president of Prentice–Hall had persuaded me to do a text on labor economics and labor relations. This book (Reynolds 1949) was an attempt to structure the subject as I saw it at that time. Many teachers apparently found my structure congenial, and the book had a substantial success. But success brings work as well as rewards. Every four years, Prentice–Hall descended on me for a new edition, and my conscience then compelled me to read what had been published since the previous edition, so as to continue pouring new wine into the old bottle. The ninth edition appeared about a year ago, and so I feel up with the literature, even though my own research in labor economics lies far in the past.

This personal account, as you will have noticed, is filled with accidental twists and turns. I never sat down deliberately and chose labor economics as my area of activity. The subject chose me, because a job vacancy appeared at a time when academic jobs were scarce. But having gotten into the field, I felt obliged to do the best I could with it. But let me turn now from personal reflections to a broader review of the development of our subject.

Labor Economics Then and Now

Labor economics is a relatively new branch of applied economics—much newer than international economics, monetary economics, or public finance, newer even than industrial organization, which dates at least from Marshall's *Industry and Trade* (1919) and was well developed by the late twenties. I would date labor economics from around 1940, which because of the war hiatus means effectively from 1945. So people of my age can claim to be first-generation labor economists.

Why do I choose 1940 rather than some earlier date? Mainly because I am talking about the *economics* of labor. There were important earlier books on trade unionism, by Sidney and Beatrice Webb, John R. Commons, and Selig Perlman, among others. But those books were mainly organizational and historical and did not make effective contact with the central core of economics. There were also college courses in the twenties and thirties, usually called "labor problems" or simply "labor." I surmise that these courses crept into the curriculum partly as an offset to the apparent inhumanity of monetary economics, international economics, and other standard courses. Many economists, from Smith onwards, have been concerned with welfare and with using economics to improve the lot of the common man. Somewhere in the curriculum these concerns needed to be packaged up and presented to students. Hence the labor course, where reformers could have their say.

I do not mean to look down on these courses, from which students must have learned a good deal. But much of their content would scarcely be recognized as economics by theoretical purists. A leading early text was Carroll Daugherty's *Labor Problems in American Industry* (1933). After an introduction, part two consists of 350 pages on "The Labor Problems." These problems include insecurity, low wages and incomes, hours and work periods, substandard workers (including southern workers and Negroes along with children and convicts), and industrial conflict. Part three consists of 500 pages headed "Attempts to Solve Labor Problems." These include trade unionism (eight chapters), personnel management (four chapters), protective labor legislation (two chapters), and laws regulating labor disputes (one chapter). In short, a great variety of topics, strung out like beads on a string, with little in the way of analytical framework. There is a 25-page discussion of wage determination, entitled "A Parade of Theories." Here we encounter the subsistence theory, the wages fund theory, the marginal productivity theory (only four pages!), the bargaining theory, and the high-wage purchasing power theory—all apparently enjoying equal status. This is followed by a section entitled "How Are Wages Actually Determined?"—a reality apparently unrelated to the theories discussed earlier.

I cite this not to criticize Carroll Daugherty, who was a good economist of his period, but simply to emphasize the formlessness of the subject at this stage. This is what people of my generation were reading in college and graduate school. This was the shaky foundation on which we first-generation labor economists tried to build a more solid structure. We did, I think, make improvements, and the years 1945–60 were a boom period in labor economics. But in the sixties the momentum slackened. The new glamour field was macroeconomics, and a bit later development economics. These eventually lost steam in their turn, and in the early seventies labor economics began to revive. But it revived in such a different form that it could almost be considered a new subject.

In this section I want to contrast the content of labor economics in the era 1945–60 with that in the era 1970–86. Most of the recent work comes from second- and even third-generation labor economists. What they are doing is distinctly different from what people of my generation were doing. These differences cannot be attributed to personal idiosyncrasies. Rather, they have been generated partly by external changes in the economy and partly by the internal evolution of economics—developments in theory, in data sources, in research techniques. All this I hope to explain.

Early Days: The Shaping of Thought

Economists of my age finished their formal training in the late twenties and early thirties. We began teaching and writing in the late thirties and then, usually after a break for wartime service, carried on in the forties and fifties. Let us begin, then, by considering the economic and intellectual milieu of those days, the factors which shaped our thinking and our research direction.

Pride of place should undoubtedly go to the Great Depression. It is hard for the present generation to realize how that event shook people's faith, and especially young people's faith, in the beneficence and viability of existing institutions. Many doubted that capitalism could long survive, and possible directions of change were eagerly debated. Radical political clubs on campus reached a height of popularity which they have never attained since.

Doubts about the viability of existing economic institutions necessarily rubbed off onto economic theory, which was supposed to explain how those institutions worked and even in some sense to rationalize and justify them. Macroeconomics, then called "business cycle theory," had signally failed to predict the onset and depth of the depression. The idea that people were unemployed because they were demanding too much in wages lost credibility. Theory was not helpful in suggesting ways out of the morass. Microeconomics, at least in its starkest version as the theory of competitive price, lends itself readily to caricature, as a rationalization that "whatever is, is right" and as an inaccurate picture of reality. These caricatures may be unfair, but in the thirties they were very popular. Gardiner Means, Charles Hitch, James Meade, and many others went about asking business men "Now, how do you *actually* set prices?," and came panting back with the news that conventional theory was misleading. What Galbraith later labeled "the conventional wisdom" has never sunk to a lower ebb.

Macroeconomics, of course, was reconstructed and rehabilitated in the late thirties and forties. After Keynes, theory once more seemed relevant both to explanation and to policy. But this reconstruction did not extend to microeconomics. Despite all the arrows directed at it, conventional price theory rode through depression and war with surprisingly little change. During the fifties, the price theory being taught in the introductory economics course was little changed from Marshall's exposition a half-century earlier. The apparent unrealism of these simple formulations inclined some of us to say: "Enough of all this. Let's go out and look at the world."

A major institutional development was the rapid growth of union organization from 1935 to 1945, which continued at a lower rate through the mid-fifties. To many of us, this growth seemed self-evidently good. Bargained terms of employment were bound to be more equitable than terms set unilaterally by the employer; and the *process* of bargaining coupled with grievance adjustment was more democratic, more liberating of worker initiative. We also tended to project union growth into an indefinite future, and to visualize an era in which collective bargaining would dominate the employment scene. One would expect such an economy to operate differently in many ways from a nonunion economy, and this stimulated work on how to reshape economic reasoning to accommodate this new institution.

Important also was the fact that many labor economists were immersed from 1941 to 1945 in wartime activities, often as officers of the National War Labor Board. It was a heady experience to find myself at age thirty-two laying down a uniform wage scale for all the unionized cotton textile mills. This produced a certain skepticism when I later heard theorists saying that such tinkering with wage rates was both harmful and impracticable. For better or worse, we had been doing it, and the skies had not fallen.

Day-to-day immersion in the realities of labor relations has an educational effect which is hard to define but is nonetheless real. I learned many things in those four years that could not possibly have been learned from books. Happily, today's labor economists have been spared this educational experience. War is an expensive way of learning.

Finally, a word on two characteristics of the period which are intellectual rather than institutional. First is the broad interpretation given to "labor economics" in the forties and fifties, evident in the content of textbooks and course outlines. It encompassed everything affecting the welfare of wage and salary earners. Conditions of life on the job, nonwage terms of employment, the benefits and costs of union organization, the hardships of unemployment and poverty, the operation of social insurance programs and government transfer payments to the poor—all were included. The determinants of the overall distribution of personal income, and the merit of redistributive programs, also formed part of the labor course. In the normal specialization and differentiation of any science, some of these things have now been hived off into separate courses on income distribution, social insurance, protective labor legislation, and the like. Labor economics has become narrower, sharper, more specialized. But as of 1950, this all lay in the future.

This broad conception of the subject gave it an inherently multidisciplinary character. There was a certain economic core, for which study of micro theory was a useful preparation. But social psychology, law, politics, and organization theory also had a good deal to say. Faced with this situation, economists react in different ways. Some stick resolutely to questions which can be attacked with economic tools. When they come to a problem which will not yield to economic reasoning, they wash their hands of it by saying, "I hereby turn this issue over to my colleague the political scientist, or the sociologist, or whatever." This is of course purely ritualistic because, as one wise man has remarked, "That other chap is never there." The alternative course, which has much to recommend it, is for the economist to stretch his faculties beyond the normal limits of his discipline and to become his own political scientist, or whatever. Of course, this lays one open to criticism. George Stigler or someone will say "Why, that's mere sociology". There can be no stronger putdown, but I don't regard that as necessarily the final word.

My second comment relates not just to labor economics but to most branches of economics at this time: Research methodology was relatively simple, even primitive. Graduate courses were called "economic statistics" rather than "econometrics." We learned about regression techniques and R^2 values, but we didn't use them very much. Research studies relied mainly on simple cross-tabulations, or on time series, from which truth was expected to leap to the naked eye. Given the relative scarcity of micro data, there was much reliance on homegrown samples of workers, employers, or whatever, who were interviewed with more or less elaborate questionnaires. A procedure which relies on believing what people tell you is obviously fallible. But it seemed useful, and often necessary, at the time.

Early Days: Research Directions

So much for background. Now what were labor economists working on and writing about in the forties and fifties? Without having counted books and articles, I feel safe in saying that the greatest volume of work was on trade unionism and collective bargaining. It is significant that the early Princeton research center and the new centers which sprang up after 1945—at Berkeley, UCLA, Illinois, Minnesota, Cornell, and other places—were typically called institutes of *industrial relations*. The focus was on union and management decision making, collective bargaining processes, and their economic impact. Much of this work related to unionism per se—general studies of union growth, histories of particular unions, studies of internal union government, and so on.

Studies with a more economic orientation took several forms. John Dunlop and others wrestled with the problem of modeling a union's economic objectives. Is it useful to regard the union as a monopolist maximizing some quantity, and if so, which of several possible quantities? Some scholars questioned the assumption of a single union decision maker reasoning in economic terms. They pointed to the political nature of wage decisions, including rivalry and imitation among unions with overlapping or neighboring job territories. We can all remember "pattern bargaining," and Arthur Ross's "orbits of coercive comparison." Another body of work examined the detailed pattern of wage rates in a company or industry. Several studies traced the way in which industry wage structures had been reshaped under union influence— in basic steel, automobiles, over-the-road trucking, cotton textiles, pulp and paper, and other industries. The question was raised whether exercise of market power by companies and unions contributes to inflationary pressure.

The "cost-push hypothesis" was advanced and debated, as in some measure it has been ever since.

Labor economists of this period would have been the first to recognize that wages aren't everything. Indeed, a major criticism of conventional theory was its fixation on the wage effects of unionism to the neglect of other important effects. Collective bargaining ranges across all aspects of the employment relation and among other things compels a reshaping of management organization and policies on labor matters. These effects were reviewed by Sumner Slichter in a trailbreaking 1941 study, which was to be revised and amplified twenty years later by younger colleagues at the Harvard Business School.

Turning from collective bargaining to more general studies, we note first a large body of work on the national wage structure. This work, in which Richard Lester played a leading role, took off from the wide variation of wage rates for different jobs. BLS reports document the fact that different employers in a local labor market pay substantially different rates for apparently similar work. Are these apparent differences genuine or spurious? To the extent that they are genuine, how can one account for them? Wage rates, corrected as they should be for living cost differences, vary considerably by size of community and region of the country. Particular attention was directed to the North–South differential (see Lester 1945)—how it had come into existence, whether it was narrowing over time, how it might evolve in the future. There was work on interindustry wage differences. Do monopolistic or oligopolistic industries with controlled pricing and relatively high profit rates tend also to pay higher wages? Do industries with above-average rates of increase in employment find it necessary to give above-average wage increases to attract the necessary labor? Finally, what about wage differences between different occupational strata? Here there is a venerable tradition of theorizing about wage differences, stemming from Adam Smith and revised and restated by later writers. To what extent does this body of reasoning give a satisfactory explanation of existing occupational differences, and changes in these differences over time?

I have already mentioned the numerous studies of local labor markets during the forties and fifties. The motivation for these studies was that the picture of a competitive labor market presented in micro texts did not fully account for the phenomena observed in actual labor markets. There is more variation in company wage levels, more misallocation of individuals among jobs, more frictional unemployment than one would expect in a world of perfectly informed choice. Since micro data on wages, employment, and unemployment are usually not available on an area basis, the studies relied heavily on questionnaire data from samples of workers and employers. I shall comment further on these studies in my concluding section on the evolution of labor market concepts.

There is not time to do justice to the variety of other issues covered in the research literature. There was much work on legal aspects of collective bargaining, on income distribution, on labor legislation, on unemployment and income maintenance programs—all regarded at the time as coming with the orbit of labor economics. As one reads the literature, one is struck by its strong empirical tone, the simple and straightforward framing of research problems, the absence of theoretical panache.

The "New Labor Economics": Conditioning Factors

At some point in the late fifties the steam began to go out of labor economics. The glamour field was macroeconomics, where it seemed that economists had helped policymakers to ward off depression. This was soon to be succeeded by the new glamour field of development economics, which attracted not only graduate students but faculty members like myself from other fields. Many of the best minds, too, were preoccupied with tool development, with pure theory and econometric method. Students choosing labor economics as a thesis field tended to be in the lower half of the class, with some brilliant exceptions.

Around 1970 the tide turned once more, and labor economics began to revive. But it revived in such a different form that it could almost be considered a new subject. Perhaps this is why it did revive and once more began to attract superior students. The transformation is seen most clearly by comparing a 1985 textbook with the texts being used in the thirties and forties. The older books are heavily historical, institutional, descriptive. In looking at my own first edition in 1949, which I had not done for many years, I was startled to find 260 pages on unionism and collective bargaining, 120 pages which could be considered labor economics, and 100 pages of policy discussion—minimum wages, unemployment, social security, and a variety of income maintenance programs. Modern texts, among which I would modestly include my ninth edition, give three-quarters of their space to labor economics rather strictly defined. The discussion is fitted into the theoretical rubrics of labor supply, labor demand, and wage determination. It is heavily studded with references to econometric studies, mostly of post-1970 vintage. The student seems to be in quite a different world from that of 1950.

How did this transformation come about? The answer, I think, lies mainly in new directions of theorizing, new data sources, and new econometric techniques, aided and abetted by computer facilities. The pace of change in these respects over the past generation has been remarkably rapid. So it is not surprising that labor economics, earlier one of the most descriptive and untheoretical branches of economics, should have experienced a drastic overhaul.

As macroeconomics became increasingly controversial and confused after the mid-sixties, microeconomics began to emerge from the shadows and to attract some of the best theoretical minds. There has been more progress in microeconomics in the last twenty years than in the preceding sixty years Consider only a few of the new directions in micro theory:

1. *Human capital theory*, which treats education and job training as analogous to investment in physical capital, with immediate costs balanced against a larger lifetime earnings stream. This has stimulated a large body of research on the interrelation of ability, training, and earnings.

2. *Theories of labor market discrimination*, prompted partly by the emergence of the civil rights movement and the women's movement in the sixties and the passage of antidiscrimination legislation. Again, this has stimulated many research studies of earnings differences by sex and race, how far these differences reflect labor market discrimination, and how much they could be reduced by effective enforcement of antidiscrimination policies.

3. *The life-cycle approach* to individual decision making. Modigliani, Duesenberry, and others were arguing a generation ago that decisions about consumption and saving, about accumulation and decumulation of capital, should logically be made in a lifetime perspective. From this it was a short step to argue that labor supply decisions—about how much to work, what occupation to choose, how much to invest in human capital, and so on— should also reflect long-term expectations and preferences. This has produced a host of testable hypotheses.

4. Analysis of labor supply has been enriched also by what is often called *the new home economics*. This recognizes that most adults live in household units, that husband–wife decisions are interrelated, and that labor supply decisions are part of the whole complex of decisions about where to live, how much to spend and save, how much to invest in children, and so on. Becker's work on allocation of time, and the work of Lancaster and others on consumption as household production, is ingenious and illuminating.

5. Recognition of *inside labor markets* and the prevalence of long-term employment commitments has also yielded many insights. In particular, it has encouraged theorizing about optimal personnel policies for the employer— investment in recruitment and screening, investment in on-the-job training, wage strategy over the employee's life cycle, optimal adjustment to short-term fluctuations in labor needs, and so on. Recognition that while long-term commitments are common, they are not universal, has led to development of "dual labor market" models and efforts at empirical tests of these models.

6. Developments in *information and search theory* have been quite fruitful as applied to the labor market. It turns out that, with limited information, a competitive labor market will not eliminate wage discrepancies among employers. It turns out that part of what appears as time lost through unemployment is actually investment in productive job search.

This burst of theorizing has somewhat blurred the distinction between who is and is not a labor economist. I'm sure that Richard Freeman and James Medoff would want to be called labor economists. Probably people like Melvin Reder and Sherman Rosen would consent to be so labeled. But what about people like Robert Hall, George Perry, Gary Becker, Jacob Mincer, George Stigler, Ted Schultz, James Heckman? These people have contributed greatly to the enrichment of labor studies, but I imagine they would want to be considered general economic theorists who happen to have taken an interest in labor supply and labor markets. One could almost say that the theorists have invaded and conquered the labor field. This does not worry me especially. A good theorist is entitled to take the whole economy as his province.

Turning from theory to data, the main development has been the increased availability of micro data on individuals and firms from government sources. Instead of running around on foot asking questions, one can now get the answers on tape—individual employment histories, company records of employment and labor costs. Some of these samples now run over periods of twenty to thirty years, so that cross-section results can be checked against longitudinal studies.

Techniques of data analysis are also considerably improved. We now know that hypotheses, instead of being outlined in a literary and often incomplete way, should be specified completely in quantitative terms. Econometricians have provided better methods for crunching the numbers and more sophisticated rules about what results we can and cannot believe. These tool developments now largely guide the choice of research subjects. The modern labor economist, confronted with an empirical question, asks first, "Do we have an applicable theory, or could one be developed?" and second, "Do we have data adequate for testing theoretical predictions?" Subjects which cannot pass these tests tend to be rejected, and research goes where the numbers are. While this has brought gains in precision, it has also brought some loss in the variety and richness of the subject. The quantitative emphasis seems mainly responsible for the "slimming down" and narrowing of modern labor economics.

The New Labor Economics: Content

Let me conclude this section with a few comments on the content of labor economics today. Trade unionism and collective bargaining occupy considerably less space in today's literature. This may partly reflect the relative decline of unionism in the private sector, so that it appears as an only moderate emendation of market theory rather than as the wave of the future. In addition, work on labor history, labor law, and collective bargaining procedures has been assigned increasingly to specialists in those areas, so that the work left for labor economists is confined to more strictly economic issues. The union impact on earnings has been debated for a long time, but new sources of micro data now permit a more penetrating analysis. The impact is highly variable—

by time period, by industry, by skill level, by age and sex of the worker. The effort to explain these differences has led to improved models of union wage and employment objectives and more careful specification of the demand for union labor.

Perhaps more interesting is the work on nonwage effects of unionism, such as those on fringe benefits, quit rates, length of job tenure, labor productivity, and company profits. These things used to be discussed in qualitative terms, usually ending with a statement that "We don't really know." Recent researchers, notably Richard Freeman and James Medoff, have made a determined effort to quantify such effects and to reach less ambiguous conclusions. The answers are certainly not all in . A decade ago, some theorists, focusing on the monopoly face of unionism, thought that they had finally destroyed any economic case for union organization. The revisionist results of Freeman and Medoff clearly has these critics worried, and lively debate will certainly continue.

Another subject which has been debated for decades and which continues to receive attention is the behavior of wages and labor costs during business cycle fluctuations. Many people continue to like "cost-push," and I regularly receive complaints that my text doesn't take it seriously enough. Related to this are discussions of how labor markets operate, why market clearing may be incomplete or sluggish, the significance of measured unemployment rates, and whether there is a "natural" rate of unemployment—all the things which Phelps labeled "the micro foundations of macroeconomics." The boundary between macroeconomics and labor economics is not nearly as clear as it was a generation ago. Many macro theorists have invaded what we used to consider our terrain, with benefit to all.

Turning to micro issues, there has been a great increase in work on the determinants of labor supply, which instead of half a chapter now occupies several chapters of a labor text. All kinds of intriguing hypotheses have emerged from the theoretical developments mentioned earlier: hypotheses about differences between male and female labor force behavior, about interaction of decisions within the household, about timing of work and nonwork over the life cycle, about decisions regarding education and job training which influence labor force quality. The growing availability of micro samples makes it easier to test these hypotheses, and researchers have rushed in to exploit these possibilities. The supply of possible dissertation subjects is almost endless. There have also been efforts to estimate the effect of income maintenance programs, and the potential effect of a negative income tax plan, on labor supply decisions.

Labor demand curves have been with us for a century, ever since the marginalist revolution. But in earlier times we drew a line on the chart without worrying about its shape. Recently there has been greater effort to estimate actual elasticities, including short-run versus long-run elasticities, and elasticities of demand for union labor as against labor in general. The new emphasis on expected continuity of the employment relation, and on employer investment in worker training, has also altered and enriched the demand discussion. It appears that what the company is hiring is largely trainability, which is estimated by a variety of imperfect indicators. Specific job skills are then inculcated through training and work experience. The existence of sunk costs in the worker, and the gap between his or her productivity and the productivity of a possible replacement, makes employer behavior distinctly different from what it would be if workers were anonymous and interchangeable units sitting on a demand curve. This insight has led to much investigation of employers' recruitment and training decisions, use of overtime and layoffs as alternatives to changing the size of the labor force, the characteristics of labor mobility, and the relation between earnings and length of job tenure.

There has also been a great increase in work on differences in earnings and differences in total compensation, including fringes. A clearer rationale for use of fringes has appeared in the literature, and reasons for the growth of fringes are now analyzed in quantitative rather than impressionistic terms. Earnings differences used to be discussed in terms of group averages for a company, an industry, an occupation. Variation within the group being averaged creates a lot of noise. Today, micro samples permit us to relate the earnings of a particular worker to the characteristics of that worker. The largest body of work is probably on the relation between education and earnings. The positive relation which usually appears then raises many subquestions: What does education actually do? Does it increase the worker's productivity—in general, or in a particular area? Or is it a proxy for intellectual ability and perserverance at a task? If so, is it a good proxy? Is the diploma mainly a certification, which causes the holder to be screened out for a better job than would be available otherwise? The answers, still not fully known, are obviously important for evaluating the social return to investment in education, as well as the efficiency and equity of labor market processes.

While formal education has received most attention, there has been much work also on the relation between earnings and such other variables as age, amount of on-the-job training, total work experience, length of tenure with present employer, continuity of employment, personal ability as indicated by such proxies as IQ scores or aptitude tests, union or nonunion status, and of course race and sex. Union wage effects now tend to be measured by the size of the union-status coefficient in earnings regressions. The race and sex coefficients are used in analyses of discrimination, which deserves a separate word.

The economics of discrimination is one of the newest and most policy-relevant branches of labor economics. It attempts to define, explain, and measure labor market discrimination, that is, unequal access to jobs and to the education which prepares for such jobs. On the policy side, it tries to appraise the effect of antidiscrimination measures. The measurement problems are complex, and the policy issues are somewhat emotional, making this a lively area for those who venture into it.

This is by no means a full account, but it may be sufficient to indicate the main frontiers of current research.

How can one characterize the new labor economics in comparison with the old? It is narrower in scope. It is scientifically-oriented, with policy conclusions as a by-product rather than a prime objective. It seems at times a bit colorless, lacking the drama of earlier writings on union–management relations. There is less anecdotal economics and more regression analysis. Research is focused more strictly on questions which can be cast in quantitative terms: Not "what would be interesting to know?" but "what can we actually prove?" It takes competitive market theory as a necessary starting point. The results tend to confirm that markets work rather well, and that hypotheses which assume economic calculation are vindicated. In contrast to the value-laden content of some earlier writings, the tone of modern labor economics is cool, detached, scientific. To the extent that any political shading can be discovered, it is usually conservative, which is in line with trends in the community generally. This is perhaps not unconnected with the fact that much of the recent work has come from faculty members and graduates of the University of Chicago, which has always been soft on markets, critical of unionism, dubious of government intervention in the economy.

These comments are not advanced in a spirit of complaint. If I was critical of some micro theorists in the fifties, it was because they seemed to be spinning the same old prayer wheels. But some of today's labor economists have invented new and better prayer wheels. I do deplore theorists who waste their ingenuity in solving little mathematical puzzles. But these are not the best of their breed. The very best theorists are trying to cut, in a rigorous way, into the core of the economy. This kind of work I respect and admire.

Some of you may have seen an amusing essay, presented originally as an after-dinner talk at Oxford and later published in *Oxford Economic Papers* (see Sargent 1963). The title was "Are American Economists Better?" The answer was "Better—but less useful." The author meant that American economists are better tooled up, and technically more skillful, than most British economists, but that they are often doing small finger exercises with little empirical or policy relevance. Observing my colleagues, I often feel some sympathy with this view. But who is to judge? The glory of academia is that each of us is free to pursue whatever line of inquiry seems most interesting. Charity toward the work of others is a great virtue. A few people in each generation are doing significant and durable work, and perhaps the others don't really matter. By 2020 A.D. it will be easier to judge what has survived from the new labor economics. Meanwhile, I applaud the vigor and imagination of younger scholars in the field. They have revived what in the sixties seemed a rather moribund subject, and have restored it as a field to which one need not be ashamed to direct the best graduate students.

The Emergence of Labor Market Theory

Is not the effort and reward from work as important as the satisfaction from consumption? Do not labor markets deserve equal billing with commodity markets? Many of us would answer yes. So it is rather startling to observe that for the first hundred and fifty years of modern economics, labor markets are almost absent from the literature.

Classical economics was preoccupied with the growth of national output and its distribution among landowners, capitalists, and workers. It was almost completely aggregative. There was endless discussion of *the* level of wages, and whether this did or did not tend toward a subsistence minimum. But there was little attention to determination of specific wage rates and the reasons for wage differences.

There was, of course, Adam Smith's famous chapter on compensating differences in wages. This implies the possiblity of occupational choice and of labor markets in which choice can be exercised; but this implication was not developed, perhaps not even recognized. Smith's discussion includes an analysis of human capital, but this insight was also to lie fallow until the 1950s.

J.S. Mill's chapter on wage differences is largely an elaboration of Smith, but there are several original contributions. Mill notes that the distinction between different grades of labor almost amounts to hereditary castes. "Consequently the wages of each class have hitherto been regulated by the increase of its own population rather than of the general population of the country." This anticipates Cairnes's later discussion of noncompeting groups, though Cairnes rightly added the influence of reciprocal demand by each group for the other's products. Mill opined that the earnings of occupations requiring education "are at a monopoly rate, from the impossibility, to the mass of people, of obtaining that education." He noted that pay for women's occupations is well below that of comparable occupations done by men. One reason, he thought, might be a supply price depressed by the fact that most women at that time were not primary wage earners. But probably most important was the restricted range of occupations open to women, causing an overcrowding of those occupations, which lowered their market wage. So the "crowding hypothesis," which figures largely in recent discussions of sex discrimination, goes back a long way.

The situation was not appreciably changed by the marginalist revolution. The new tools were still employed only at an aggregative level. In J.B. Clark's theory of distribution we find again *the* rate of wages and *the* rate of interest.

The rate of wages is determined by an aggregate real demand schedule for labor and the number of homogeneous, equally efficient workers available. Eventually, of course, marginalist concepts were to provide a foundation for industry and company demand curves for labor. But this was a much later development.

So we come to Alfred Marshall, whose book (Marshall 1890) was long the bible of microeconomics—indeed, almost the origin of that subject. The term *labor market* appears only rarely in Marshall. But there is a great deal about *wage determination*—six chapters rather than the traditional one—and much more concern with wage differences. There are all the nice Marshallian touches: the mutual interdependence of demand, supply, and wage rates; the distinction between short and long periods, and the difference between short-run market wages, which are influenced mainly by demand, and the "normal equilibrium" attained over periods long enough for supply to have its full effect. He thought that the long-run was longer for labor than for commodities because "labor is slowly produced and slowly worn out."

Even where Marshall is elaborating earlier themes, as he often does, he adds depth and sharpness to the discussion. Three examples will suffice. He generalizes Smith's reasons for wage differences into a theory of "net advantage." "The attractiveness of a trade depends not on its money-earnings but on its net advantages"—presumably to workers on the margin of decision, though he does not say this explicitly. He restates Smith's assertion that any occupation must yield enough to repay the costs of training for that occupation plus a normal rate of return on cost. But he adds that, because training periods are long for many occupations, supply adjustments are correspondingly slow, just as they are for long-lived physical capital. Thus specialized workers may earn positive or negative quasi rents for a long time.

Marshall was preoccupied with the importance of education, which recurs frequently in his chapters. In the case of labor, unlike that of capital, those who make the investment decisions are not those who reap the reward. Educational decisions are made by parents. This presents no serious problem in the higher income levels. "The professional classes especially, while generally eager to save some capital for their children, are even more on the alert for opportunities of investing it in them." But working-class parents typically underinvest, because of both limited resources and limited foresight. The disadvantage thus imposed on working-class people is not merely temporary but can become cumulative.

Like Mill, Marshall accepts the marked stratification of British society as a fact of life. His strata are workingmen, artisans, and "the well-to-do." Mobility between these levels is quite limited, though he notes that "small streams of labor" can have an eroding effect over long periods. If there were not movememt at all among grades, and if the population growth rate in each grade was due to noneconomic causes, then their relative earnings would depend solely on product demand.

Turning to bits of analysis which seem original with Marshall, we can again note three examples. First, he gives a precise statement of the principle that, in equilibrium, a producer will employ each factor up to the point at which its marginal product equals its price. Thus "the wages of every class of labor tend to be equal to the net product due to the additional labor of the marginal laborer of that class." Moreover, since the wage paid by each employer tends to be equalized by competition, it follows that marginal products will also be equalized, yielding an optional allocation of the labor force.

A second contribution consisted in taking account of differences in labor quality through the concept of *efficiency wages*. What competition tends to equalize is not wages but rather efficiency wages in a particular occupation. This equalizing tendency is stronger the greater the mobility of labor, and he emphasizes the need for alertness of parents in directing their children to the most advantageous occupations.

Perhaps the most celebrated passage in Marshall is the statement that the lower grades of labor, having small cash reserves, are under the necessity of selling their labor quickly, which puts them at a disadvantage in negotiating with employers. "It is, however, certain that manual laborers as a class are at a disadvantage in bargaining; and that the disadvantage wherever it exists is likely to be cumulative in its effects." What can this possibly mean? It sounds like haggling over prices in some kind of market. And one might have expected Marshall to proceed to a discussion of actual wage setting. But he does not do this, apparently regarding his bold statement as one of those stylized facts with which everyone should be familiar. To me, the statement is more puzzling than illuminating.

All in all, one comes out of Marshall with a collection of shrewd insights rather than with a labor market theory. The treatment of wages in Book VI does not approach in completeness and rigor the treatment of prices in Book V. There are, incidentally, no diagrams in the wage chapters, and the Mathematical Appendix also stops short before Book VI. Labor had not really been rescued from the realm of anecdotal economics.

There is not time to take account of Pigou's contribution in *The Economics of Welfare* (1932). His part III, "The National Dividend and Labor," consisting of 18 chapters in 230 pages, could almost be regarded as a treatise on labor economics. But it is labor economics with a special twist. Since his focus is on maximizing the national dividend, his concern here is with conditions that may reduce the national dividend, and with the desirability of public intervention to correct such conditions. This motivates his discussion of legal limits on hours of work; of ways of adjusting workers' earnings more closely to services rendered, particularly by use of piece rates; of the various obstacles to labor mobility, and the extent to which it is socially efficient to override these obstacles at public expense; of the consequences of intervention to raise wages where they are "unfair," and in other cases where they are already fair; of the effect of a national minimum time wage. This is sophisticated policy discussion, still worth reading today. But analytically, it does not carry us much beyond Marshall.

Thus I date the appearance of modern labor market analysis at around 1930. Around this time several things happened with remarkable speed. Most important was the sudden appearance of a theory of the firm. Up to this point, price theory had been industry economics. Pure competition was the standard case, and by definition a competitive industry consists of many firms, whose identities and decisions are not very interesting because they are constrained by the market. Marshall's "representative firm" was a convenient analytical device, not a real flesh-and-blood business.

Now with Edward Chamberlin (1933) and Joan Robinson (1933), the shoe was suddenly on the other foot. The firm, with some degree of market power, and with its own downward-sloping demand curve, came to center stage. Pure competition was pushed to the sidelines. Profit-maximizing diagrams for the firm became a staple of the introductory course. Naturally enough, some economists, who considered these diagrams too good to be true, began going around to businesses asking, "Now, what do you actually do? How do you decide prices and output? How, for that matter, do you reach decisions on wage rates and employment?" Questions were asked which no one had thought to ask before. This set up a fruitful interaction between observation and theorizing which continues to the present day.

Edward Chamberlin's book was devoted entirely to product markets; but Joan Robinson went beyond this to analyze and diagram labor markets. Along with John Hicks, who published his *Theory of Wages* (1932) almost simultaneously, she was the first to do this. She invented monopsony, though she gives credit for the label to a Cambridge colleague. Here we find a battery of productivity diagrams (gross and net, average and marginal), an analysis of the labor demand schedules of the firm and industry, a discussion of the meanings which can be given to "exploitation of labor." This is strict, concise analysis, without any real world comments à la Marshall. The conceptual approach and the diagrammatic style found their way quickly into the infant study of labor economics.

The other seminal work of the period was John Hick's *Theory of Wages*. What a lovely and original book this is. Hicks was mainly responsible for importing indifference curves from the Continent to Britain. So we find the now-standard analysis of the relation between the wage rate and the hours of work offered by the individual employee. In part one, entitled "The Free Market," we find also a discussion of individual productivity differences and the ways in which wage systems can accommodate these differences; an analysis of employers' wage policies over the business cycle; the new concept of elasticity of factor substitution and its impact on factor shares of national income; and the effect of differing types of invention on output and distribution. Part two, on "Regulation of Wages," contains Hicks's celebrated wage bargaining diagram, the first of its kind in the literature. There is also an analysis of the generally adverse effects of wage regulation, and a discussion of the possibility that union pressure may reduce hours of work below the optimum level.

By the early thirties, then, the foundations of modern labor market analysis had been laid. They were laid by general economic theorists rather than by people calling themselves labor economists; and the demand side was much more fully developed than the supply side, which remained rather shadowy. There were, to be sure, many studies of labor mobility in the thirties, particularly by Gladys Palmer (1941) and her colleagues at the University of Pennsylvania. But this work amounted mainly to "counting moves" or, to borrow Koopmans's phrase, "measurement without theory." There was little effort to test hypotheses about labor supply and wage determination.

In my *Structure of Labor Markets* (1951) I tried to examine wages and mobility *together* and to explore the relations between them. In this effort I was partly reacting against the simple competitive diagrams which appeared, for example, in the first edition of George Stigler's *Theory of Competitive Price* (1942). In this model, "wage determination and movements of labor are intimately related. They are, in fact, simply different aspects of a single process by which members of the labor force are distributed to the points at which they can make the greatest productive contribution. Movements of labor are induced by wage differences. The wage structure in turn is conditioned by potential movement of labor" (Reynolds 1951: 1).

But looking at actual labor markets, I seemed to see two distinct processes. Voluntary movement of labor seemed rather haphazard and uninformed, conditioned more largely by differences in the availability of jobs than by differences in wage levels. On the other side, people engaged in setting wages often made little explicit reference to mobility as an influence on their decisions. This led me to ask: How close is the relation between labor mobility and wage determiniation? Do we need one theory or two?

The fieldwork, as I mentioned earlier, involved interviews with a large number of industrial workers, employers, union officials, and Employment Service people in New Haven over the years 1946–48. You can discover the factual findings either by looking at the book or by reading a recent review by Richard Freeman (1984), which he titled "The Structure of Labor Markets: A Book Review Thirty Years Later." With typical diligence, Freeman sorted out thirty findings of fact and compared my conclusions with the findings of subsequent research. I was pleased to see that my box score was twenty-five out of thirty. The recent findings, of course, are much better grounded in econometric analysis, and on some points the shadings of emphasis and interpretation differ from my own.

In retrospect, it appears that I understated the extent of workers' labor market information and the degree of rationality in job search. I should not have overgeneralized from a sample of factory workers, who are a minority of the labor force. Other studies of clerical workers, and of college students bound for professional and managerial occupations, show a higher level of information and more purposeful choice of jobs. But in addition to limitations inherent in the scope of my sample, I'm afraid that my interpretation was influenced a bit by an emotional bias against accepted theory, a bias from which I should have struggled harder to free myself. As a convinced trade unionist, I could not quite believe Henry Simons and George Stigler when they asserted that unions can do only harm. And since these assertions relied on the competitive market model, I thought it necessary to put down the competitive model. This effort now strikes me as largely misguided. It would have been better to follow the Freeman–Medoff (1984) approach of accepting the "monopoly face" of unionism and balancing this against the positive effects of union "voice" in the workplace.

Past Accomplishments and Directions for Future Research

It has been more than fifty years since labor market theory was opened up by Robinson and Hicks. It has been thirty years since the local labor market studies of the fifties. What have we learned over that course of time? There has been a marked development of labor market analysis in recent decades, and the subject has moved increasingly to the center of the labor course. A labor text of 1950 vintage usually had a single chapter entitled "The Labor Market." (My own first edition did not have even that!) Today's texts are structured largely around market concepts—the demand for labor, the supply of labor, market structure, wage determination. Labor demand alone gets three or four chapters, and so does labor supply. This suggests progress in both concepts and research.

Without repeating what I said earlier about broad trends in labor economics, let me make several points:

1. We have had to think harder about what we mean by a labor market. We used to speak loosely of "the labor market," usually connoting an areawide market for a particular occupation. Today it is clear that there is a multiplicity of market types, and that we need to specify which of these we are discussing. The "inside market," a concept which appears in my *Structure* study and which John Dunlop (1966) elaborated and cemented into the literature, has turned out to be very important. It is a characteristic feature of what others have called the primary labor market. But there are also areawide markets: for

common labor and other jobs which constitute "ports of entry" to the inside market; for skilled crafts, which are sometimes said to have a distinctive "guild market," and for workers and employers in the so-called secondary market. Primary and secondary seem to me most meaningful, not as mutually exclusive categories but as polar concepts, with actual jobs arrayed along a spectrum in between. Finally, we are increasingly conscious of regional, national, even international markets for higher-level skills.

2. On the demand side, the most important development has been a great enrichment of the meaning of demand for an employer with an inside market. Such an employer makes a substantial investment in recruitment, screening, and training, and investment which he hopes to recoup over a long period of future employment. This has all kinds of implications for hiring criteria, for managing a worker's lifetime wage progression, for layoff and rehiring procedures, and for other aspects of personnel policy. Related to this, there has been increased investigation of actual hiring decisions, how far "ability" (however defined) can be estimated in advance of employment, and whether screening criteria may involve overt or inadvertent discrimination against particular race, sex, or age groups.

3. There have been even more substantial developments on the supply side, producing a better balance between demand and supply analysis than existed a generation ago. Consider, for example, the large body of work on investment in education, job choices by college-trained people, and the interrelations of education, ability, and earnings. Other important and active areas include: workers' job search behavior, the factors determining their reservation wage, and the relation of this to unemployment rates; the supply behavior of important subgroups in the labor force, such as women workers and black youths; and efforts to test the Smithian principle of compensating wage differentials by examining jobs with unattractive features such as health risks, loss-of-life risks, strenuous conditions, irregular employment.

4. We have already mentioned wages in connection with employer strategy in the inside market, the returns to investment in education, and compensating wage differentials. In addition, there has been much multiple regression analysis of differences in individual earnings, usually from cross-section data but sometimes including longitudinal studies. A difficulty is that the observed differences do not speak for themselves but have to be interpreted in terms of presumed labor market processes, and often more than one interpretation is possible. This is notably true of wage differences related to sex and race, which are still under active debate.

5. Finally, while collective bargaining has now retreated from center stage, there is a continuing stream of work on union-nonunion wage differentials. Along with this have been ingenious efforts at improved modeling of a union's economic objectives, a kind of analysis pioneered by John Dunlop long ago, and efforts to quantify some important nonwage effects of unionism,

where Richard Freeman, James Medoff, and their colleagues at the National Bureau's labor project have played a leading role.

While these accomplishments are encouraging, it is useful also to ask: What do we still not know about labor markets? What areas are still underinvestigated? Let me suggest a half-dozen such areas.

1.   I have not heard much lately about company wage decisions. In the dominant nonunion sector of the economy, management takes the initiative on wages. Even in the union sector, management efforts to counter union pressure and even to demand rollbacks are stronger than they were in earlier periods. How much autonomy does management have in wage decisions? How effective are labor supply constraints? These questions, actively investigated by Lester and others in the fifties, have rather dropped out of sight, and we need to take a fresh look at them.

2.   To a considerable extent, the labor force is now being replenished by immigrant groups, notably from Mexico but also from other Latin American countries and from Asia. At the higher occupational levels, there is the familiar "brain drain" of doctors, engineers, scientists, and other professionals from the less developed countries. At the bottom of the occupational structure, legal and illegal immigrants perform somewhat the function of "guest workers" in Western Europe, taking jobs which the native-born are no longer willing to perform. But unlike guest workers, who can be shipped home when no longer needed, most of our immigrants prefer to stay. What are these people doing, and what are they earning? Does their entrance to the U.S. labor market adversely affect workers already established there? What are the costs and benefits to the national economy? These questions are not new, but we have not faced them on the present scale since the massive immigration of 1880–1914.

3.   Studies of the economic impact of unionism might well devote greater attention to the public sector, where unionism is still expanding rather than retreating. The economics of public employment differs in obvious ways from that of private employment. Demand for labor and employer ability to pay are differently determined. Government workers are voters and taxpayers as well as employees. How does the appearance of unions change the balance of forces? Do public-sector unions have a substantial effect on the size and allocation of government budgets? Do they succeed in shifting demand for their services to the right? Does the wage–employment trade-off influence union policy in the same way as in the private sector? We are far from knowing the answers to such questions.

4.   The educational system is a central labor market institution. It is the main channel of intergenerational mobility. While there has been much work on the relation of education to earnings, other important areas remain

underinvestigated. For example, there is a set of problems involving the transition from school to work. Many students drop out before finishing high school. Others graduate without any vocational plans or marketable skills. There is often no effective linkage between teachers and school counselors on one side and employers and employment service officials on the other. Research is needed to discover what goes on in this murky area, and to devise more effective linkages between the schooling system and the world of employment.

Another example: when we speak of *equal opportunity*, we must mean mainly equal access to education, especially college and graduate education. To what extent are students with good academic ability still screened out by educational costs? How are costs divided at present between taxpayers, parents, and students? Is this division socially efficient? There is now an extensive loan system in which students operate, and how could it be improved? It is wrong to consign such important issues to the professional educators. Economists have sharper tools, and there are few places where they could be more usefully employed.

5. Modern microeconomics has become *very* micro, and we have tended to lose sight of some broader issues which interested earlier economists. Major theorists such as Mill and Marshall, and sophisticated textbook writers such as F.W. Taussig, were concerned with the stratification of the population into self-perpetuating social and occupational classes. Being well-intentioned, they hoped that social mobility was increasing over time and that class barriers were being eroded. This is probably true. And it is probably true also that social stratification is less marked in the United States than in Britain and other European countries. But do we really know? Why should the study of such an important issue be left to Marxists and others in the underworld of economics?

6. Finally, let me note a curious "two worlds" approach to labor markets, evident in all of the leading texts. At the outset there is a chapter on the operation of a competitive labor market, with monopsony and collective bargaining usually added as departures from competition. This exposition is admittedly highly simplified and introductory. The author then turns to how the world really works. There are several chapters on labor supply and several on labor demand, covering a wide variety of analytical issues and empirical findings. After all this, one might expect to find a synthetic chapter on real-world labor markets, as a contrast to the intial simplified view. But this capstone chapter is typically missing. Instead, the discussion trails off into a miscellany of policy issues such as unemployment, income inequality, and discrimination.

We should be able to do better. Of the many underlying assumptions of the simplified model, which are relatively innocent and which can do positive harm? Among the many findings about real-world labor markets, which are crucial for clear thinking and for policy judgments? Facts are not created equal. Which are highly important, which moderately important, which relatively trivial? The student is entitled to some perspective on these questions at the end of the course.

References

Chamberlin, Edward. 1933. *The Theory of Monopolistic Competition.* Cambridge: Harvard University Press.

Daugherty, Carroll. 1933. *Labor Problems in American Industry.* New York: Harper.

Disraeli, Benjamin. 1845. *Sybil; or, the Two Nations.* London: Colburn.

Dollard, John. 1937. *Caste and Classes in a Southern Town.* New York: Harper.

Dunlop, John. 1966. "Job Vacancy Measures and Economic Analysis." In National Bureau of Economic Research, *The Measurement and Interpretation of Job Vacancies,* 27–47. New York: National Bureau of Economic Research.

Freeman, Richard. 1984. "The Structure of Labor Markets: A Book Review Three Decades Later." In Gustav Ranis, Robert West, Mark Leierson, and Cynthia Taft Morris, eds., *Comparative Development Perspectives: Essays in Honor of Lloyd G. Reynolds.* Boulder: Westview.

Freeman, Richard, and James Medoff. 1984. *What Do Unions Do?* New York: Basic Books.

Hicks, John. 1932. *The Theory of Wages.* London: Macmillan.

Kerr, Clark, John Dunlop, Frederick Harbison, and Charles Myers. 1960. *Industrialism and Industrial Man; The Problems of Labor and Management in Economic Growth,* Cambridge: Harvard University Press.

Lester, Richard. 1945. "Trends in Southern Wage Differentials Since 1890." *Southern Economic Journal* 3 (April): 317–44.

Marshall, Alfred. 1890. *Principles of Economics.* 1st ed. London: Macmillan.

———. 1919. *Industry and Trade.* London: Macmillan.

Macdonald, Robert. 1963. *Collective Bargaining in the Automobile Industry.* New Haven: Yale University Press.

Myers, Charles, and Rupert Maclaurin. 1943. *The Movement of Factory Workers.* New York: John Wiley.

Myers, Charles, and George Shultz. 1951. *Dynamics of a Labor Market.* New York: Prentice–Hall.

Palmer, Gladys. 1941. "Mobility of Weavers in Three Textile Centers." *Quarterly Journal of Economics* 55 (May): 460–87.

Pigou, Arthur. 1932. *The Economics of Welfare.* 4th ed. London: Macmillan.

Reynolds, Lloyd. 1935. *The British Immigrant: His Economic and Social Adjustment in Canada.* Toronto: Oxford University Press.

———. 1940. *The Control of Competition in Canada.* Cambridge: Harvard University Press.

———. 1949. *Labor Economics and Labor Relations.* 1st ed. Engelwood Cliffs, N.J.: Prentice–Hall.

———. 1951. *The Structure of Labor Markets.* New York: Harper.

Reynolds, Lloyd, and Cynthia Taft. 1956. *The Evolution of Wage Structure.* New Haven: Yale University Press.

Robinson, Joan. 1933. *The Economics of Imperfect Competition.* London: Macmillan.

Sargent, J.R. 1963. "Are American Economists Better?" *Oxford Economic Papers* 15 (March): 1–7.

Slichter, Sumner. 1941. *Union Policies and Industrial Management.* Washington, D.C.: The Brookings Institution.

Stigler, George. 1942. *The Theory of Competitive Price.* New York: Macmillan.

Webb, Sidney, and Beatrice Webb. 1894. *The History of Trade Unionism.* London: Longmans, Green.

———. 1897. *Industrial Democracy.* London: Longmans, Green.

5

The Postwar View of Labor Markets and Wage Determination

Bruce E. Kaufman

The Postwar Labor Economists

The period from the end of World War II to 1960 is one of the most interesting and influential chapters in the history of labor economics. Before the war, labor economics was badly fragmented with the institutionalists on one side of the intellectual divide and the neoclassical theorists on the other. The institutionalists knew much about the realities of working life but rejected the orthodox theory of the day as largely irrelevant for explaining what they saw. The neoclassical economists, on the other hand, knew much about how labor markets work in theory but made little effort to check the predictions of the theory against the facts of the real world. The result was that labor economics was a house divided, having no common frame of reference or mode of analysis.

With the return of peace in 1945, a new and younger generation of labor economists soon began to exert their influence on the field. From among this new generation arose one group of young scholars in particular who were to dominate the intellectual scene in labor economics for the next decade and a half. The most prominent names among this group were John Dunlop, Clark Kerr, Richard Lester, Lloyd Reynolds, Charles Myers, and Arthur Ross.[1] These economists undertook the task of integrating theory and practice. They were, in the words of one of their contemporaries, the "Bridgers of the Gap" (Killingsworth 1949: 103). These economists were uniquely equipped for this task, for not only had they been well trained in the neoclassical theory of Marshall and Hicks, but they had also been introduced to real life labor markets through their experience as labor arbitrators and staff members with the War Labor Board.

Following Marshall, the new labor economists of the 1940s made the labor market and the forces of demand and supply their basic conceptual frame of reference. Their research centered on two issues: the process of wage

The author benefited greatly from comments by Glen Cain on an earlier draft of this paper.

determination in union and nonunion labor markets and the relative importance of market versus institutional forces in the determination of wages, hours, and working conditions.[2] To obtain evidence on these issues, they followed the lead of the institutionalists and conducted painstaking case studies of local labor markets and union wage policies. The result of their research was a new view of how labor markets work—a view somewhere in the middle between the competitive labor market of Hicks and the institutional market of Commons. Their research also yielded many insights into the nature of union wage policy and the impact of collective bargaining on the labor market, and a general feeling that collective bargaining was more of a plus for society than a minus.

After 1960, labor economics entered a new phase in its development. Due both to historical events and to new theoretical insights, the "new" view of the labor market of the 1940s and 1950s was gradually replaced by the "new-new" view of the 1960s and 1970s, a view which has continued to dominate in labor economics to the present day. This view was chiefly associated with the University of Chicago and economists such as H. Gregg Lewis, Gary Becker, George Stigler, Milton Friedman, Jacob Mincer, Melvin Reder, and Albert Rees. The ascendency of the Chicago school was in many ways a counterrevolution in both theory and methodology. The competitive model, viewed with skepticism in the 1950s, now became the standard frame of reference in the 1970s. Not coincidentally, labor unions and government wage standards, once perceived as largely beneficial (or at least benign) in the 1950s, had, twenty years later, become a source of market inefficiency. Finally, the institutional "go and see" case study approach gave way to an empiricism based on large survey data sets and the statistical tools of econometrics.

Although the 1950s or "postwar" view of the labor market has now been largely supplanted (or in some case absorbed) by the neoclassical model of the Chicago school, there are a number of reasons why it is useful and interesting to take another look at it. One, of course, is to gain a better appreciation for the evolution of thought in labor economics. A second and more compelling reason is to draw attention to issues, concepts, or empirical findings from the literature of the 1950s that present-day labor economists have either neglected or forgotten. Finally, the 1950s view of the labor market offers at least one alternative theoretical base that critics of neoclassical theory could build and expand on. The dual labor market literature of the 1970s represents one such effort (see Cain 1976).

In what follows, I attempt to sketch the postwar view of the labor market.[3] In doing so, I rely primarily on the publications of Dunlop, Kerr, Lester, and Reynolds (henceforth referred to as DKLR), since they are, in my opinion, the most influential of the labor economists of that period. The work of other researchers of that period is, however, also introduced where relevant. Primary attention in this discussion is given to the operation of labor markets as described by DKLR, and particularly the process of wage determination. The impact of unions and collective bargaining on the labor market is also considered, but writings by DKLR on other industrial relations topics are of necessity omitted. After describing the 1950s view of the labor market, I briefly consider the reasons for the eclipse of the postwar view of the labor market by the Chicago school, what school of thought in labor economics (if any) DKLR belong to, and an assessment of the contributions of the 1950s research program on labor markets.

Historical Background

Probably the most important contribution of the postwar labor economists was to make the operation of the labor market the core subject of analysis in labor economics. This represented a fundamental shift in emphasis. The study of labor in the United States in the 1920s and 1930s generally focused on two separate topics: a descriptive analysis of various "labor problems" (for example, inadequate wages, excessive work hours, instability of employment) and possible solutions to them, and a discussion of the history, objectives, and institutions of trade unionism (McNulty, 1980: 127–176). Although both labor problems and trade unionism were portrayed as an outgrowth of, or reaction to, the capitalist system, little attempt was made to analyze the mechanics of the market process itself.[4] This neglect of labor market theory resulted from several factors. One was the antipathy that many institutionalists had towards neoclassical theory. On positive grounds, the institutionalists rejected the hedonistic conception of "economic man" and the perfectly competitive markets of neoclassical theory as patently unrealistic, while on normative grounds they objected to the antiunion, laissex-faire implications derived from the theory by economists such as Friedrich von Hayek and Henry Simons. A second factor militating against the development of labor market theory was that few labor economists had much training or aptitude for it. They tended to be far more convsersant with history, law and sociology than mathematics and price theory.

Although labor market theory was largely neglected in the United States before World War II (with certain notable exceptions such as the work of Paul Douglas), the same was not true in England. At the turn of the century, Alfred Marshall (1890) developed the neoclassical theory of competitive markets, showing how supply and demand determine wage rates and employment levels. The model of competitive markets was further developed by A.C. Pigou (1912) and J.R. Hicks (1932), both of whom also made valuable contributions to the theory of bargaining. England was also the home of two other important theoretical breakthroughs. The first was the development by Joan Robinson (1933) of models of imperfect competition in the labor market such as monopsony and oligopsony; and the second was J.M. Keynes's (1936) macroeconomic theory of underemployment equilibrium.

The approach of DKLR to labor economics was heavily influenced by this diverse range of theoretical perspectives which they received in graduate school in the mid-1930s (see Kerr 1983). The neoclassical theory of Marshall and Hicks became their standard frame of reference in analyzing the operation of labor markets. Following on Keynes and Robinson, however, DKLR also gave far more weight to the role of imperfections in the labor market such as rigid wages, persistent unemployment, and employer domination of local labor markets. Finally, their view of how labor markets work was also greatly impacted by intellectual developments in the newly emerging field of industrial relations. Of particular importance was the research of Sumner Slichter on the work rules and group relations that structure the organization of work and the distribution of rewards in the workplace. The interest of DKLR in industrial relations research also brought them into contact with diverse theoretical perspectives such as social psychology and organizational behavior, with their more behaviorally oriented theories of human behavior, and sociology, with its stress on status and social stratification (see Kerr and Fisher 1957).

Events as well as ideas also played a significant role in shaping the research interests and outlook of the postwar labor economists. One was the Great Depression. The persistence of mass unemployment for over a decade seemed to provide stark evidence that the price mechanism did not function nearly as effectively or automatically as competitive theory predicted. A second was the surge in union membership in the 1930s and the replacement of individual bargaining with collective bargaining across a wide range of industries. The spread of industrial unionism not only opened up many new questions about the structure and process of collective bargaining but it also called into question the relative importance of market forces as the principal control mechanism in the labor market. Perhaps of most importance, however, was the experience gained by DKLR as staff members and directors of the National War Labor Board during 1943–1945.

The goal of the War Labor Board was to stabilize wage rates and settle labor disputes. In pursuit of the first objective, the board attempted to determine the "going" wage for workers in specific occupations in a local area and then apply this standard across firms. To the surprise of the labor economists on the board, when they went looking for the going rate predicted by Hicks, they found instead a range of wage rates that varied in an unsystematic way 50 percent or more around the man (see Lester 1946a; Kerr 1950). It was this discrepancy between theory and fact that, more than anything, shaped the research agenda of the postwar labor economists. The experience gained by DKLR in adjudicating disputes over the board's wage standards was also instructive, for they were introduced firsthand to the different concerns and perspectives of union and management officials and the pervasive influence that considerations of equity had in wage determination (Kerr and Fisher 1950).

Wage Determination in Nonunion Labor Markets

Although Marshall and Hicks had written extensively on the determination of wages, their work remained largely in the world of theory. It was not until the 1940s that economists such as DKLR took the theory and compared it with the operation of real world labor markets. Insight into the operation of labor markets came not only from the sources mentioned above (labor arbitration, the War Labor Board), but also from detailed case studies of local labor markets. The most influential of these case studies were done by Reynolds (New Haven, Connecticut), Lester (Trenton, New Jersey), and Myers and Maclaurin (Fitchburg, Massachusetts).[5] Through extensive interviews with management officials and individual workers (primarily blue-collar factory workers), they studied the relationship between labor mobility and wage determination, the hiring practices and recruiting methods of firms, the job search methods of workers, and the policies and impact of unions.

In carrying out these studies, the postwar labor economists used the competitive model of Marshall and Hicks as their basic conceptual framework. In this theory, the competition forces of demand and supply in the labor market yield an equilibrium or going wage for similar workers and jobs and an optimal structure of wages and allocation of labor across industries and occupations. On the supply side, any firm that pays a wage less than the going rate will lose its workers as they quit and seek work elsewhere, while on the demand side no firm would be willing to pay more than the going rate because of its desire to maximize profits. Given the usual assumptions of maximizing behavior, many buyers and sellers, perfect information, and free and costless mobility, the twin competitive pressures of labor mobility and profit maximization insure that in the long run all noncompensating wage differentials are competed away, and that labor is employed in its most efficient use.

This of course is the outcome in a perfect world, but the real world is imperfect. The importance issue, as recognized by DKLR, was not whether the operation of labor markets matched the theoretical ideal but the *degree* to which they approached this standard (Reynolds 1951: 2). Hicks argued in *The Theory of Wages* that the competitive model does well on this score, since its predictions are approximated fairly closely by actual behavior.[6] Of the predicted "one wage" of competitive theory, for example, he says (1932: 3): "For the general tendency for the wages of labourers of equal efficiency to become equalised in different occupations (allowance being made for other advantages or disadvantages of employment) has been a commonplace since

,lthe days of Adam Smith . . . . The movement of labour from one occupation to another, which brings it about, is certainly a slow one; but there is no need to question its reality."

From their case studies, the postwar labor economists obtained a substantially different view of how labor markets operate. Although there was some disagreement among them on points of fact, emphasis, or interpretation, on the basics of the market process their conclusions were remarkably alike. The substantive differences between the postwar model of the labor market and the neoclassical competitive model can best be illustrated by focusing on four major features of the market process.[7]

Labor Mobility. In the competitive model, the movement of workers in search of the best possible employment results in an equalization of net advantages among jobs in the labor market. This is a long-run outcome, however, and at any point in time there may exist some wage differentials that are noncompensating due to factors such as imperfect information and costs of mobility. If the competitive model is a reasonably close approximation to real world labor markets, it should nevertheless be the case that the size of any noncompensating wage differentials should be relatively small and that these differentials should decrease over time in a stable market.

Neither of these conditions was found by the postwar labor economists in their case studies. After taking into account various nonwage factors such as worker productivity, working conditions, and fringe benefits, Reynolds (1951: 234) concluded, "it would appear there remain substantial differences in labor cost per efficiency unit and even larger differences in job attractiveness. Nor is there much reason to think that these differences tend to diminish over the long run."[8] The explanation for the market's apparent failure to equalize net advantages was found to lie with two aspects of the process of labor mobility. The first aspect was the highly constricted nature of the manual worker's job-search process; the second was the relative immobility of the large majority of the employed work force.

For competition to yield a determinate going wage, it is necessary that some (but not necessarily all) workers be reasonably well informed about alternative job opportunities and that they engage in some sort of systematic search in pursuit of the job with the highest net advantage. The postwar labor economists found that only a relatively small number of blue-collar factory workers reasonably satisfied either criteria (see Myers and Shultz 1951: 45–73; Reynolds and Shister 1949; Palmer 1954; Parnes 1954). From worker interviews, they concluded that most blue-collar workers (and particularly the unskilled) were largely ignorant or misinformed about even the most general features of wage rates, fringe benefits, and working conditions at other plants in the local area. Reynolds (1951: 84) found, for example, that when asked where they would go to look for work if out of a job, three-quarters of the workers in his sample were either unable or unwilling to name a specific plant. In a similar vein, 80 percent of those workers questioned by Reynolds who were employed by firms in the lower half of the wage distribution stated that the wages paid by their company compared favorably with other plants in the area (p. 214).

Several reasons were thought to account for this lack of information about alternative job opportunities. One was that to acquire detailed information on a job, the worker generally has to personally visit each firm, making the process of job shopping a costly and time-consuming activity. A second factor was that nonpecuniary conditions of employment are quite difficult to ascertain without actually working at the job for a time. A third was the deliberate policy of many firms not to publicly reveal the specifics of their compensation program, in order to minimize overt wage competition in the market. Finally, and perhaps of most importance, the great bulk of employed workers were reasonably satisfied with their jobs and neither paid much attention to nor sought out information on other employments.

The method of job search used by workers also limited the degree to which labor mobility could put competitive pressures on wage differentials. If confronted with two similar jobs, one of which paid better, workers would choose the higher paying job much as the economists' model of rational behavior would predict. The postwar labor economists found, however, that the exercise of rational choice in this manner was severely limited or "bounded" by the lack of job information and the costs of job shopping. Workers, therefore, developed an alternative search process where they contacted one firm at a time and accepted the first job offer that exceeded their subjectively determined minimum standard (Reynolds 1951: 110–111). The workers' minimum standard, in turn, was positively related to the earnings level on their previous job and negatively related to the length of unemployment already incurred.

Although this sequential method of job search is consistent with some recent neoclassical models (McCall 1970), several factors caused the actual outcome of the search process to be considerably less than optimal. One was that many workers picked the first firm to contact in a largely random or haphazard way, or on the basis of where friends or relatives worked (Parnes 1954: 162–165). A second was that the great majority of job seekers accepted the first job offer without looking further. Among first-time job seekers, for example, Reynolds and Shister (1949: 57) found that seven-eighths took the first job offer they received, while Myers and Shultz (1951: 62–66) found that among displaced textile workers the proportion of those who accepted the first job offer was 60 percent. Finally, once employed, workers gradually developed a strong attachment to their employer and rarely quit to search for better work, particularly after acquiring job tenure beyond one or two years.

This last point directly leads to another aspect of labor mobility that significantly reduced the competitive pressure on wage differentials. Even if the job search process is highly constricted, employers will still face effective competition for labor as long as there is a sufficiently large number of workers who are willing to quit one firm and move to another in search of a higher net advantage. The postwar labor economists found contradictory evidence on this subject. Surveys (see Parnes 1954) revealed that there was a substantial amount of turnover among the labor force, and that two-thirds to three-fourths of all job separations were voluntary. These results seemed to be supportive of the competitive model. On closer examination, however, it was found that the great proportion of turnover was accounted for by a relatively small group of workers who typically were young and unmarried, with little job experience. Thus, Lester (1954: 60) discovered that among the firms he interviewed it was rare for an employee with as little as one to three years of seniority to voluntarily quit for another job with a competitor. Reynolds (1951: 21) likewise concluded: "The propensity to move . . . is slight after three years and negligible after ten years of work in the same plants." Most workers, therefore, were part of what Kerr (1950: 281) called the "hardcore employed," meaning they were no longer active market participants. The relative lack of mobility on the part of the experienced work force, in turn, significantly reduced the competitive pressure on wage differentials among jobs that were above the entry level in the firm.

DKLR cited a number of reasons for the strong job attachment of manual workers. One was the importance of seniority in layoffs and promotions. A second was that fringe benefits such as pensions and vacations increased with job tenure. A third was the widespread policy of firms to hire new workers only for entry-level jobs. A fourth was that many firms discouraged voluntary turnover by adopting a formal or informal anti-pirating policy in which they refused to hire away a worker employed with another firm. Most important, however, was the desire of blue-collar workers for security, and their deep-seated aversion to gambling a satisfactory job for one that might prove worse or even nonexistent.[9]

The fact that most experienced workers were relatively immobile significantly reduced not only the pressure of competition on wage differentials but also the role of wage differentials in allocating labor. The effective labor supply of most firms was found to be largely comprised of unemployed workers who were new entrants into the labor force, had voluntarily quit a job because they were dissatisfied with it, or had been involuntarily separated from a job due to layoff (Reynolds 1951: 105). For reasons cited above, the labor supply of experienced workers came disproportionately from the latter group, and for them the evidence indicated that movement in the market was principally guided by the availability of jobs rather than relative wages. The new jobs that were obtained by the laid off were, in fact, often at a lower rate of pay than the ones they left (Reynolds 1951: 214–215). Thus, for a wide range of jobs the major source of labor mobility in the market was the result of an involuntary separation from a job and a movement to a new job at a lower rate of pay, not a voluntary quit and movement to a higher paying job as envisioned in the competitive model. As Reynolds (1951: 244) put it, "There is certainly no difficulty in getting workers out of places where they are no longer needed; they are simply laid off. In order to get them into places where they are needed, it is usually necessary only to place a Help Wanted sign on the plant gate."

The upshot of this discussion is a view of the supply side of the labor market that is distinctly different from that of the competitive model. Wage competition for "good" jobs is present, but in a much attenuated form, due to the restricted nature of the job search process and the relative lack of mobility among the great bulk of the employed work force One result is that the twin processes of wage determination and the allocation of labor become partially disjointed, or in the words of Kerr (1950: 278; 1977: 6), the "wage market and job market go their own not so merry way." Thus, because of the weak competitive pressure exerted by labor mobility, firms gain some discretion in their pay policies—they can pay either above or below the going rate without undue repercussions on their labor supply. The converse is also true: To a significant degree the allocation of labor across industries and occupations takes place without reference to the structure of relative wages. While the wage structure may facilitate the allocation of labor, it does not play a central or indispensable role. The outcome is that changes in wage rates and changes in employment and unemployment levels are only weakly impacted by each other.[10]

A final implication of the postwar research on labor mobility concerns the nature of the labor supply function to the firm. In competitive theory, the firm's labor supply curve is a horizontal line at the equilibrium market wage. This means that at the going wage the firm can hire all the labor it desires, but at any lower wage its workers will quit and seek work elsewhere. The labor supply curve in the postwar model differs in two important respects. First, rather than a line it becomes a band, illustrating that there is a range of possible wage rates the firm can pay and still attract a supply of labor (Lester 1952; 1964: 263–268; Reynolds 1951: 233–235). The lower bound to the supply curve is determined by the minimum supply price of the unemployed. The upper bound is defined, not by the highest wage the most prosperous firm in the area could pay, but rather by the maximum which it can pay without being considered "unethical" by other employers. Within this upper and lower bound is an area of indeterminancy in wages within which the firm can choose the wage it desires to pay. Lester (1964: 267) and Reynolds (1951: 235) suggested this area of indeterminancy might be on the order of 10–20 percent of the mean wage in the market.

Besides being a band, the shape of the labor supply curve to the firm also differs in the postwar model. According to Reynolds (1946a, 1946b), at "full employment" (the equilibrium point in the competitive model) the labor supply curve to the firm is generally upward sloping, reflecting the fact that it takes higher wage offers to pry workers away from their current employers. In the more usual state of less than full employment, the labor supply curve is kinked at the firm's present level of employment. If the firm wishes to expand employment, it can generally attract the additional labor from among the unemployed at whatever wage it is currently paying, suggesting that the labor supply curve is horizontal. At employment levels below the present amount, on the other hand, the labor supply curve is downward sloping, showing that a firm could pay a lower wage and yet keep most of its workers. The downward sloping portion of the supply curve reflects the limitations placed on worker mobility by factors such as fringe benefits, seniority rights, and specific training. These barriers to mobility give firms some monopsony power over their employees, particularly over those that are "inframarginal." Firms, therefore, possess a certain degree of market power over wage rates in a nonunion labor market, both because of the willingness of unemployed workers to accept less than the competitive rate and because of the relative immobility of the employed work force. Although it is difficult to diagrammatically represent the process of wage determination in this situation (for an attempt, see Bronfenbrenner 1956), Reynolds and Lester claimed that the reality of employer power over wages is manifest in the ability of firms to pay significantly less than the average market rate (see Lester 1954; Reynolds and Taft 1956: 369).

Company Wage Policy. The relatively weak competitive pressure exerted by labor mobility on the supply side of the labor market provides a necessary condition for the existence of noncompensatory wage differentials. For such differentials to actually occur, however, it is also required that individual firms in the labor market pursue different wage policies so that similar workers are paid unequal wages.

In the competitive model, firms have a wage policy, but the policy is identical for all of them. In deciding what to pay for a particular type of labor, the firm's discretion is bounded on the lower end by the need to pay the going market wage if it is to keep its work force. On the upper end, the firm's wage policy is shaped by its goals and ability to pay. If the firm has the single goal of maximizing profit, it will want to pay the lowest wage possible consistent with market conditions—meaning the going market rate. An important implication of the profit maximization assumption is that the firm's wage policy is not affected by the structure of the product market (for example, competitive or monopolistic), for regardless of the size of its profits the firm always desires to minimize labor cost. If the firm has other goals besides maximizing profit, ability to pay may then influence its wage policy. This possibility is usually rendered moot in neoclassical theory, however, by assuming that the product market is also perfectly competitive. In this case, regardless of the firm's other goals it must minimize labor cost if it is not to go bankrupt in the long run.

The evidence accumulated by DKLR in their case studies and management interviews painted a significantly different picture of company wage policies than depicted above. They found that companies chose to pay widely different wages for roughly similar jobs (Dunlop 1957; Kerr 1950; Lester 1948a, 1954; Reynolds 1951). Instead of all firms paying a wage close to the market minimum, there was a distribution or range of firms in the market based on the size of their wage offers. Some firms did pay wages as low as labor supply conditions would permit, but others paid near the community average, while others paid well above the average. Variability in company wage policies, therefore, gave rise to a marked dispersion in wage rates in the labor market.

As noted by the postwar labor economists, the observed dispersion in wage rates was not in itself necessarily inconsistent with competitive theory. Net advantages among jobs could be equal even though money wage rates differed if high wage firms offered relatively fewer fringe benefits or had more disagreeable working conditions. The evidence indicated, however, that just the opposite was actually the case. A second way the dispersion in money wages could be rationalized to fit the competitive model is if firms that pay high wages gain a corresponding reduction in unit labor cost due to reduced turnover, lower search costs, higher employee morale, or their ability to hire more productive workers. These factors were clearly operative and did tend to reduce—but not eliminate—the variability in total labor cost per hour across firms.

After these adjustments, the evidence still pointed to the existence of significant noncompensating wage differentials in the local labor market. The obvious question, then, was why some firms would voluntarily pay a higher wage than was necessary to obtain a supply of labor. Lester (1951: 63–64) cited four reasons. The first was that management had multiple objectives. One objective was larger profit, but others included a good community image, fair treatment of employees, and the exercise of wage leadership. A second consideration was the firm's ability to pay. Marginal producers and firms in competitive industries generally earned little profit, so to survive they had to pay as low a wage as possible. Larger size firms and companies in sheltered product markets, on the other hand, tended to make large profits, and these could be used to pay higher wages in pursuit of the nonprofit objectives noted above. A third consideration was management strategy and outlook. The reason some firms paid low wages, for example, was that the management was interested only in short-term results or had a basically adversarial perspective on labor relations. Finally, part of the explanation for nonuniform wage scales is history and custom. Some firms start out with a high wage scale because they are expanding rapidly. If the firm's high position in the community wage structure becomes established and customary, it cannot easily let this position erode in later years because of the widespread dissatisfaction and low morale it would cause among employees.

The findings of the postwar labor economists with respect to company wage policy have several important implications for the process of wage determination. The first is that the wage structure among firms in a local labor market is shaped primarily by demand-side factors. Reynolds (1951: 35) perhaps stated it best when he said, "Under nonunion conditions, then, the wage structure of an area is shaped mainly by the labor demand curves of firms in the area. The supply situation is such that each firm, instead of being faced with a market wage rate, is faced with a considerable range of possible wage levels. Depending on the height of its demand curve, it can select a higher or lower position in the area wage structure and can shift this position gradually over the course of time." This position contrasts markedly with the neoclassical model of competitive labor markets where wage differentials are explained almost totally by supply-side considerations (for example, demographic characteristics of workers, human capital variables, and so on).

A second implication that flows from the first concerns the important linkage that exists between product markets and labor markets. The variation in labor demand curves noted by Reynolds was not random among firms but rather directly reflected each firm's competitive position in its product market. Dunlop (1957) attempted to formalize this relationship through the concept of a "wage contour." A wage contour is a group of firms that pay a similar wage for a particular type of labor. In competitive theory, there should be only one wage contour in a local area for a specific occupation such as truck driver, assuming that truck-driving jobs are identical with respect to working conditions, commuting distance, and so on. The actual situation, however, was that there were many wage contours and, thus, wage rates for workers that were otherwise similar. Dunlop argued that competitive conditions in the product market were the major determinant of which wage contour a firm was on, with firms in more profitable industries being on higher contours. Firms can rise or fall to lower wage contours, but this is also largely due to product market developments (or unionization). Thus, Dunlop (1944: 122–148) noted that during the depression wages fell first in those industries where the product market was most competitive, not where unemployment was necessarily the highest. The implication is that it is product market pressures, not excess supplies of labor as envisioned in the competitive model, that are the dominant force in causing wage changes, particularly in the downward direction.

Finally, the work of the postwar labor economists points to the importance of management objectives as a factor in wage determination (Lester 1952). From a short-run perspective, it simply was not true that all firms seek to maximize profits as depicted in traditional theory. Where competitive conditions permitted, managers sacrificed profits in pursuit of their own objectives, be they the "easy life" or the satisfaction obtained from being a wage leader in the community. On a theoretical level, this result argued in favor of adopting a more behaviorally-oriented theory of the firm in labor economics, such as that later developed by Herbert Simon (1962). From a policy perspective, it suggested that outside intervention in wage setting such as collective bargaining or minimum wage laws would not necessarily lead to a greater misallocation of resources, since many firms were not cost minimizing to begin with (Lester 1947b: 144–145).

Labor Market Structure. A third distinctive feature of the postwar model of wage determination is the emphasis given to the unique structural characteristics of the labor market. The term *structure* is used here to connote all those factors that determine the size of labor markets, who is able to compete in the market, and how the exchange process is organized.

First consider the technical organization of trading in the labor market. In a perfectly competitive labor market, wages are determined much as are prices of stocks and bonds or commodities such as wheat. The market in this case is a bourse, where many buyers and sellers circulate among each other trading a homogeneous good. Every market participant knows each bid and offer or the terms of each transaction and may alter his proposals in the light of this information. Wages, like stock prices, would rise and fall on a daily basis in response to shifts in demand and supply.

Are wages determined in this way? Literally speaking, the answer is obviously no. Neoclassical economists have often assumed in their models of the labor market, however, that it resembles a bourse, on the argument that over the longer run, wages are bid up and down by the forces of demand and supply much as they would be in a regular commodity market (Dunlop 1984). The bourselike nature of the labor market is clearly evident in Hicks's *The Theory of Wages*, for example, when he says (1932: 4–5): "Wages . . . tend to that level where demand and supply are equal. If supply exceeds demand, some men will be unemployed, and in their efforts to regain employment they will reduce the wages they ask to that level which just makes it worthwhile to take them on. If demand exceeds supply, employers will be unable to obtain the labor they require, and will, therefore, offer higher wages in order to attract labor from elsewhere." He went on to say that "so far as general tendencies are concerned, wages do turn out on the whole very much as if they were determined in this manner."

The postwar labor economists rejected this view of the labor market as seriously misleading. Dunlop (1944: 8–15), for example, argued that a more realistic conception of the labor market is where a limited number of buyers quote a fixed price to a much larger number of sellers who can "take it or leave it." This conception of the labor market has several implications for wage determination. With a bourse, the organization of the market is seemingly neutral with respect to the price negotiated between the buyers and sellers. In a quoted price market, however, the price fixer (the firm) gains a strategic advantage because it can start the trading at the price most favorable to it. This is especially true when, as in the case of labor, information about other quoted prices is difficult to obtain and the process of shopping around is costly. A second implication concerns the downward rigidity of money wages. In a bourselike labor market, an excess supply of labor should quickly lead to a bidding down of wage rates. As is well known, however, money wages tend to be sticky even in the face of considerable numbers of unemployed workers. Dunlop attributed this phenomenon, in part, to the fact that in the labor market, wages are quoted prices. While the willingness of the unemployed to work for lower wages may eventually induce the firm to cut its wage offer, in the short run there simply is no way for an unemployed person to successfully underbid someone who is working at the quoted rate.

A second structural characteristic of the labor market that is quite important in the postwar model is the segmentation of the market by the policies of institutions such as unions and corporations. In the competitive model, the boundaries of labor markets are defined by the limits placed on the sphere of competition by the flow of information, the transferability of skills, and the costs of mobility. Institutions, however, introduce rules and regulations that further define the dimensions of labor markets. These rules and regulations may either be formal (written) or informal (customary). In either case, they effectively delineate who can compete for particular jobs, who is most preferred, and which business firms can compete in the bidding. These rules are established in the form of corporate personnel policies, union contracts, and government legislation, among others.

According to DKLR, one of the most important sources of labor market segmentation is the internal labor market. The classic description of the concept of an internal labor market is contained in Kerr's (1954a) "The Balkanization of Labor Markets," although the idea of an "inside market" can also be found in the writings of the other three postwar labor economists (Dunlop 1957; Lester 1954; Reynolds 1951). Kerr observed that many firms prefer to fill higher-level job vacancies by promotion from within the firm rather than by canvassing outside the firm in the "external" labor market for job applicants. The principal reason for such an in-house bidding system is that the necessary job skills tend to be specific to the firm, due to the importance of on-the-job training and unique features of the production process. Thus, as workers above the entry level leave to retire or take new jobs, vacancies are created on the firm's "job ladder." Because workers in the external labor market do not have the skills or knowledge to fill those jobs, the firm limits the competition to those workers employed within the company. As these workers move up the job ladder, vacancies appear at the bottom of the job ladder or "port of entry." It is here that the sheltered internal labor market is connected to the external labor market as the firm recruits new people for its entry-level positions.

The fragmentation of the labor market is a consequence not only of corporate personnel policies but also of union hiring and promotion rules. According to Kerr, labor unions reduce the sphere of competition for jobs in two alternative ways, depending on whether the union is a craft or industrial union. A craft union claims an ownership of jobs over a carefully defined occupational and geographical area. The port of entry into the internal labor market is the union hiring hall. Once admitted, a worker can move from firm to firm in an essentially horizontal direction. Industrial unions, on the other hand, create an internal labor market that is organized in a vertical direction within a single plant or firm. The firm in this case controls admittance to the internal labor market by its choice of whom to hire into entry-level positions at the bottom of the job ladder. Competition for the rest of the jobs that fall under the union's jurisdiction, however, is strictly controlled by detailed seniority provisions that make movement up the job ladder a function of length of service.

By delineating and narrowing the group of workers that have access to jobs, institutions restrict the process of labor mobility and lessen the economic pressure on wage rates. The weakness of competition on the supply side of the market due to poor information and the abbreviated method of job search of manual workers is thus aggravated by institutional barriers to mobility. These barriers to mobility not only open up a range of indeterminancy of wages, they also tend to stratify the work force into the "ins" and the "outs." Kerr, writing in 1954 (p. 103), observed that the control over job opportunities by unions and firms was likely to bring forth more government intervention to insure that all groups had equal access to "good" jobs. In this he anticipated the civil rights and affirmative action policies of the 1960s by a decade.

A final aspect of labor market structure that concerned the postwar labor economists was the impact of social stratification and class lines on mobility in the market. Although they disavowed any strict Marxian definition of class or theory of class conflict, the postwar labor economists did believe there was a distinct, if not easily defined, working class and that the interests and outlook of the working class were substantially different from those of the owner/ manager/professional class (see Lester 1951; Reynolds 1954). One result of this split was the emergence of the adversarial relationship between workers and managers. A second result of the division of the work force along class lines was the emergence of noncompeting groups in the work force.

Probably the most intensive research on this subject was done by Reynolds, who investigated occupational mobility among manual workers. He reached several conclusions. Within the working class (which he defined to include manual, service, and agricultural workers), there is a fair amount of opportunity for both upward and downward movement on the occupational ladder. He found, for example, that of the workers he interviewed who had started as laborers, one-third had since worked up to semiskilled jobs and another third had worked up to skilled jobs (Reynolds 1951: 137). While upward movement within the working class was common, few manual workers ever crossed the divide into professional and technical occupations during their working life. Reynolds attributed this barrier to mobility to several factors. The most important was that manual workers did not have the necessary level of education to compete for professional and technical jobs, and once employed as manual workers they seldom had the money or time to re-enroll in school. A second factor was more social and psychological in nature. Most manual workers, he found, had a well-developed sense of their "social place," and due to both limited aspirations and aversion to change they seldom desired to venture into the higher occupational ranks.

Among employed workers, therefore, there seemed to exist fairly strong barriers to mobility between blue-collar and nonclerical white-collar jobs. This being the case, Reynolds turned to the issue of intergenerational mobility. Even if manual workers were unlikely to ever enter a professional or managerial occupation, what about their sons and daughters? Here, too, Reynolds concluded that the labor market was strongly segmented. He said (1954: 507), for example, "the people doing the higher managerial and professional jobs in the economy form a relatively closed group which is hard for people not born into that group to enter." The major explanation for the limited amount of intergenerational mobility between classes was, in his opinion, again to be found in the educational system. The passport to professional and technical careers was a college degree. This, however, involved an expense which many working-class families could not afford. Because of unequal opportunity in access to funds for investment in education, therefore, the stratification between the working class and managerial and professional class tended to perpetuate itself over time. A second result was that the supply of labor to these upper-class occupations was also smaller than what would exist if there were more perfect capital markets, leading to noncompensating wage differentials among occupations. As Reynolds (1954: 510) stated it, "Earnings in many of the higher occupations appear to be well above the equilibrium level, which means there are too few people in these occupations for social efficiency."

The Importance of the Human Factor.   A final element of the postwar model of nonunion labor markets is the importance that the "humanness" of labor has for the operation of the market. It has been recognized since the days of Adam Smith that the market for labor differs in certain respects from the market for a commodity such as wheat. The most unique property of labor is that it cannot be separated from the person owning it and, thus, the worker and employer must have a direct, on-going relationship. This causes the seller of labor to be much more concerned about the physical and social conditions of the workplace, since he or she will have an intimate contact with them on a daily basis. The fact that labor is embodied in a human being also makes the management of labor a far more complex task than that of an inert input such as capital or land. While a machine will provide the same flow of services regardless of the human relations skills of the employer or the price paid for others of its kind, the amount of labor provided by a worker is significantly affected by the full range of human emotions such as envy, insecurity, and a desire for equity and due process.

Although Alfred Marshall gave considerable weight to the "peculiarities" of labor, later neoclassical writers tended to minimize their importance. Hicks (1932: 4), for example, argued that "the general working of supply and demand is a great deal more important than the differences between markets." The postwar labor economists such as DKLR, on the other hand, gave considerable emphasis to the unique aspects of the labor market. They did not reject the application of microeconomic theory to the study of labor markets, but did feel that micro theory should be used with considerable circumspection. The problem with demand/supply analysis, in their view, is that it treats the labor market as if it were a commodity market. By neglecting the human dimension of labor, this is likely to lead to significant error. Representative of this position is the following admonition by Lester (1951: 38): "Economists, especially in formal analysis, may not distinguish labor services from material products, contending that in principle there is no difference between selling labor and selling commodities. In practice, however, the differences are often so marked and significant that to reason by analogy from commodities to labor may be completely unrealistic and erroneous."

Two examples with regard to wage determination will illustrate Lester's point. The first concerns the downward rigidity of money wages. The fact that money wages seldom fall even in the face of considerable excess supplies of labor represents one of the most important deviations between the predictions of competitive theory and the facts of real-world labor markets. DKLR offered several explanations for the rigidity of money wages. The first has already been cited—the fact that the labor market is not a bourse. A second concerns the reaction of workers to a wage cut (Lester 1951: 46–48). The firm pays a certain wage per hour for labor, in return for which it obtains an hour of a person's time. It is not the hour of time, however, that alone determines the amount and quality of output produced, but also the effort and diligence devoted by the worker to the job. The exchange negotiated in the labor market, therefore, is really a wage/effort bargain, with the wage determined by the firm and the level of effort determined by the worker. Thus, the problem for management in cutting wages is that it unilaterally changes the agreed-upon terms of the wage/effort bargain, leading to retaliation by workers in the form of reduced work effort, shirking, inattention to quality, and so on.[11] Money wages do not readily fall in the labor market, therefore, because employers find it counter-productive to do so, since worker productivity declines commensurately with the cut in wages.[12] Were labor a commodity, such a problem would not exist.

A second way the human factor enters into wage determination is through the concepts of equity and fairness. Neoclassical theory has never found a place for the concepts of equity and fairness because of its individualistic conception of human behavior and the analytic complications introduced by interdependent utility functions (see Kahneman, Knetsch, and Thaler 1986). In the postwar model, however, equity and fairness play a major role in wage determination at the level of both the firm and the market.[13] At the firm level, for example, the concern of employees for fair treatment led companies to develop in the 1940s formalized pay plans that established common wage rates or wage scales for all workers in a particular job classification (Kerr and Fisher 1950; Lester 1948). Before such plans, many firms allowed foremen or department managers to assign wage rates to individual workers, leading to numerous irrational or discriminatory wage differentials and much dissatisfaction among workers (see Jacoby 1985).

At the market level, the importance of relative wage comparisons was manifested by the development of wage imitation and pattern setting. Even in nonunion labor markets, DKLR found that wage increases often seemed to be dictated more by the timing of wage changes in nearby communities or industries than by competitive conditions in the labor market (Lester 1951: 44). Considerations of fairness also seemed to explain the importance that custom had on market wage rates, particularly with respect to occupational wage differentials such as between firemen and policemen or locomotive engineers and conductors (see Ross 1957: 200–201).

Wage Determination in Unionized Labor Markets

The postwar labor economists also gave considerable attention to the process of wage determination in unionized labor markets. They sought to understand the operation of collective bargaining and, in particular, the determinants of union wage policy. They were also much interested in the impact of unionism on the structure of wages and whether unionism was beneficial or harmful to economic efficiency and social welfare. The research of the postwar labor economists on these subjects was trailbreaking in several respects. They provided, for example, the first analytical treatment of unions as economic and political organizations. Their empirical research also provided the first systematic investigation of the impact of unions on the various dimensions of the wage structure.

The picture of unionism that emerged from studies of the postwar labor economists was in many ways antithetical to that held by neoclassical economists, both then and now. These differences, as well as the pioneering aspects of the work by DKLR, are well illustrated by consideration of three topics related to unionism and the labor market.

The Effect of Unions on Economic Efficiency and Social Welfare. Labor unions affect the operation and outcomes of the labor market in many ways. Some of these are economic, such as raising wages or reducing turnover, and some are social in nature, such as providing workers with protection against arbitrary dismissal. Ever since the first unions were formed in the late eighteenth century, economists have debated the relative benefits and costs of unionism. From an economic perspective, the central issue has been the impact of unions on economic efficiency (that is, the amount of output produced given the available inputs and state of technology). From a social perspective, the central issue is whether unions contribute to or subtract from the attainment of social goals such as fair treatment at the workplace, respect for individual rights, and reduction of economic inequality. Both critics and proponents of unionism recognize that on a scale of zero to ten, collective bargaining rates neither total condemnation (zero) nor unqualified support (ten)—the actual situation is somewhere in between. The controversy is over where on this spectrum unionism falls. Is it a one, a five, or a nine?

Opinion on this matter is principally shaped by two considerations. The first is the relative competitiveness of the labor market; the second is the goals and functions of unions. Based on these considerations, most neoclassical economists would probably give labor unions a score of two–four (see Rees 1962: 195; Freeman and Medoff 1984). One reason is that they view the labor market as relatively competitive. The importance of this assumption is severalfold. First, if workers have relatively free mobility in the market and there are a number of buyers of labor, firms have little opportunity to practice monopsonistic exploitation. Second, in a competitive economy, market forces act as an "automatic policeman" on the social conditions of labor. If a firm requires excessive work hours or has unhealthy working conditions, workers can quit and seek employment elsewhere, providing not only an escape valve for workers but also an incentive for the firm to improve its employment policies. Finally, in a competitive labor market, wage rates accurately reflect the opportunity cost of labor, leading to an optimal allocation of workers across industries and occupations and an efficient combination of factor inputs in production.

The low regard most neoclassical economists have for labor unions is also shaped by their perspective on the function and objectives of unions. While they recognize that unions confer important noneconomic benefits, neoclassical economists typically assume that the union's primary objective is to raise the wage rate for its members above the market level (Hirsch and Addison 1986: 21–22, 180–187). To do so, the union acts much as a monopoly seller of labor, forcing up the price of labor by restricting the availability of workers to the firm through the strike threat or control of entrance to the trade. Like monopolies, therefore, unions are regarded by neoclassical economists as a market imperfection that leads to artificially high wages and a consequent misallocation of resources. The inefficiency engendered by the wage effect of unionism is compounded, in this view, by the harmful effects unions have on productivity through restrictive work rules and strikes.

The postwar labor economists arrived at a significantly different view of unionism. On their scorecard, collective bargaining rated a six-eight. One reason for this relatively high rating had to do with DKLR's view of the competitive nature of labor markets. Lester (1941: 43) stated, for example, "Generally speaking, labor markets are by their nature some of the most imperfect markets in our economy." One imperfection was that employers tended to dominate local labor markets. In this regard, Reynolds and Taft (1956: 369) stated, "There can be no doubt of employers' monopsony power over wages under nonunion conditions." As discussed earlier, the monopsony power of employers did not stem in most cases from there being only one or several firms in the market, but rather from their tacit collusion to avoid wage competition and the relative immobility of the experienced factory work force.

A second defect of nonunion labor markets was the failure of competition to give rise to a going wage for labor. Because of limited labor mobility, the constricted nature of workers' job search, and employers' wage policies, at any one point in time there existed a bewildering array of wage rates paid to similar workers both within a firm and across firms. Thus, Lester (1951: 279) stated, "Nonunion wage structures usually contain all kinds of diversity, inequity, and irrationality. Collective bargaining does not, therefore, serve to distort a well-balanced wage structure and to cause a malallocation of labor resources."

A third defect of the market system, in the view of the postwar labor economists, was that it did not offer adequate protection to workers against unsafe working conditions or deleterious management practices such as discrimination and arbitrary discipline (Lester 1951: 7). In the case of working conditions, wage rates did not adequately compensate workers for disagreeable features of employment, such as risk of injury or excessive heat and noise, because of market imperfections such as limited information and mobility and the fact that some types of working conditions (for example, cleanliness in the plant) are public goods. The market also failed to adequately protect workers against abuses of management because factors such as seniority, fringe benefits, and internal labor markets inhibited workers from quitting and moving to a new firm.

The postwar labor economists also adopted a different view of the function and objectives of labor unions. They recognized that one goal of unions was to raise wages, and that in some cases they were able to do so considerably in excess of the market level. DKLR also noted that unions engaged in various anticompetitive practices such as featherbedding and restriction of apprenticeship training. Far more so than neoclassical economists, however, DKLR also stressed the positive functions of unionism. Lester (1951: 22), for example, argued that the four most important desires of workers are: economic security, a chance to better oneself, fair treatment, and a sense of community. In each case, the labor market either works against accomplishment of the goal, such as with security and a sense of community, or does not adequately protect the workers' interest, such as with fair treatment and equal opportunity. Because of the limitations of the market mechanism and individual bargaining, therefore, workers turn to unions and collective bargaining.

It is seen, then, that from the point of view of neoclassical economists, labor unions act as a monopolistic element in an otherwise competitive labor market. The impact of unions from this perspective is largely harmful, since they distort relative prices and reduce productivity. While unions may in some ways yield positive economic and social effects, these are outweighed by the overall loss of economic efficiency. The postwar labor economists, on the other hand, took a different perspective on collective bargaining. Because labor markets contain numerous imperfections, the level of wages, hours, and working conditions in a nonunion situation may significantly diverge from the ideal of a competitive market. In this case, collective bargaining may move the labor market closer to the competitive ideal rather than away from it. In some instances, the opposite may also happen, however. Quite apart from economic effects, collective bargaining is also a net plus because it affords workers dignity and due process in the work force.

Union Wage Policy. A second issue that concerned the postwar labor economists was union wage policy. The key questions about union wage policy were, first, how do unions decide on the wage rate to demand in bargaining and, second, what environmental factors are important in determining the union's choice of a wage rate.

The subject of union wage policy proved to be a contentious one and represented the most important area of disagreement among the postwar labor economists. The debate over union wage policy revolved principally around the "economic" model advanced by Dunlop and the "political" model put forward several years later by Ross. In 1944, Dunlop published *Wage Determination Under Trade Unions*. In chapter 3, he developed several alternative economic models of union behavior. His basic approach was to model the union as if it were a business firm. Following on the theory of the firm, Dunlop argued (1944: 4), "An economic theory of a trade union requires that the organization be assumed to maximize (or minimize) something." He then considered several possibilities, concluding (p. 44) that "the most suitable generalized model of the trade union for analytical purposes is probably that which depicts the maximization of the wage bill for the total membership." Given this objective, the firm's labor demand curve, and the union's wage membership function, Dunlop was able to derive a unique wage rate that the union would choose as its bargaining goal.

Four years later, Ross (1948) published *Trade Union Wage Policy*. According to Ross (p. 43), "to conceive of the union as a seller of labor attempting to maximize some measurable object (such as the wage bill) is a highly misleading formulation. Although comparable with a business firm in some respects, it is so dissimilar in other respects that the analogy is of questionable value." The problem with the business firm analogy, Ross argued, was severalfold. First, unions do not sell labor; rather they set the wage, and firms then purchase labor from individual workers. Second, if the union has any single economic objective, it is maximization of the membership's economic welfare, but the concept of economic welfare is so amorphous as to be useless for analytical work. Finally, the relationship between the union and its members is quite different from the relationship between the corporation and its stockholders. It is to the interest of stockholders for the firm to maximize profits, since each receives a share of the total; it is not to the interest of union members for the firm to maximize the wage bill, however, since there is no internal transfer device in most unions that evenly distributes the benefits and costs of such a wage policy among those members who remain employed and those who may lose their jobs.

What, then, determines a union's wage policy? On this, Ross (p. 12) says, "The central proposition . . . is that a trade union is a political agency operating in an economic environment." The political nature of the union comes from the fact that it is divided into two groups: an elected set of union leaders and the rank-and-file members. According to Ross, the union leadership is primarily responsible for formulating the union's wage policy. The wage policy they choose will be influenced by three objectives: insuring their own reelection to office, insuring the survival and growth of the union as an institution, and advancing the membership's economic welfare. Ross's model does not lead to any precise prediction about the wage rate that the union will choose as its bargaining goal. He did argue, however, that political pressure on the union leadership to go "all out" in bargaining arises in several situations. The most important is when a closely related group of workers in another plant, industry, or union gain higher wages than the membership's own union has obtained. Ross claimed that relative wage comparisons and concepts of equity and fairness pervade the wage determination process. Thus, union wage demands get locked into "orbits of coercive comparison" as workers in one plant pressure their union leaders to keep up with wage increases won elsewhere. With regard to economic variables, Ross claimed that they were important only to the extent they generated political pressure on the leadership to change the union's wage policy. Perhaps most controversially, Ross denied that most unions either perceive an inverse relationship between the level of wages and employment or take it into account in determining their wage goal.

The other postwar labor economists staked out a middle ground in the Ross/Dunlop debate, in effect offering a reconciliation of the opposing points of view[14] Following Ross's position, Kerr, Lester, and Reynolds argued that union wage policy was best analyzed as the outcome of a political process. Maximization of the wage bill, therefore, was not a valid union wage objective (see Reynolds 1957: 196–199). With regard to the relative importance of economic versus political influences on union wage policy, however, they tended to side more with Dunlop. Kerr (1977: 15) said, for example: "I have always felt that Ross rather overdid the political side. He was too concerned with conditions of new and rival unionism . . . and too little concerned with economic constraints." The economic constraints alluded to by Kerr were represented in Dunlop's model by the firm's labor demand curve, the union's wage membership function, and the variables that underlie both, such as profit, price, level of sales, and labor cost as a percentage of total cost. As Ross argued, these variables only affect the union's wage policy indirectly as they generate political pressure on the union leadership. Kerr, Lester, and Reynolds believed, however, that particularly in the longer run the relationship between price, profit, sales, the size of the union's wage demand, and the survival and growth of the union were sufficiently clear and immediate that in most cases union wage policy would be primarily shaped by the economic environment, as Dunlop claimed.

The empirical evidence from several case studies of union wage policy in the 1950s seemed to offer support for the positions of both Ross and Dunlop. In a study of the shoe industry, Shultz (1951) found that the union's wage demands were closely attuned to economic conditions in the product and labor market. Levinson (1960), however, concluded that in the auto industry the wage policy of the UAW was little affected by considerations of any possible negative employment effect from raising wages. In the area of union wage policy, then, it seems that the postwar labor economists made significant advances in knowledge but were unable to fully resolve the dispute between Dunlop and Ross[15]

The Effect of Unions on the Wage Structure. The third union-related topic investigated by the postwar labor economists was the impact of collective bargaining on the wage structure. Three issues were of chief concern. The first was factual in nature: To what extent, if any, had collective bargaining altered various dimensions of the wage structure? The second was a natural extension of the first: If collective bargaining had in some way changed the wage stricture, was it, on net, harmful or helpful to economic efficiency? Finally, the postwar labor economists attempted to determine the relative importance of market versus institutional forces in shaping the wage structure.

The nation's wage structure can be divided into five different types of wage differentials: interpersonal, interfirm, interarea, interoccupational, and interindustry. The postwar labor economists examined each of these dimensions of the wage structure, seeking to determine for each the answers to the three questions noted above (see Kerr 1957; Lester 1947a, 1951; Reynolds and Taft 1956). Their conclusions are briefly summarized below.

1. *Interpersonal.* Collective bargaining resulted in a significant reduction in interpersonal wage differentials. Unions discouraged incentive rate wage systems and replaced separate time rates paid to each employee with standard wage schedules that based pay on the characteristics of the job, not the person. The success of unions in reducing interpersonal differentials reflected their overriding concern with equity (equal pay for equal work) and security (ending wage competition among workers). The benefit of wage leveling was the reduction of irrational and discriminatory wage differentials; the cost was that wage rates could not always reflect differences in productivity among workers. On the whole, the impact of collective bargaining was moderately beneficial.

2. *Interfirm.* The dispersion in interfirm and interplant wage rates was significantly reduced by collective bargaining, particularly among firms in the same product market. In nonunion labor markets, interfirm wage differentials reflected differences in ability to pay among firms, with low-wage firms generally being the marginal producers. Unions placed great emphasis on establishing common wage scales across firms in order to "take wages out of competition." The cost of wage standardization was that some firms were forced out of business. The benefits were severalfold. First, pressure was brought to bear on high-cost, inefficiently managed firms to modernize and rationalize production (the shock effect). Second, forcing the marginal producers out of business allowed capital and labor resources to be allocated to more efficient uses. Third, from both an economic and an equity perspective, it was seen as undesirable to use low wages and substandard working conditions as a means to keep inefficient producers in business. On net, then, the narrowing of interfirm wage differentials was beneficial.

3. *Interarea.* The union impact on interarea (geographic) wage differentials was slight. Unions attempted to narrow interregional wage differentials, particularly between the low-wage South and high-wage North. The impetus was to protect organized firms in the North from the competitive threat posed by lower-cost, nonunion firms in the South. This effort was handicapped, however, by the inability of unions to effectively organize the South. Since wage rates in the South were believed to be considerably below what they would have been in a competitive market, the reduction in geographic wage differentials by unions was seen as beneficial.

4. *Occupational.* Collective bargaining had only a minor impact on

occupational wage differentials. Reynolds and Lester felt that unionism had led to a narrowing of occupational wage rates, while Kerr concluded that unions, had, if anything, maintained existing skill differentials. All agreed that market forces were primarily responsible for the historic narrowing of occupational differentials.

5. *Interindustry.* The effect of collective bargaining on interindustry differentials was small. Reynolds believed that, on net, unionism caused a gradual widening of the interindustry wage structure. The reason was that union organization was greatest in concentrated industries with a high ability to pay. He argued that the widening of interindustry differentials was harmful. Kerr believed that the effect of unions on interindustry wage rates varied over the business cycle with little net impact over the long run.

All in all, what is the net impact of collective bargaining on the wage structure? According to Reynolds (1957: 221):

> First, there has been a widespread tendency to overstate the net effect of trade unionism on wage structure. Curiously enough, this error has been committed in equal measure by the friends of trade unionism and by its critics . . . Second, from the standpoint of conformity to competitive norms of wage structure, collective bargaining has clearly had a mixed effect—"improving" the wage structure in some respects and "worsening" it in others. The doctrinaire view that trade unions, being "monopolies," must by definition have an adverse effect on the wage structure, does not stand up well in the light of empirical studies, for one can make at least as good a case for the contrary opinion.

The Firm's Internal Wage Structure

A third aspect of wage determination focused on by the postwar labor economists was the determinants of the internal wage structure of business firms. The internal wage structure refers to the set of wage rates and wage differentials paid to workers employed in the various jobs within the firm. In their research on this issue, the postwar labor economists attempted to determine the environmental factors that shape a firm's internal wage structure, the relative role of market forces versus administrative decision in the setting of wage rates within a firm, and the ability of administrative techniques such as job evaluation to satisfy the twin demands of equity and efficiency.

The writings of DKLR and the other postwar labor economists on the internal wage structure were truly pioneering, for this facet of wage determination had received little attention from other economists. There were two reasons for this neglect (Hildebrand 1963). One was the belief that the process of wage setting within the firm was largely an administrative issue and thus of more relevance to scholars in management than in economics. A second reason was that neoclassical economists saw little in the subject to merit separate investigation. From their perspective, wage rates for particular types of labor are determined by the market forces of supply and demand, and firms, acting as passive wage takers, pay whatever the going price for labor happens to be. The internal wage structure is thus a reflection of the types of occupations or job skills which firms seek employees for and the wage rate which the market sets for each occupation and skill level.

The postwar labor economists rejected both of these arguments. The first was dismissed because, in their view, wage setting, whether by market forces or administrative decision, is inherently of interest to economists, since it affects the remuneration and allocation of labor resources. The second argument was also rejected, for reasons alluded to in the discussion of nonunion labor markets. As noted there, DKLR found that in most labor markets the forces of supply and demand are sufficiently impeded by various imperfections that there is no deterministic going wage for labor but rather an area of indeterminancy in which the firm has room to choose the wage rate to be paid. This being the case, it is impossible to treat the market structure of wage rates and the firm's internal wage structure as one and the same thing.

Because the internal wage structure of most firms has a life of its own, the postwar labor economists set out to describe the forces that shape the internal wage structure and cause it to change. In so doing, they developed a number of new theoretical concepts, as well as a generalized perspective on wage setting in the firm which is distinctively different from anything in the neoclassical tradition. These concepts and the overall perspective on wage determination within the firm are briefly sketched below.

The Job Structure. The starting point in the postwar model of the internal wage structure is a concept known as the "job structure" (Livernash 1957). The job structure refers to the set of jobs in terms of skill and function required by the firm, and their organizational relationship to each other. The importance of the job structure is twofold. First, it defines the types of jobs for which wages must be assigned. The internal wage structure, therefore, takes many of its features from the underlying job structure. Second, many job structures contain vertical and horizontal segments across which there is only limited worker mobility, with the result that the wage rates paid to one group of workers in the firm may be only loosely connected to the wage rates paid to another group.

The job structure of a firm is heavily influenced by the nature of the product produced, and particularly the technology of production. The production of cotton yarn or railway freight transportation, for example, requires a specific set of occupations and job skills that are generally organized together in much the same configuration by all the firms in that industry. Although technology is the dominant force in shaping the job structure, it is not the sole influence. To some degree, management can shape the job structure through its capital investment decisions, as can collective bargaining through manning requirements and restrictions on the implementation of new technology.

There are two aspects of the job structure that the postwar labor economists identified as significant structural influences on the internal wage structure. The first is what Dunlop (1957) labeled as "job clusters." A job cluster is a set of jobs related to a common activity. One of the hallmarks of modern technology is specialization and the division of labor, reflected in the organization of the business firm into functional departments and subunits thereof. As discussed more in a moment, the similarity of tasks and close physical proximity of the workers in each job cluster makes them a natural focal point for wage determination in the firm.

The second important feature of many job structures is the existence of well-defined job ladders (Dunlop 1966). As noted previously, a job ladder is a vertical hierarchy of jobs along which workers are promoted upwards from the least skilled to the most skilled job. The impetus behind the creation of job ladders is again the technology of production. In many manufacturing industries, for example, there are certain job clusters in which the jobs to be performed build one onto another in terms of the skill and experience required. Because the skills tend to be firm-specific and are best learned through on-the-job training, firms find it advantageous to establish formal lines of progression (such as delineated by seniority districts) so that job vacancies above the port of entry position on a job ladder are filled by internal promotion rather than hiring from the external labor market, or even from different job clusters within the firm. It is these job ladders which give rise to the internal labor market.

The Role of Market Forces versus Administrative Decision. The job structure defines the various types of occupations and job skills for which the firm must recruit employees. The next issue concerns how the wage rate paid to each worker in the job structure is determined.

According to the postwar labor economists, the internal wage structure is the product of three elements (Hildebrand 1963): the market forces of supply and demand, the range of administrative discretion afforded by market forces, and the particular wage setting techniques or practices used by management (possibly in conjunction with a labor union) in exercising this discretion. In most cases, the internal wage structure is determined by some combination of market forces and administrative decision, although there is wide variation within a firm and across firms in the degree to which discretion can be exercised.

The labor market exerts its major influence upon the internal wage structure through "market-oriented" jobs. These are jobs that are fairly uniform in their duties and involve training that is general in nature. Such jobs allow both job candidates and incumbents to compare wages and other employment conditions across firms and to choose the job that is most advantageous. In this situation, competitive pressure from the external labor market largely (but seldom completely) determines the wage rate the firm can (must) pay.

In most firms, some jobs are more market-oriented than others, although the degree to which this is true varies greatly by industry and union status. As an example, a job cluster in which most jobs are market-oriented is the clerical department of a firm. Clerical jobs are usually fairly standard in duties and requirements, and there exist few barriers to mobility between employers. The result, as shown in a case study of secretaries in Boston by George Shultz (1962), is that employers are quite conscious of being in competition for labor and adjust their wage rates fairly quickly to shifts in demand and supply. The internal wage structure in the clerical job cluster, and for most jobs in smaller size retail and service establishments, is thus largely market determined.

Among production jobs in a factory, on the other hand, there are generally far fewer market-oriented jobs, a fact which necessarily diminishes the influence of supply and demand in wage determination. It is here that the job structure gives rise to job ladders and the internal labor market. Because these jobs tend to involve idiosyncratic skills and firm-specific training, the competitive pressures arising from comparison and mobility are weakened. As DKLR intuited, and Walter Oi (1962) and Gary Becker (1964) later showed more rigorously, firm-specific training creates its own area of indeterminancy in wage rates—competition places upper and lower limits to the wage bargain, but within these limits the wage is indeterminant until explicitly set by unilateral management decision, individual bargaining, or collective bargaining.

A third type of internal wage structure analyzed by the postwar labor economists involved firms in industries such as construction or printing where craft unionism is prevalent (Kerr 1954a). Like the job structure in the clerical job cluster, there are relatively short job ladders in the job structure of a firm in a craft industry, and the job skills are largely transferable across firms. As a consequence, the internal wage structure in such firms in a nonunion market would be largely market determined. Craft unionism substantially changes the process of wage determination in such firms, however. The first impact of craft unionism is to increase the horizontal segmentation of the firm's work force as each craft union seeks to define and protect its jurisdiction. In the craft case, therefore, each individual job cluster becomes a formal unit for wage determination. A second impact of craft unionism is to greatly reduce the impact of market forces on wage determination within the firm. By controlling entry to the trade through the hiring hall and enforcing the single rate across firms through the strike threat, craft unions lead to an internal wage structure that is not market-oriented by "union-oriented." Discretion again plays a significant role, but in this case it is the union, not management, that is the effective authority in wage determination.

Wage Setting in the Internal Labor Market.   Since there are relatively few market-oriented jobs in the internal labor market, it becomes necessary for management to fashion, either unilaterally or in consultation with a union, an explicit wage structure within these job clusters. The specific form of the internal wage structure and the rates of pay that are earned in each job are thus a function of the personnel and compensation practices of the firm. As the postwar labor economists discovered, the methods used by management in deriving the internal wage structure have a number of important consequences for the operation of labor markets.

As part of their work with the War Labor Board and other related wartime agencies, DKLR became heavily involved in resolving disputes over wage differentials among job classifications within and across firms. They soon discovered that in many nonunion firms it was not unusual for there to exist a host of seemingly irrational wage differentials that had no apparent relation to either differences in job content or personal abilities (Lester 1951: 65). The haphazard nature of these internal wage structures was the product of two factors: the loose constraints imposed by the external labor market on wage rates in many job clusters of the firm, and a lack of any type of formal, systematic plan for determining rates of pay, the order of layoff and promotion, and other such issues. Not infrequently, these matters were handled on an informal case-by-case basis by individual supervisors, department heads, or upper-level management.

One consequence of such management practices was a high degree of dissatisfaction among the workers over perceived inequities in the firm's compensation policies. The union policy of "equal pay for equal work" was thus a powerful inducement for workers to organize, and helped to explain the surge of unionization in the 1940s and early 1950s. As companies sought to rationalize their wage structures, either under the pressure of collective bargaining or with the desire to remain nonunion, they began to search for more formalized methods to determine wage rates. One such method was job evaluation.

Job evaluation is a technique that assigns wage rates to particular jobs based on the number of points awarded for factors such as skill, responsibility, risk of injury, and so on (see Wallace and Fay 1983). It is particularly useful, for example, in establishing a set of pay differentials for positions arrayed along a job ladder. Since job evaluation provides only a relative ranking of jobs in terms of job worth points, to derive an explicit wage structure it is necessary to select one or more jobs and their associated wage rates as reference points for developing the wage scale. These reference points were called "key jobs" by the postwar labor economists (Dunlop 1957). Key jobs might be particular positions in the job cluster that were market-oriented and for which a going wage could be determined. In other cases, key jobs might be selected on the basis of their importance to total labor cost or their prominence in the production process.

The virtue of job evaluation is that it provides management a technique to develop a rational structure of pay differentials in situations where the market does not. The gradations of pay along a job ladder, however, are not equilibrium wage rates in the sense that they balance demand and supply (Livernash 1957). As the postwar labor economists noted, there is always a shortage of positions on the upper reaches of a job ladder relative to the number of people who desire to be promoted into them. Promotion and training opportunities in the internal labor market, therefore, must be rationed through some type of administrative rule such as seniority. According to Dunlop (1984), this fact also means that human capital theory errs when it assumes that the amount of on-the-job training required by workers is determined by some equilibrium economic process where workers and firms balance the prospective benefits and costs of investment in training.

Although pay rates in the internal labor market are not strictly market determined, market forces do set upper and lower bounds to the range of management discretion. A continual problem for management is to derive an internal wage structure that satisfies the internal constraint of equity and ease of administration and the external constraint of consistency with demand and supply conditions. Perhaps the classic illustration of this problem is the analysis by Kerr and Fisher (1950) of the experience with job evaluation during World War II in the West Coast airframe industry. Because of the serious labor shortages in the industry, certain job rates established under the job evaluation plan were substantially below the corresponding market rates. To attract and hold people in these positions required a substantial revision in the job rate, but doing so then set off demands from workers in other positions for similar raises on equity grounds. The fundamental lesson, according to Kerr and Fisher, is that the internal wage structure is a function of both the external economic environment and the internal demand of the work force for equity, and the difficult task of management is to structure the wage scale to satisfy both.

The Attack on Marginal Analysis

In addition to their work on various aspects of wage determination, the postwar labor economists also wrote on a variety of other subjects pertaining to economic theory and labor markets. Of these, the one that proved to be the most controversial was the attack by Lester on the usefulness of marginal analysis for understanding labor market behavior. Lester's critique of marginalism was most forcefully stated in his 1946 article "Shortcomings of Marginal Analysis for Wage-Employment Problems," an article which set off a now-famous debate between himself, Fritz Machlup, and George Stigler.[16] Even though Dunlop, Kerr, and Reynolds stayed largely outside this particular controversy, the issue raised by Lester—the alleged lack of correspondence between neoclassical theory and real-world behavior—followed firmly in the postwar tradition.

Lester's critique of marginal analysis was directed specifically at the marginal productivity theory of labor demand, although it indirectly called into question the entire neoclassical theory of the firm. The marginal productivity theory provides an answer to the question of how much of a factor input such as labor a firm should hire. The answer given by the theory is that to maximize profit a firm should hire additional labor as long as each worker's marginal revenue product is greater than or equal to the worker's marginal labor cost (the wage rate in a perfectly competitive labor market). The theory also predicts that a firm's quantity demanded of labor will decline in response to an increase in the wage rate, other things equal. Assuming diminishing returns to labor in the short run and continuous marginal product and marginal revenue schedules, a firm will face a smooth, downward sloping short-run demand curve for labor. An increase in the wage rate, therefore, will cause a decline in employment as the firm moves up the labor demand curve, laying off those workers whose marginal revenue product is less than the wage.

The basic thrust of Lester's critique was to deny that in the short run there is necessarily any consistent negative relationship between the wage rate and level of employment. He claimed that for a modest (for example, 10 percent) increase in the wage, a firm's employment might decline, remain the same, or even increase.[17] This was possible, in his view, because the assumptions of the marginal productivity theory are frequently violated in the real world. He attacked four of the theory's assumptions, in particular:[18]

1. *Profit Maximization.* The most important behavioral assumption in the neoclassical theory of the firm is that the objective of firms is to maximize profits. As noted earlier, however, Lester and the other postwar labor economists argued that a more realistic assumption is that managers strive only to achieve a satisfactory level of profit, after which they either pursue other goals such as market share or harmonious labor relations, or willingly tolerate inefficiency and slack in the operation of the firm. If firms do not maximize profits, this weakens the marginal productivity theory in two ways, according to Lester. The first is that it reduces the motivation for managers to either make marginal calculations or to reduce employment in response to a wage increase. Second, and more important, the existence of inefficiency and slack gives the firm a buffer in which it can absorb the cost impact of a wage increase through

improved methods of production or management rather than layoffs (the "shock effect").

2. *Limits to Human Cognition.* A second objection raised by Lester was that managers frequently do not have the required information or cannot make the relevant computations to operationalize the marginal productivity theory. He claimed, for example, that managers often cannot distinguish each worker's contribution to production, particularly where there are joint products or in multiprocess industries. Likewise, interviews with managers reveal that they have little knowledge of product demand elasticities and the marginal revenue associated with alternative output levels. Finally, business accounting methods are not able to provide managers with data on the costs of incremental units of production. For all these reasons, Lester argued that most business firms are precluded from using marginal calculations and, thus, will not make incremental changes in employment as the theory presumes.

3. *Increasing Returns.* A fundamental assumption of marginal productivity theory is that labor is subject to diminishing returns in the short run, giving rise to a downward-sloping marginal physical product schedule and labor demand curve. Lester noted, however, that much of the available empirical evidence contradicted this assumption. Rather than diminishing returns, statistical studies found that in many manufacturing firms, labor was subject to increasing returns, implying that marginal cost and average variable cost actually declines until the full capacity level of production is reached. He argued that this fact would be likely to significantly change a firm's response to a modest wage increase. According to the marginal productivity theory, a wage increase shifts up the firm's marginal cost curve, causing it to curtail production and employment until the marginal revenue product of the last worker employed again equals the wage rate[19] Lester argued, however, that the actual response of a firm to an upward shift of the marginal cost curve is not to curtail output but rather to increase output through a greater sales effort. The reason is that by increasing production the firm is able to move down the declining marginal cost curve, offsetting the higher marginal cost due to the wage increase with a lower marginal cost due to a more efficient level of production. The net result, according to Lester, is that employment might not change at all or might actually increase in response to a wage increase.

4. *Fixed Capital/Labor Ratios.* A fourth assumption of the theory criticized by Lester was that capital and labor can be used in variable proportions in production. While he admitted that this was a realistic assumption for agricultural goods and certain other products, Lester argued that in most manufacturing industries production requires a relatively fixed number of workers for a given size of plant, implying a fixed proportions-type production technology. This fact, combined with the relative stickiness of prices in the industrial and regulated sectors of the economy, causes the firm's

demand for labor, according to Lester, to be relatively independent of wage rates in the short run.

In his paper, Lester attempted to buttress these criticisms of the marginal productivity theory with empirical evidence. The data he used came from a survey questionnaire mailed to 430 southern business firms and returned by 58 of them. The survey results revealed:

1.   The executives of the firms ranked sales as a far more important determinant of the level of employment than wage rates.
2.   The majority of executives reported that average variable cost declined with increased production up to 100 percent of the plant's capacity level.
3.   Southern firms did not use relatively more labor than their northern counterparts, even though the relative cost of labor in the South was lower.
4.   When asked what their response would be to a wage increase, few of the business executives cited curtailment of output, while the majority said they would increase sales effort, attempt to improve efficiency, or raise prices.

In support of his criticisms of the marginal productivity theory, Lester also cited other evidence that he claimed was difficult to reconcile with the notion of a downward-sloping labor demand curve. One example was the impact of the hike in the minimum wage on employment in a number of southern industries. Because wage rates were, on average, considerably lower in firms in the South, Lester reasoned that the increase in the minimum wage between 1937 and 1941 should have caused a relatively greater decline in employment among those firms than in northern firms. He found, however, just the opposite— employment actually grew considerably faster among southern firms despite the relatively greater increase in labor cost.

Lester's attack on marginal analysis set off a lively and spirited debate in the economics profession. He obtained at least qualified support from some economists such as Reder (1947) and Gordon (1948), but also evoked considerable opposition from others, particularly Machlup (1946, 1947, 1967) and Stigler (1947). On a conceptual level, Machlup and Stigler claimed that Lester had either misrepresented or misinterpreted the marginal productivity theory, while on an empirical level they argued that his survey results both failed to refute the theory and were of questionable content validity. Given below is a brief summary of their rebuttal to the specific points raised in Lester's paper.

1.   Machlup admitted that businessmen are motivated by more than a pecuniary quest for profit but denied that this fact invalidates marginal analysis. He cited three reasons. First, although managers may wish to pursue

various nonprofit objectives, the forces of competition are sufficiently strong that in most cases they are forced to focus on the maximization of profits if the firm is to survive in the long run. Second, nonpecuniary considerations can be incorporated into neoclassical theory by assuming that managers maximize a utility function rather than a profit function. Third, Machlup claimed that the major purpose of the theory is not to explain all aspects of firm behavior but only the probable change in certain key variables such as output and employment in response to a change in some other variable. He did not believe that the accuracy of such predictions was likely to be much affected by the various nonpecuniary factors that may enter into business decision making.

2. Machlup also disputed Lester's contention that managers do not have the cognitive ability to make marginal-type calculations. In a well-known analogy, Machlup compared a business manager to the driver of a car. Just as the driver of a car does not make explicit mathematical calculations in deciding whether to pass another automobile, the same is true for business managers when they decide on how many workers to hire. The end result, however, is likely in both cases, he claimed, to closely approximate the outcome predicted by a formal model such as the marginal productivity theory. Machlup also claimed that the lack of objective data on marginal productivity and marginal revenue does not invalidate the theory, for it is always assumed that the data are in the form of "subjective estimates, guesses, and hunches."

3. With respect to the issue of increasing returns to labor, Machlup denied that this phenomenon necessarily invalidates marginal productivity theory. Even if the marginal physical product schedule is upward sloping, Machlup pointed out that the labor demand curve could still be downward sloping if the product demand curve were sufficiently inelastic. Both Machlup and Stigler claimed that Lester's survey data with respect to the behavior of average cost were highly suspect because of the ambiguous definition of "full capacity" and the apparent failure of some of the respondents to separate fixed from variable costs.

4. Machlup also disputed Lester's criticism concerning the importance of fixed capital/labor ratios in production. He claimed that fixed proportions is a special case which is much less common than alleged by Lester. Machlup further disputed Lester's empirical evidence on the lack of substitution in production. For example, the fact that executives rated output demand as far more important than wage rates in determining the firm's level of employment did not, according to Machlup, invalidate the theory, for all it illustrated was that output was far more variable than wage rates. Similarly, Machlup noted that although few firms said they would deliberately restrict output in response to a wage increase, many did report they would raise the product price, which would indirectly lead to the same result. Machlup concluded, therefore, that the labor demand curve is likely to be downward sloping, as hypothesized by the theory.

5.   Finally, Machlup and Stigler denied that Lester's evidence concerning the minimum wage disproved the validity of a downward-sloping labor demand curve. Machlup claimed, for example, that the negative employment effect caused by the increase in the minimum wage was obscured by the growth in employment that occurred due to the increase in industry sales.

Having reviewed both sides of the debate, it is useful to attempt some assessment of Lester's critique of marginalism and its ultimate impact on economic theory. Perhaps the most basic lesson from the debate is that no matter how cogent are one's criticisms of a theory, in the final analysis it takes a theory to beat a theory. Although the design of Lester's survey questionnaire and his interpretation of some of the data obtained from it can justifiably be faulted, taken as a whole his article did raise fundamental questions about the validity of the marginal productivity theory. Nor, in my opinion, were Machlup and Stigler entirely successful in rebutting Lester. Machlup, in particular, came close to making the theory an irrefutable tautology by equating whatever the business manager does as somehow consistent with marginal-type analysis, while his attempt to stretch the theory to include such factors as increasing returns and non-profit maximizing behavior is ingenious but unconvincing. It is evident from textbooks and scholarly articles written in the 1950s that a majority of labor economists agreed with Lester's view, for discussions of the marginal productivity theory tended to emphasize the unrealistic nature of its assumptions and the limited applicability of its conclusions to actual labor market behavior (see Shister 1956; Reder 1958).

From a longer-run perspective, however, it is clear that Lester lost the battle, for today the marginal productivity theory (and marginal analysis in general) continues to be a mainstay of economic analysis. The reason for the theory's resurgence is not due to new empirical evidence that contradicts Lester's criticisms. Forty years later, economists are still debating whether firms maximize profits, the phenomenon of increasing returns has yet to be fully explained (see Hazeldine 1979), and little evidence has ever been presented that large-scale business firms use marginal-type decision rules to determine their desired level of employment. What, then, accounts for the ascendancy of marginalism? The answer entails two parts. The first is the failure of Lester and the other postwar labor economists to develop a formal theory of input demand that could replace the marginal productivity theory. The second is the attack by Milton Friedman and others on realism in theory. Both of these factors are discussed in more detail in the next section.

Reasons for the Decline in Influence of the Postwar Labor Economists

The influence of the postwar labor economists in labor economics reached its high watermark in the early to mid-1950s. During this period their research program effectively defined the intellectual center of gravity in the field. In terms of topical areas of interest, this meant that research in labor economics was primarily focused on the process of wage determination in local labor markets, patterns of labor mobility, internal wage structures, union wage policy, the process and structure of collective bargaining, and the impact of unions on wages, productivity, strikes, and other outcomes of collective bargaining. With respect to theory, the result was a mild to moderate hostility towards microeconomic theory in general and competitive labor market theory in particular, counterbalanced by an openness towards more multidisciplinary perspectives.[20] Finally, the outlook in labor economics in the mid-1950s was generally sympathetic towards collective bargaining and government regulation of the labor market, and sharply critical of free market ideologues.

What a difference twenty years makes! By the mid-1970s the big names of the postwar period such as DKLR were replaced on graduate readings lists and conference proceedings by a new group of labor economists who in large part drew their training and inspiration from the University of Chicago. The economists of the Chicago school breathed new life into neoclassical theory, and in so doing completely changed the field of labor economics from what it had been in the 1950s.

The hallmark of the Chicago approach was the rigorous and unflinching application of microeconomic theory to all aspects of labor market behavior. Essential assumptions of the theory were maximizing behavior, stable preferences, and competitive markets (Becker 1976: 3–14). In terms of the research focus in labor economics, by the 1970s attention had shifted to a substantially different set of topics, including determinants of hours of work and labor force participation, investment in human capital (for example, education, on-the-job training), discrimination, and the economics of the family. Conversely, some topics that were big in the 1950s (for example, company wage policies) faded completely from sight, while others (for example, all aspects of collective bargaining) received considerably less attention (see Johnson 1975). Labor economics also became far more analytical in its approach to research with the widespread use of mathematics and statistics. Finally, the ideological perspective of most labor economists did an about-face from the 1950s. Collective bargaining and government regulation of labor markets were now seen as undesirable sources of inefficiency, while a much greater faith was put on the ability of free markets to achieve desired economic and social outcomes.

What accounts for the eclipse of the postwar labor economists and their point of view on theory and policy? Specific factors included:

1. *Loss of Research Momentum.* The dominant position that the postwar labor economists had in the field during the years 1945–1955 was built directly on the quantity and quality of their research. After 1955, their research

output on labor market issues slackened considerably, and with it so did their influence in the field.

One factor behind the decline in research activity was that by 1955 there was a perception that the research program of the postwar labor economists had encountered diminishing returns. In a survey of research on wages, for example, Reynolds (1953: 235) said, "The law of diminishing originality seems to have set in, and new writings seem mainly to be ringing the changes on reasonably familiar themes. . . . I would argue that work on company wage levels and wage structure has been pushed to the margin of usefulness for the time being." In the search for more fertile ground, DKLR moved on to other research interests. In the 1960s Reynolds and Kerr gradually shifted into completely different fields (economic development, education) while Dunlop and Lester wrote on more industrial relations–type topics (for example, dispute resolution, the evolution of unions as organizations). A second factor was that their talents also led them on to nonresearch activities. Dunlop and Lester became faculty deans, while Kerr went on to become president of the University of California. Public service also beckoned, particularly in the case of Dunlop, who served as an administrator in four wage-and-price-control programs and as secretary of labor in the Ford administration.

2. *Failure of the Postwar Labor Economists to Develop Theory.* A second important factor contributing to the decline in influence of the postwar labor economists was their failure to develop their insights into more formal models or theories. Economists, like all scientists, are hungry for analytic models that yield testable hypotheses. The postwar labor economists demonstrated in their case studies that real-world labor markets worked substantially differently from what would be predicted from conventional microeconomic theories. The challenge, then, was to construct analytic models that could better explain reality. By and large, the postwar labor economists failed to do so. They showed, for example, that demand-side factors were primarily responsible for wage differentials in local labor markets, but they were unable to construct a theory of the firm to explain this phenomenon. Similarly, Ross and others argued persuasively in favor of a political model of union behavior, but they never developed a formal model that could yield testable hypotheses about the relationship between the economic environment or the union's institutional structure and the size of its wage demand. A third example is Lester's failure to develop an alternative nonmarginal theory of labor demand.

Not only did the postwar labor economists largely fail to develop formal models of their own, but they also had relatively little success in stimulating their graduate students to carry on the task of theory building. Perhaps the major exception was the work of Doeringer and Piore (1971) in the late 1960s on internal labor markets and dual labor market theory.[21] Although these models caused a considerable flurry of excitement at first, their proponents never successfully developed either into a viable alternative to neoclassical theory, and the appeal of each has since faded.

3. *The Attack on Realism in Theory.* A third development that had much to do with the decline in influence of the postwar labor economists and the revival of the neoclassical school was the methodological attack staged by Milton Friedman (1953) and others on realism in theory. According to Kerr (1983: 311), the guiding principle behind the work of the postwar labor economists was "fidelity to reality." On a theoretical level, fidelity to reality meant two things: a rejection of competitive theory because its assumptions and predictions seemed to be frequently violated in real-world labor markets and, second, an emphasis on developing new theoretical models that gave greater emphasis to market imperfections, the influence of institutions and social convention, and more behaviorally oriented theories of human psychology.

As long as realism was an important criterion in theory, the proponents of competitive theory were inevitably on the defensive. In a brilliant counterstroke, Friedman not only freed neoclassical theory from the strictures of realism but actually used the issue of realism to undercut rival theories of imperfect competition. In his 1953 essay, "The Methodology of Positive Economics," Friedman argued, first, that the ultimate goal of theory is to yield testable hypotheses and, second, that the criterion by which to judge a theory is its ability to predict, not the realism of its assumptions. Friedman's argument dealt a blow to the position of the postwar labor economists in several ways.

The first was to blunt much of their criticism that the competitive model was not descriptively accurate. As noted earlier, there was much discussion during the 1950s about the fact that firms actually pursued other objectives besides maximum profits, that labor demand and supply curves had gaps, kinks, or were bands instead of lines, and that labor mobility was only weakly related to wage differentials. According to Friedman, all of the facts might well be true, but they are also irrelevant to whether or not competitive theory is useful. The purpose of theory is to predict behavior, not describe reality. Thus, in his view, as long as firms act "as if" they maximize profits or wage rates change "as if" there are well-defined demand and supply functions, then competitive theory is a fruitful tool, even if it is a poor representation of how firms actually make business decisions or how wage rates are actually determined.

While Friedman's argument did much to defang the critics of competitive theory, of even more importance was the apparent carte blanche that the "as if" assumption gave neoclassical economists in their application of competitive theory to any and all aspects of labor market behavior. Since realism of assumptions was no longer a controlling factor, it became impossible to rule out the use of competitive theory for any given subject because of a lack of congruence between the model's assumptions and the objective facts of the situation. Thus, for example, even though many workers in the short run do not have discretion in their work hours, this fact does not, in Friedman's view, invalidate use of the neoclassical labor/leisure model, for the only admissible criterion on which to judge is whether the change in hours of work match the predictions of the theory. Similar reasoning has been used to justify the expansion of economic theorizing to areas (for example, fertility, marriage) that were once outside the pale of labor economics.

A third consequence of Friedman's attack on realism in theory was to undercut the viability of alternative behavioral theories or models of imperfect competition (also see Stigler 1949: 12–24). In his essay, Friedman argued that when two theories have the same predictive ability (that is, *ex ante* ability to correctly explain events), the preferred one is the theory which is most parsimonious in its assumptions. Competitive theory clearly wins on this score because its assumptions with regard to both the nature of human behavior and the economic environment are far simpler than those in, say, the conventional model of oligopsony or DKLR's model of wage determination. Competitive theory, in Friedman's view, also does better with regard to a second dimension of "predictive ability"—the ability of a theory to give rise to testable hypotheses. Because of its relatively uncomplicated structure, the competitive model is far more analytically tractable than alternative theories of imperfect competition, allowing both a higher degree of formalization and the derivation of a greater number of unique solutions to comparative static problems. The impact of both arguments has been to displace the middle ground of imperfectly competitive labor market theories such as DKLR's with models that occupy the extreme ends of the theoretical spectrum, one being the model of perfect competition, the other being monopsony. Since monopsony is seen as largely irrelevant to today's labor market (see Viscusi 1980), the net result is that the model of perfect competition has gradually become the standard frame of reference in labor economics.

Since Friedman made the ability to explain events the desideratum for choosing among theories, at least from the perspective of the early 1950s it still might have been thought that on this ground alone the competitive model would be rejected. There were, after all, such things as rigid wages, persistent unemployment, and noncompensating wage differentials that all conflicted with the predictions of the theory. Neoclassical economists have so far successfully immunized the theory from these deviant observations in several ways, however.

One line of defense has been to argue that these deviant observations (for example, noncompensating wage differentials) are short-run phenomena, while the predictions of the theory apply only to the longer run when market forces have time to work themselves out (Reder 1958). A second has been to argue that the predictions of competitive theory apply only to aggregate behavior and not to the behavior of individual people or firms (Machlup

1967). A third has been to co-opt the critics by showing that the various imperfections thought to be so damaging to the theory are really themselves the product of rational, economizing behavior and, thus, are fully consistent with the theory (for example, the sequential nature of job search, the immobility of labor due to specific on-the-job training). A fourth has been to redefine concepts so that what was once a deviant observation no longer is (for example, involuntary unemployment became part of the "natural rate" of unemployment; see Brown 1983). A fifth has been to add unobservable or unmeasurable variables to the theory (for example, risk aversion in implicit contract theory) so that the predictions now fit the facts (Azariadis 1975). A sixth has been to simply ignore the evidence (for example, the large degree of wage dispersion in occupational wage rates in local labor markets), or to argue (Smith and Ehrenberg 1983) that inconsistent results are due to data problems (for example, the inability to find a negative correlation between wage rates and fringe benefits). A final line of defense, and one that has carried the day with most economists, I believe, is the pragmatic argument that while competitive theory may not lead to correct predictions in all cases, it is still able to explain a broader range of labor market behavior than its alternatives (Cain 1976).

4. *New Developments in Labor Supply Theory.* A fourth factor that contributed to the decline in the influence of the postwar labor economists was the series of theoretical breakthroughs by neoclassical economists in the theory of labor supply. Writing in 1957, Dunlop (1957: 128) observed, "Wage theory has tended historically to disintegrate on the supply side. . . . In a sense the pivotal task of wage theory is to formulate an acceptable theory on the supply side." His words were prophetic, but for a variety of reasons the postwar labor economists never explored this side of the intellectual terrain[22] Chicago economists, on the other hand, seized the initiative and rigorously developed a host of new theoretical constructs that significantly strengthened labor supply theory. Examples are H. Gregg Lewis's (1956) pioneering work on the labor/leisure model and its application to the long-run trend in hours of work, Jacob Mincer's (1962) work on labor force participation and the household model of labor supply, and the theories of human capital and allocation of time developed by Gary Becker (1964, 1965). The allure of these theories was further heightened by their usefulness for analyzing various public policy issues which came to the fore in the 1960s. A prominent example was the labor supply impact of tax and transfer programs.

These new theoretical developments in labor supply had several repercussions on the development of labor economics. One was to shift the research momentum away from the postwar labor economists and towards their neoclassical rivals. A second was to shift the analysis of wage determination away from the demand side of the labor market which DKLR had emphasized and toward the supply side. The standard tool in analyzing wages became the human capital earnings function, and the variables included in it were supply side in their orientation (for example, years of schooling and job experience, demographic characteristics, pecuniary and nonpecuniary aspects of work). Finally, a third effect was to make the tools and concepts of microeconomics the standard theoretical framework for analyzing labor market behavior.

   5. *The Development of Econometrics and Large Survey Data Sets.* Much of the inspiration for the research of the postwar labor economists and many of their insights came from personal contact with union leaders and management officials and personal observation of the mechanics of wage setting and collective bargaining. Their link to the real world and its complexities was further nurtured by the nature of the principal research tool of the 1950s—the case study by the participant/observer. After 1960, however, the method of empirical research changed greatly in labor economics due to the development of computers, econometrics, and large survey data sets.

   In principle, the innovations in the technology of research need not have diminished the influence of the 1950s view of the labor market, but in practice they have. Econometrics, for example, has led economists to focus disproportionately on those aspects of labor market behavior that can be quantified (for example, the impact of unions on wages), at the expense of topics for which data are either hard to obtain or are more qualitative in nature (for example, the effect of unions in reducing arbitrary discipline and discharge of workers). Unfortunately for the postwar view of the labor market, it is the latter type of topic that was often an important part of the theory.

   Of perhaps more harmful consequence has been the growing reliance of labor economists on secondary data sources, particularly large survey-generated data sets. Although these data sets have permitted labor economists to intensively explore many aspects of labor market behavior once outside their reach, they have also caused researchers to become cut off from personal contact with real-world labor markets. It can be argued with some validity that because DKLR had such intimate knowledge of how actual labor markets work that their writings gave undue emphasis to short-run imperfections and indeterminacies and insufficient weight to the long-run power of competitive forces. The opposite charge can be leveled against most labor economists of the 1970s and 1980s, on the other hand. The only labor markets known to them are the ones of theory, for few researchers ever venture out of the computer room and library to do a case study or interview employers, workers, or union officials. The result is that recent research in labor economics has overemphasized the power of rational behavior and competitive market forces in giving rise to an optimal allocation of resources, with a concomitant neglect of short-run imperfections in the market process, the importance of organizations, and the pervasive influence of social norms. The lack of contact with real-world labor markets also manifests itself, according to Dunlop (1977), in the irrelevance that much of empirical research has for policymakers.

6. *Historical Events.* A sixth factor that has worked, on net, to diminish the influence of the postwar model of the labor market is the tide of historical events. Labor markets today differ in a number of important respects from those of the 1950s—the geographic mobility of the work force is greater, workers have a much higher level of education, the work force is now more female and concentrated in the service industries and white-collar occupations instead of blue-collar manufacturing jobs, the percentage of the work force unionized has shrunk considerably, part-time workers and two-career families have proliferated, the amount of instability in employment and unemployment has been reduced by government management of fiscal and monetary policies, government regulation of the terms and conditions of employment has grown greatly, the personnel programs of most companies are far more professional than thirty years before, and the importance of fringe benefits in the compensation package has grown.

It is difficult to sort out the precise impact of each of these events on the popular view of how labor markets work, but arguably the net affect has been to swing opinion towards a more competitive, free market perspective. In support of the position of DKLR, the labor market today is even less of an auction market than it was thirty years ago as internal labor markets and fringe benefits have grown in importance and as firms have turned from a commodity conception of labor to a welfare-human resource concept. The emphasis of the postwar labor economists on the limitations to labor mobility and the concomitant lifetime nature of jobs has, accordingly, gained renewed attention in labor economics (see Hall 1982). The labor market is also a more "managed" market than it was in the 1950s because of increased government regulation (particularly in the civil rights area) and the greater emphasis given to human resource management by business firms.

Working against the 1950s view of labor markets, however, are several other factors. One is the rise in the proportion of women and minorities in the labor force and the concomitant interest of economists in explaining race and sex differences in wages. DKLR wrote relatively little on these subjects, and their model of wage determination has seemed less relevant to these issues than alternative neoclassical theories such as the human capital model and Becker's (1957) model of discrimination. A second consideration is that labor unions have fallen out of favor with the public and the economics profession alike. Although to the postwar labor economists, unions were often "monopsony reducing" in their impact on wage rates, most economists today regard unions as primarily "monopoly creating" and, thus, a source of inefficiency. The long-term increase in the union/nonunion wage differential has undoubtedly helped to foster this view. A similar change in heart has affected the perspective of economists on the desirability of government regulation of the labor market. The minimum wage, for example, had considerable support among labor economists in the 1950s as a means of preventing exploitation of unskilled workers and a downward spiral of wages during a depression (see Lester 1951: 361–69). Today most economists are critical of the minimum wage in the belief that its main impact is to reduce employment and training opportunities for the very segment of the labor force it is meant to help.[23] Although there is nothing in the postwar model that conflicts with the view that collective bargaining and government regulation can be carried to excess, the sympathy of the postwar labor economists towards both forms of organized intervention in the labor market has nonetheless tended to diminish the allure of their theory of the market process.

A second aspect of the postwar model that has lost support over time is the stress on the imperfect nature of the labor markets. It is possible that this shift in opinion reflects more the power of ideology than fact, but historical events give at least some credence to the view that market imperfections have diminished in importance. Probably the clearest case has to do with the job search process and geographic labor mobility. The job search process among today's workers is undoubtedly more efficient than described by DKLR because of workers' greater education, increased geographic mobility, a wider dissemination of information, and the availability of unemployment compensation. Various forms of market segmentation have also been reduced due to civil rights and affirmative action programs. As a result, the labor market is now more open to women and minorities than it was in the 1950s. Finally, through fiscal and monetary policies the federal government has been able to avoid the calamitous levels of unemployment such as experienced in the Great Depression.

All of these factors help the labor market work more efficiently today than was the case in the 1930s–1950s. It is important to note, however, that many of these improvements did not automatically occur as a result of the competitive market process but rather were at least in part the result of institutional forces in the form of collective bargaining and government intervention. Should deregulation of the labor market and a union-free environment become a reality in coming years, it will be interesting to see if a truly free market works as well as its proponents believe. If not, the 1950s view of the labor market would gain additional credence.

Are the Postwar Labor Economists "Institutionalists"?

An interesting question is what school of thought in labor economics, if any, the postwar labor economists belong to. Opinion on this subject varies widely.

The postwar labor economists have been variously labeled as institutionalists, neoinstitutionalists, post-institutionalists, neorealists, and antimarginalists. Others have argued that the postwar labor economists belong to no particular school of thought more specific than the "mainstream." About the only consensus that has developed on the subject is what the postwar labor economists are *not*, which is members of the Chicago version of the neoclassical school.

Since the major alternative to the neoclassical school has been the institutional, a number of writers have put DKLR in that camp, either as full-fledged institutionalists or neoinstitutionalists. In his tribute to H. Gregg Lewis, for example, Albert Rees (1976) states that when Lewis began teaching (the early 1940s), the institutional approach dominated the field and, by implication, continued to do so until displaced by the "analytical" labor economics pioneered by Lewis and his colleagues at Chicago in the 1950s and 1960s. Rees uses the word *analytic* to connote the use of microeconomic theory and econometrics in labor research. Glen Cain (1976) argues, on the other hand, that it is better to consider DKLR as "neoinstitutionalists." In this view, the postwar labor economists are clearly distinct from the prewar institutionalists such as Commons and Hoxie, but nevertheless are in the institutional tradition because of their skeptical view of competitive theory and their attempt to construct a more realistic alternative in its place.

Other writers have argued that the postwar labor economists are not members of the institutional school or one of its offshoots. Martin Segal (1986), for example, claims that the research of the postwar labor economists has little in common with that of the institutionalists in terms of either theoretical orientation or topical coverage. As he sees it, the institutionalists were primarily interested in labor history, collective bargaining, and personnel management, and in their research used mostly the tools of history, sociology, and the law. The postwar labor economists, on the other hand, focused on labor market topics such as wage determination and relied primarily on economic theory as the basic conceptual framework in their research. Segal prefers to call DKLR "post-institutionalists."[24]

In their writings on the subject, it is clear that DKLR also reject the institutional (or neoinstitutional) label. In this regard, Kerr (1983: 302–303) has said, "I think that terminology [i.e., neoinstitutionalist] is inaccurate. Many [of the postwar labor economists] shared a sympathy with the institutional school, with its concern for history, with its emphasis on real life, even with its sympathy for unions and ameliorative legislation. But the people who contributed to the integrative effort were not, as the neoinstitutionalist label implies, a new version of the Wisconsin school . . . they were more the descendants of Smith, Marshall, and Pigou than of Commons and Perlman . . . they did not reject theory, as did the institutionalist . . . rather, they respected theory and wanted to make it more useful in understanding practice." He suggested a better label for the postwar labor economists might be that of "neorealists."

It is apparent from the above discussion that much of the controversy on this subject stems from the vague and ill-defined meaning of the word *institutional*. Institutional clearly means different things to different people. To judge whether the postwar labor economists were or were not institutionalists, it is necessary, therefore, to arrive at some accepted definition of what institutional means. Although this paper is hardly the place for an extended discussion of this subject, I would like to offer a few brief thoughts on it.

If institutional is to have any substantive content as a distinct school of thought, it must connote a body of theory or a paradigm that purports to explain the key outcomes generated in the labor market such as the determination of wages, allocation of labor, the conditions of work and so on. It cannot simply be a methodology or way of doing research (for example, does or doesn't use econometrics). In my view, such a paradigm requires three components: first, a theory of human behavior; second, a theory of how labor markets work; and third, an assumption about the relative importance of nonmarket (institutional and social) forces in the determination of labor outcomes. The neoclassical school is a paradigm in this sense, since its theory of human behavior is the model of economic man, the theory of how markets work is the competitive model (variously amended and qualified), and the usual assumption about nonmarket forces is that they are relatively unimportant in shaping most labor outcomes (for example, hours of work).

Using these criteria, is there an institutional school of thought? Although it is difficult to discern from the writings of the institutionalists, I believe the answer is yes. John R. Commons, the founder of the institutional school in labor economics, rejected the model of economic man because it was too rational and hedonistic, and attempted to substitute in its place a more humanistic conception of man (see Commons 1934: 90–93; Kaufman 1987). Likewise, Commons rejected the model of perfect competition since, in his view, labor markets and product markets were highly imperfect and, in the case of the former, most often dominated by employers. Finally, Commons gave the most emphasis in his writings to the role of institutions (for example, unions, government legislation, the family, social custom) in economic affairs, *not* because he rejected the notion of markets or supply and demand, but rather because institutional forces, in his view, were the most important in determining labor outcomes.

The institutionalists were admittedly much better at identifying what they objected to in orthodox theory than in formalizing an alternative. Particularly the work of Commons, however, was directed not only at exposing the weaknesses of neoclassical theory but also in the constructive task of revising (not replacing, as is often charged) the theory so that it better explained the facts of the real world. In this spirit, Commons (1919: 5, 17) said, "Demand

and supply determine wages . . . . The ebb and flow of the labor market is like the ebb and flow of the commodity market." He goes on to say, however, that "the commodity theory of labor is not false, it is *incomplete*" (emphasis added).

What I am arguing, therefore, is that the word *institutional* is most properly interpreted as meaning an attempt to develop an economic theory that is built around a model of man more congruent with the principles of social psychology, a model of markets that is grounded in the economics of imperfect competition, and a conception of the market process that gives considerable weight to the role of institutions (broadly defined). If this definition of the word *institutional* is accepted, we may then ask: Are the postwar labor economists institutionalists? My answer would be that it is incorrect to call them institutionalists per se. With respect to specific aspects of their research, Commons and DKLR were worlds apart. As Kerr and Segal argue, the postwar labor economists were more receptive to conventional labor market theory, gave it a greater place in their research, and were far more analytical in their research than was Commons.[25] There is also no question that DKLR view themselves as more the lineal descendants of Marshall than of Commons.

If the postwar labor economists were not institutionalists, what about neoinstitutionalists? Here I think there is a better case. The key point is that, whatever their differences, Commons and DKLR were critical of neoclassical theory for much the same reasons and attempted to revise it in the same direction. Based on the three criteria noted above (that is, the model of man, the model of markets, and the relative importance of organizational influences), the revisions to competitive theory proposed by the postwar labor economists were solidly in the institutional tradition. Under this interpretation, then, the postwar labor economists are second-generation institutionalists (or neoinstitutionalists), just as dual labor market theorists are third-generation institutionalists (see Cain 1976). The goal of each generation has been the same, even if the methods and sources of inspiration have differed considerably.

Although I think there is a certain amount of logic behind the term neoinstitutional, it admittedly has problems of its own. The term implies, for example, a more direct lineage both personally and philosophically between the institutionalists and the postwar labor economists than there was. It may be that the differences between the two groups so outweigh the similarities that the term is more misleading than helpful. This view is the one held by DKLR and, the arguments presented above notwithstanding, it may be the right one.

The Contributions of the Postwar Labor Economists to Economic Science

From a historical perspective, the 1940s and 1950s represent a great transitional period in the development of labor economics. The labor economists of that era such as DKLR affected a fundamental reorientation of the field, moving it away from a preoccupation with the pathologies of the market process and towards a more analytical study of how actual labor markets work. In doing so, the postwar labor economists made a significant contribution to economic science, for not only did this serve to integrate labor economics more closely with its parent discipline, but it also made the labor market the central conceptual device around which the study of labor is organized. In a real sense, then, the labor economists of the 1940s and 1950s are the founding fathers of the field as it is conceived by most practitioners today.[26]

The postwar labor economists made a number of other contributions to labor economics as well. One is in the area of theory. Although their work was primarily empirical in nature, several theoretical concepts emerged which have proven to be quite influential. Chief among these are the idea of the internal labor market, the long-term nature of the employment relationship, wage imitation and pattern setting, and the economic and political models of union wage policy. Several other theoretical concepts which were given much emphasis in the 1950s, such as wage contours and range theories of wage determination, have not had the same success, however.

A second area in which the postwar labor economists made significant contributions was the empirical study of labor markets. Their research on wage determination in local labor markets provided the first systematic analysis of the process of job search, company wage policies and hiring practices, the relationship between wage differentials and labor mobility, and the nature of the firm's labor demand and supply functions. They also provided the first systematic evidence on the determinants of wage growth among industries (see Dunlop 1948b: Ross and Goldner 1950) and the impact of collective bargaining on the various dimensions of the wage structure.

Out of the research of the postwar labor economists came a unique view of how labor markets work. Some labor markets, such as those for day laborers or migrant workers, correspond closely to the competitive model described in textbooks. Here wage rates truly are set by the impersonal forces of supply and demand. In most labor markets, however, competitive forces are strong but not overwhelming—they set outside limits to the wage bargain, but within is an area of indeterminacy where there is room for nonmarket forces to operate. The limits to competition are partly the work of nature in the form of limited information, costs of travel, and personal inertia. To a greater extent, however, the limits to competition are man-made, partly for reasons of economic efficiency as firms attempt to train and keep a dedicated work force, and partly because the desire of workers for security and equity demands it. One result is that wage rates in most sectors of the labor market are administered prices. They are not immune to market forces, but they respond slowly to competitive conditions. A second result is that the expansion and contraction of jobs has only a loose connection to the wage-setting process. It is possible for wage rates to keep rising even in the face of slackening demand.

This was the labor market as seen by DKLR in the 1950s. Is it the labor market as it exists today? Did it ever exist? Perhaps the greatest legacy of DKLR to the present generation of labor economists is to confront us with these questions, to force us to square the reality of the market process as they saw it with the theory as we teach it. The implications are large. Let me close by listing three.

There is currently a widespread feeling in the economics profession that something is "wrong" with macroeconomics, that the existing theory does not adequately explain the behavior of output, prices, employment, and wages over the business cycle (see Thurow 1983). Economists are split on the diagnosis of the problem, however. On one side are monetarists and rational expectationists who argue that macro is in trouble because it is not solidly built on the foundations of micro theory; hence the attempt to reconstruct macro theory to be consistent with the micro model of auction markets where wages and prices clear the market instantaneously (Barro 1984). On the other side are Keynesians, post-Keynesians, and, as Paul Samuelson (1985) would have it, those other economists who are members of the mainstream. From their point of view, what is wrong with macro theory is that the underlying micro theory is itself wrong, or if not wrong, at least incomplete. As they see it, the beginning of wisdom is to recognize that the prices in many markets, and particularly the labor market, are sluggish and change only slowly in response to shocks to demand and supply. The result, as Keynes showed long ago, is that quantities take much of the brunt of adjustment.

What light can the research of the postwar labor economists shed on this debate? Clearly, if their view of the market process is an accurate one, then the more fruitful approach for macroeconomists is to explore the latter option—to build into their macro theories the structural and behavioral features of labor and product markets that inhibit wage and price responsiveness. These features include the administered nature of wage rates, the long-term nature of the employment relation, the separation of the job market from the wage market, and the process of wage imitation and pattern setting.

A second implication of the 1950s view of the labor market concerns the impact of collective bargaining and government regulation of the labor market on economic efficiency. The standard conceptual framework used today by most neoclassical labor economists to analyze the impact on efficiency of collective bargaining, minimum wage laws, or occupational safety and health regulations is the model of perfect competition. In some cases the model is qualified to take into account various market imperfections (for example, labor immobility, public goods), or nonmarket considerations (for example, equity and due process), but in many others the analysis proceeds unencumbered by these considerations. It is clear that the more perfect is the economy assumed in the theory, the greater the likelihood that outside intervention in wage setting will be pernicious on efficiency grounds. Not unexpectedly, therefore, it is a rare journal article that concludes that (1) unionization of a firm could improve resource allocation, (2) the minimum wage should be raised, or (3) occupational safety and health regulations should be strengthened.

There is nothing in the 1950s view of the labor market that implies that on *a priori* grounds (1)-(3) above are desirable or likely to be true. It does not, on the other hand, rule them out. That is the big difference. Because the labor market described by DKLR is not a perfect market, there is room for collective bargaining and government intervention to do good as well as bad. The labor economists of the 1950s would, I think, urge their counterparts in the 1980s to take this lesson to heart and be less doctrinaire in their policy conclusions. A fundamental prerequisite for such a change in consciousness, in turn, is that the younger generation in labor economics seek out more personal contact with flesh-and-blood labor markets so that their policy recommendations take into account not only the insights of theory but also the complexities and imperfections of real life.

A third implication of the 1950s view of the labor market concerns the state of theory and theorizing in labor economics. A common theme in the work of DKLR is that the study of labor markets is more than a study of demand and supply. Competitive market forces and the rational, economizing behavior of individual people play an important part in explaining wage determination and other market outcomes, but they are by themselves seriously incomplete. To account for the full range of reality in labor markets, it is necessary to broaden one's perspective beyond traditional microeconomic theory (see Dunlop 1984; Kerr 1983). This means incorporating into the theory the rules and regulations of the workplace that ration jobs and set wages. It also means broadening the theory to account for the influence of relative income comparisons and considerations of equity and justice. Finally, it means opening up the theory of the firm to incorporate a richer set of management objectives. The bottom line for DKLR is that labor economics cannot lead a separate life from its sister discipline of industrial relations for the problems and concerns of the two fields are inextricably linked together.

So far, labor economics, or at least one branch of it, has gone in the opposite direction. The emphasis has been on seeing how far the "economic approach" of maximizing behavior, stable tastes, and competitive markets can take us in explaining labor market and many other forms of human behavior (see Becker 1976; Stigler and Becker 1977). Is this likely to be a fruitful approach in the long run, or would labor economics be better served by a broader theoretical perspective? The position of DKLR is clear on this question. Writing in 1944, Dunlop (p. 5) said, "One of the more dangerous habits of mind that economic theory may create is an imperialism that insists that all aspects of behavior, particularly any activity related to markets, can be explained by models with the usual economic variables. . . . A fundamental tenet . . . is that models of behavior that are broader than economic theory contribute materially to the understanding of wage determination."

Notes

1. Other important scholars affiliated with this group were E. Wight Bakke, Neil Chamberlain, Lloyd Fisher, Frederick Harbison, Frederic Meyers, Herbert Parnes, Joseph Shister, George Taylor, and Lloyd Ulman. The influence of several of these men on labor economics is larger than indicated by the amount of attention given in this paper to their work. This is particularly true of Chamberlain. The primary reason for this neglect is that most of their research was devoted to the study of collective bargaining, while the focus of this paper is on wage determination and the operation of labor markets. On Chamberlain's contribution to labor economics see Kuhn, Lewin, and McNulty (1983); Ulman's contribution is discussed in Brown, Flanagan, and Strauss (1983).

2. Dunlop's research is an important exception to this statement, for he also wrote extensively on more macro-oriented labor subjects such as the cyclical behavior of real wages (Dunlop 1938), the nature of the labor demand and supply functions in the Keynesian model (Dunlop 1948a), and the impact on wage determination of wage/price controls (Dunlop 1947).

3. A number of the topics discussed in this paper are also reviewed in Freeman (1984) and Segal (1986). Although we agree on most points concerning the postwar view of labor markets, in several respects I reach different interpretations or conclusions than they do.

4. Labor textbooks of the 1930s amply illustrate the preoccupation of labor economists with a descriptive analysis of labor problems and their lack of attention to the operation of markets. As an example, in the introductory chapter of his labor text *Labor Economics and Labor Problems* (1933: 1–22), Dale Yoder provides an extensive discussion of the subject matter of labor economics and the origins of labor problems without once mentioning the terms *labor market* and *supply and demand*. By way of contrast, Lester states on page 5 of his *Economics of Labor* (1941), "The focal point of labor problems is the labor market, where such issues as wage rates, hours of work, conditions of work, and job tenure are supposed to be solved."

5. Other local labor market studies included Kerr (1942), Myers and Shultz (1951), Fisher (1953), Pierson (1953), and Wilcock and Sobel (1958).

6. In describing the neoclassical theory as it existed in the 1930s and 1940s I use Hicks's *Theory of Wages* as the standard reference, since it was regarded by DKLR as such (see Kerr 1983: 299). In fairness to Hicks, it must be pointed out that in later pages of the book he qualifies some of the statements cited here which come from the first chapter, and that in the second edition (1963) Hicks disowns parts of his earlier writings altogether.

7. In the description of "the" postwar model that follows, it must be borne in mind that it is a composite drawn from the diverse writings of DKLR and other economists of the period. Some aspects of the model described here are drawn much more from the writings of one of the group than the others, as the ensuing citations indicate. The best summary of the postwar model is given in Lester (1951: 37–73) and Reynolds (1951: 207–256).

8. In a similar vein, Myers and Maclaurin (1943:59) concluded "The persistence of wage differentials for jobs requiring comparable skill and training was not due to compensating differences in working conditions or in other perquisites such as welfare plans. Generally, the companies with superior working conditions, comprehensive welfare programs for their employees, and few or no wage cuts were *also* those which paid relatively high wages." In the 1960s and 1970s, most economists were reluctant to admit that the wage structure contained large and persistent noncompensating wage differentials, as claimed by the postwar labor economists. Recent research by Krueger and Summers (1987) and Dickens and Katz (1987), however, has found considerable evidence in support of the position of DKLR on this subject.

9. The amount of voluntary movement between jobs also seemed to be decreasing over time, as suggested by the long-term decline in the quit rate in manufacturing. Shister (1950) interpreted this as evidence that a growing proportion of the labor force was effectively immobilized, a conlusion that further called into question the relevance of the competitive model. Ross (1958) agreed that a long-term decline in the quit rate had taken place but denied that competition was seriously threatened by labor immobility.

10. Reynolds (1951) emphasized that the degree to which wage rates and the allocation of labor are interconnected depends critically on the level of unemployment, but that even with low levels of unemployment the two processes are still substantially disjoint, as evidenced by the continued existence of large noncompensating wage differentials. Myers (1954; 1957) dissented from this view, however, arguing that when the labor market is close to full employment, labor mobility does respond to wage differentials much as envisioned in the competitive model. Reynolds (p. 246) argued that of all the imperfections in the labor market, the presence of persistent involuntary unemployment is the most damaging one with respect to the predictive ability of the competitive model.

11. The interdependency between the wage rate and worker effort and productivity has recently been rediscovered and popularized in the form of "efficiency wage" theories of the labor market (see Katz 1986).

12. Even if money wages are rigid downward, equilibrium in the labor market may be restored by a fall in the real wage brought on by an increase in product prices. During the Great Depression, however, the opposite actually happened as prices between 1929 and 1933 declined by over 30 percent. See Bailey (1983).

13. The importance that equity considerations play in wage determination is further attested to by the central role that equity plays in both the theory and practice of industrial relations and compensation management. See, respectively, Barbash (1984) and Wallace and Fay (1983).

14. A close reading of Dunlop and Ross reveals that their positions were actually closer together than is generally recognized (see Borland 1986). If the microeconomic models of union wage determination developed in chapter 3 of Dunlop's book are considered in isolation, they seem far more neoclassical in their conception than anything else contained in the published work of DKLR (a fact which may well explain the criticism these models received from other postwar economists in the 1950s, and the models' continued popularity among neoclassical economists today). In chapter 4, however, Dunlop went on to discuss a wide variety of other factors besides maximization of the wage bill that influence union behavior, and in several places (for example, pp. 57–61) noted how union wage policy is affected by the organizational and political makeup of the union. Similarly, Ross (1948: 12–16) clearly stated that economic

variables, as well as political considerations, were important in shaping union wage policy. The qualifications by both authors tended to be forgotten, however, in the ensuing debate. That Dunlop recognized the importance of pattern bargaining and union rivalries is also illustrated in a later article (1947) in which he discusses the impact of these factors on the World War II wage stabilization program. Finally, it is worth pointing out that both Dunlop and Ross used the term *political* to mean two separate things. One was as a description of the internal decision-making process in unions; the second was as a synonym for interunion rivalries. This proved to be a great source of confusion, since Dunlop's critique of Ross had much more to do with the latter interpretation than the former.

15. Other attempts to resolve the Ross/Dunlop debate include Myers and Shultz (1950), Reder (1952), Mitchell (1972), and Kaufman and Martinez-Vazquez, 1987).

16. Also see Lester (1948b, 1949).

17. It is well known that a wage increase in a monopsony market may result in an increase in employment, but this is not what Lester had in mind. In keeping with his skepticism concerning marginalism, Lester claimed (1964: 281) that the textbook monopsony model is "misguided academic speculation" because managers in such firms do not determine wage and employment levels by any type of marginal comparison of revenue and cost.

18. There were two other criticisms of the marginal productivity theory often mentioned in the 1950s that Lester did not discuss in his article. The first grew out of the oligopoly kinked demand curve model. Since the marginal revenue schedule in that model has a large gap in it, the labor demand curve would have a similar gap, causing the relationship between the wage rate and level of employment to be indeterminant over a certain range. The second criticism was that the marginal physical product schedule is not independent of the wage. A wage increase, for example, might cause the labor demand curve to shift to the right if productivity increased due to higher morale or better employee health. In this case, a wage increase might lead to a net rise in employment.

19. Lester contended that the theory assumes a firm will deliberately reduce output in response to a wage increase. If the firm is competitive and the wage increase is limited to that one firm, Lester is correct. In other situations, however, he overstated the case. An imperfectly competitive firm, for example, may react to a wage increase by raising its product price. Output and employment will again decline, although the reduction in output may not be "deliberate" as deemed necessary by Lester.

20. It should be stressed that the postwar labor economists were not "anti-theory" as sometimes suggested (Rees 1976; Bellante and Jackson 1979: 46), nor did they entirely reject microeconomic theory (as is well illustrated by Dunlop 1944 and Reynolds 1946a). The principal thrust of their criticism of microeconomic theory was that its assumptions were too simplistic and narrowly conceived and, thus, the theory was unable to explain many important labor market outcomes.

21. Thurow's (1975) job competition model is another example of a more recent theory that builds on the ideas of the postwar labor economists. Thurow was a graduate student at Harvard, but did not write his dissertation under Dunlop.

22. One important explanation is that they did not believe individuals typically have the room for choice that neoclassical labor supply models assume. Thus, with respect to hours of work, Reynolds (1955: 6) stated "The individual can sometimes make a crude adjustment by holding more than one job, by seeking overtime work, or by shifting between long-hour and short-hour occupations. To a large extent, however,

the size of the national labor force and the input of labor effort is set by organizational decisions rather than by individual decisions." By way of contrast, Lewis (1956), in his application of the labor/leisure model to hours of work, argued that to consider employer's preferences "would only complicate the theory . . . without substantial gain in interpreting the data" and that "the economic role of unions in the long-run decline of average hours worked . . . is surely a minor one." Having assumed away the importance of institutional factors, Lewis then explained the long-term decline in hours of work in terms of the income and substitution effects set off by the secular rise in wage rates. Lewis's application of microeconomic theory to labor supply behavior in his article is trailbreaking and represents, in my opinion, the beginning of the neoclassical revival in labor economics in America. Others might choose a different benchmark, however, such as the publication of Becker's (1957) book on discrimination.

23. A different form of government intervention in labor markets is manpower and training programs. During the 1960s these enjoyed widespread support among labor economists, only to fall into disrepute in the 1970s.

24. A weakness of the term *post-institutional* is that it serves to link DKLR with institutionalism at the same time that it denies such a link.

25. At a more philosophical level, Commons and the postwar economists did share a common belief in the social efficacy of pluralism. Taft (1950: 140) states, for example, "Rejecting the notion of market equilibrium resulting from the competition of atomistic units, Commons attempted to show that modern economic life can be explained and even promoted, by allowing large and powerful aggregates to compete, negotiate, and work out a relationship. His view of the market is not atomistic, but pluralistic." Kerr (1954: 6) defined pluralism as "a multiplicity of power centers" and went on to say "most of us are probably practicing, if not theoretical pluralists. We reject state absolutism as inimical to freedom and an atomistic approach as inimical to industrialization."

26. There are several other acknowledged "fathers" of labor economics. John R. Commons is often cited as the founding father of labor economics in America (Kerr 1954b: 3), and H. Gregg Lewis has been called the father of "analytical" or "modern" labor economics (Rees 1976; *American Economic Review*, September 1982, front piece). The terms *analytical* and *modern*, if they are to correctly apply to Lewis, must be interpreted to mean the thoroughgoing application of competitive neoclassical price theory to labor markets. If modern and analytical are interpreted more broadly to mean the study of labor markets in a supply/demand framework, the work of Paul Douglas and DKLR qualify equally well.

References

Azariadis, Costas. 1975. "Implicit Contracts and Underemployment Equilibrium," *Journal of Political Economy* 83 (December): 1103–1202.
Bailey, Martin N. 1983. "The Labor Market in the 1930s." In James Tobin, ed., *Macroeconomics, Prices, and Quantities: Essays in Honor of Arthur M. Okum,* 21–61. Washington, D.C.: Brookings Institution.
Barbash, Jack. 1984. *The Elements of Industrial Relations.* Madison, Wi.: University of Wisconsin Press.
Barro, Robert J. 1984. *Macroeconomics.* New York: Wiley and Sons.

Becker, Gary. 1957. *The Economics of Discrimination.* Chicago: University of Chicago Press.

———. 1964. *Human Capital.* New York: National Bureau of Economic Research.

———. 1965. "A Theory of the Allocation of Time." *Economic Journal* 75 (September): 493–517.

———. 1976. *The Economic Approach to Human Behavior,* Chicago: University of Chicago Press.

Bellante, Don, and Mark Jackson. 1979. *Labor Economics.* New York: McGraw–Hill.

Borland, Jeff. 1986. "The Ross-Dunlop Debate Revisited," *Journal of Labor Research* VIII (Summer): 293–307.

Bronfenbrenner, Martin. 1956. "Potential Monopsony in Labor Markets" *Industrial and Labor Relations Review* 9 (July): 577–588.

Brown, Clair. 1983. "Unemployment Theory and Policy, 1946–1980," *Industrial Relations* 22 (Spring): 164–185.

Brown, Clair, Robert Flanagan, and George Strauss. 1983. "In Honor of Lloyd Ulman." *Industrial Relations* 22 (Spring): 135–140.

Cain, Glen. 1976. "The Challenge of Segmented Labor Market Theories to Orthodox Theory: A Survey." *Journal of Economic Literature* 14 (December): 1215–1257.

Commons, John R. 1919. *Industrial Goodwill.* New York: McGraw–Hill.

———. 1934. *Institutional Economics.* New York: Macmillan.

Dickens, William, and Lawrence Katz. 1987. "Inter-Industry Wage Differences and Industry Characteristics." In Kevin Lang and Jonathan Leonard, eds., *Unemployment and the Structure of Labor Markets,* pp. 48–89. New York: Basil Blackwell.

Doeringer, Peter, and Michael Piore. 1971. *Internal Labor Markets and Manpower Analysis.* Lexington, Mass.: Lexington Books.

Dunlop, John. 1938. "The Movement of Real and Money Wages." *Economic Journal* 48 (September): 413–434.

———. 1944. *Wage Determination Under Trade Unions.* 2d edition, 1950. New York: McGraw–Hill.

———. 1947. "A Review of Wage/Price Policy." *Review of Economics and Statistics* 29 (August): 154–160.

———. 1948a. "The Demand and Supply Functions for Labor," *American Economic Review* 38 (May):340–350.

———. 1948b. "Productivity and the Wage Structure." In *Income, Employment, and Public Policy, Essays in Honor of Alvin Hansen,* 341–362. New York: Norton.

———. 1957. "The Tasks of Contemporary Wage Theory." In George Taylor and Frank Pierson, eds., *New Concepts in Wage Determination,* 117–139. New York: McGraw–Hill.

———. 1966. "Job Vacancy Measures and Economic Analysis." In National Bureau of Economic Research, *The Measurement and Interpretation of Job Vacancies.* New York: Columbia University Press.

———. 1977. "Policy Decisions and Research in Economics and Industrial Relations." *Industrial and Labor Relations Review* 30 (April): 275–282.

———. 1984. "Industrial Relations and Economics: The Common Frontier of Wage Determination." In Industrial Relations Research Association, *Proceedings of the*

Thirty-Seventh Annual Meeting, 9–23. Madison, Wis.: Industrial Relations Research Association.

Fisher, Lloyd. 1953. *The Harvest Labor Market in California*. Cambridge: Harvard University Press.

Freeman, Richard. 1984. "The Structure of Labor Markets: A Book Review Three Decades Later." In Gustav Ranis, et al., eds., *Comparative Development Perspectives*, 201–226. Boulder, Col.: Westview.

Freeman, Richard, and James Medoff. 1984. *What Do Unions Do?* New York: Basic Books.

Friedman, Milton. 1953. *Essays in Positive Economics*. Chicago:University of Chicago Press.

Gordon, R.A. 1948. "Short-Period Price Determination in Theory and Practice," *American Economic Review* 38 (June): 265–288.

Hall, Robert E. 1982. "The Importance of Lifetime Jobs in the U.S. Economy." *American Economic Review* 72 (September): 716–724.

Hazeldine, Tim. 1979. "Employment Functions and the Demand for Labor in the Short Run." In *Economics of the Labour Market*, 149–181. London: Her Majesty's Stationery Office.

Hicks, John R. 1932. *The Theory of Wages*. 2d edition, 1963. New York: Macmillan.

Hildebrand, George. 1963. "External Influences and the Determination of the Internal Wage Structure." In J.L. Meij, ed., *Internal Wage Structure*, 260–299. Amsterdam: North Holland.

Hirsch, Barry, and John Addison. 1986. *The Economic Analysis of Unions*. Boston: Allen and Unwin.

Jacoby, Sanford. 1985. *Employing Bureaucracy: Managers, Unions, and the Transformation of Work in American Industry, 1900–1945*. New York: Columbia University Press.

Johnson, George. 1975. "Economic Analysis of Trade Unionism." *American Economic Review* 65 (May): 23–28.

Kahneman, Daniel, Jack Knetsch, and Richard Thaler. 1986. "Fairness and the Assumptions of Economics." *Journal of Business* 59 (October): S285–S300.

Katz, Lawrence F. 1986. "Efficiency Wage Theories: A Partial Evaluation." In Stanley Fischer, ed., *NBER Macroeconomics Annual 1986*, pp. 235–75. Cambridge, Mass.: MIT Press.

Kaufman, Bruce E. 1987. "Models of Man in Industrial Relations Research." Atlanta: Georgia State University Discussion Paper.

Kaufman, Bruce E. and Jorge Martinez-Vazquez. 1987. "The Ross/Dunlop Debate and Union Wage Concessions: A Median Voter Analysis." *Journal of Labor Research* 8 (Summer): 291–306.

Kerr, Clark. 1942. *Migration to the Seattle Labor Market Area, 1940–1942*. Seattle: University of Washington Press.

———. 1950. "Labor Markets: Their Character and Consequences." *American Economic Review* 40 (May): 278–291.

———. 1954a. "The Balkanization of Labor Markets." In Social Science Research Council, *Labor Mobility and Economic Opportunity*, 92–110. New York: John Wiley.

———. 1954b. "Industrial Relations and the Liberal Pluralist." In Industrial Relations Research Association, *Proceedings of the Seventh Annual Meeting*, 2–16. Madison, Wis.: Industrial Relations Research Association.

———. 1957. "Wage Relationships—The Comparative Impact of Market and Power Fores." In John Dunlop, ed., *The Theory of Wage Determination: Proceedings of a Conference Held by the International Economic Association*, 173–193. New York: Macmillan.

———. 1977. *Labor Markets and Wage Determination*. Berkeley: University of California Press.

———. 1983. "The Intellectual Role of the Neorealists in Labor Economics." *Industrial Relations* 22 (Spring): 298–318.

Kerr, Clark, and Lloyd Fisher. 1950. "Effects of Environment and Administration on Job Evaluation." *Harvard Business Review* 28 (May): 77–96.

———. 1957. "Plant Sociology: The Elite and the Aborigines." In Mirra Komarovsky and Paul Lazarsfeld, eds., *Common Frontiers of the Social Sciences*, 281–309. Glencoe, Ill.: Free Press.

Keynes, John Maynard. 1936. *The General Theory of Employment, Interest, and Money*. New York: Harcourt.

Killingsworth, Charles. 1949. "Discussion," Industrial Relations Research Association, *Proceedings of the Second Annual Meeting*, 103–107. Madison, Wis.: Industrial Relations Research Association.

Krueger, Alan, and Lawrence Summers. 1987. "Reflections on the Inter-Industry Wage Structure." In Kevin Lang and Jonathan Leonard, eds., *Unemployment and the Structure of Labor Markets*, pp. 17–47. New York: Basil Blackwell.

Kuhn, J.W., David Lewin, and Paul McNulty. 1983. "Neil W. Chamberlain: A Retrospective Analysis of His Scholarly Work and Influence." *British Journal of Industrial Relations* 21 (July): 143–160.

Lester, Richard. 1941. *The Economics of Labor*. New York: Macmillan.

———. 1946a. "Wage Diversity and Its Theoretical Implications." *Review of Economics and Statistics* 28 (August): 152–159.

———. 1946b. "Shortcomings of Marginal Analysis for Wage/Employment Problems." *American Economic Review* 36 (February): 63–82.

———. 1947a. "Southern Wage Differentials: Developments, Analysis, and Implications." *Southern Economic Journal* 13 (April): 152–159.

———. 1947b. "Marginalism, Minimum Wages, and Labor Markets." *American Economic Review* 37 (March): 135–148.

———. 1948a. *Company Wage Policies: A Survey of Patterns and Experience*. Princeton: Industrial Relations Section, Princeton University.

———. 1948b. "Absence of Elasticity Considerations in Demand to the Firm." *Southern Economic Journal* 14 (January): 285–289.

———. 1949. "Equilibrium of the Firm." *American Economic Review* 36 (March): 783–787.

———. 1951. *Labor and Industrial Relations: A General Analysis*. New York: Macmillan.

———. 1952. "A Range Theory of Wage Differentials." *Industrial and Labor Relations Review* 5 (July): 483–500.

————. 1954. *Hiring Practices and Labor Competition.* Princeton: Industrial Relations Section, Princeton University.

————. 1964. *Economics of Labor,* 2d edition. New York: Macmillan.

Levinson, Harold. 1960. "Pattern Bargaining: A Case Study of the Automobile Workers." *Quarterly Journal of Economics* 74 (May): 26–317.

Lewis, H. Gregg. 1956. "Hours of Work and Hours of Leisure." In Industrial Relations Research Association, *Proceedings of the Ninth Annual Meeting,* 196–206. Madison, Wis.: Industrial Relations Research Association.

Livernash, E. Robert. 1957. "The Internal Wage Structures." In George Taylor and Frank Pierson, eds., *New Concepts in Wage Determination,* 140–172. New York: McGraw-Hill.

Machlup, Fritz. 1946. "Marginal Analysis and Empirical Research." *American Economic Review* 36 (September): 519–555.

————. 1947. "Rejoinder to an Anti-Marginalist." *American Economic Review* 37 (March): 148–154.

————. 1967. "Theories of the Firm: Marginalist, Behavioral, Managerial." *American Economic Review* 57 (March): 1–33.

Marshall, Alfred. 1890. *Principles of Economics.* London: Macmillan.

McCall, John. 1970. "Economics of Information and Job Search." *Quarterly Journal of Economics* 84 (February): 113–126.

McNulty, Paul. 1980. *The Origin and Development of Labor Economics.* Cambridge: MIT Press.

Mincer, Jacob. 1962. "Labor Force Participation of Married Women." In H. Gregg Lewis, ed., *Aspects of Labor Economics,* 63–105. Princeton: Princeton University Press.

Mitchell, Daniel J.B. 1972. "Union Wage Policies: The Ross-Dunlop Debate Reopened." *Industrial Relations* 11 (February): 46–61.

Myers, Charles. 1954. "Labor Mobility in Two Communities." In Social Science Research Council, *Labor Mobility and Economic Opportunity,* 68–79. New York: John Wiley.

————. 1957. "Labor Market Theory and Empirical Research." In John Dunlop, ed., *The Theory of Wage Determination,* 317–326. London: Macmillan.

Myers, Charles, and Rupert Maclaurin. 1943. *The Movement of Factory Workers: A Study of a New England Industrial Community.* New York: John Wiley.

Myers, Charles, and George Shultz. 1950. "Union Wage Decisions and Employment." *American Economic Review* 40 (June): 362–380.

————. 1951. *The Dynamics of a Labor Market.* New York: Prentice–Hall.

Oi, Walter. 1962. "Labor as a Quasi-Fixed Factor." *Journal of Political Economy* 70 (December): 538–555.

Palmer, Gladys. 1954. *Labor Mobility in Six Cities: A Report on the Survey of Patterns and Factors in Labor Mobility.* New York: Social Science Research Council.

Parnes, Herbert. 1954. *Research on Labor Mobility.* New York: Social Sciences Research Council.

Pierson, Frank. 1953. *Community Wage Patterns.* Berkeley: University of California Press.

Pigou, A.C. 1912. *Wealth and Welfare*. London: Macmillan.

Reder, Melvin. 1947. "A Reconsideration of Marginal Productivity Theory." *Journal of Political Economy*. 55 (October): 450–458.

———. 1952. "The Theory of Union Wage Policy." *Review of Economics and Statistics* 34 (February): 34–45.

———. 1958. "Wage Determination in Theory and Practice." In Neil Chamberlain, Frank Pierson, and Theresa Wolfson, eds., *A Decade of Industrial Relations Research, 1946–1956*, 64–99. New York: Harper.

Rees, Albert. 1962. *The Economics of Trade Unions*. Chicago: University of Chicago Press.

———. 1976. "H. Gregg Lewis and the Development of Analytical Labor Economics." *Journal of Political Economy* 84, pt. 2 (August): 53–57.

Reynolds, Lloyd. 1946a. "The Supply of Labor to the Firm." *Quarterly Journal of Economics* 60 (May): 390–411.

———. 1946b. "Wage Differences in Local Labor Markets." *American Economic Review* 36 (June): 366–375.

———. 1951. *The Structure of Labor Markets*. New York: Harper.

———. 1953. "The State of Wage Theory." In Industrial Relations Research Association, *Proceedings of the Sixth Annual Meeting*, 234–240. Madison, Wis.: Industrial Relations Research Association.

———. 1954. *Labor Economics and Labor Relations*, 2d edition. Englewood Cliffs, N.J.: Prentice-Hall.

———. 1955. "Research and Practice in Industrial Relations." In Industrial Relations Research Association, *Proceedings of the Eighth Annual Meeting*, 2–13. Madison, Wis.: Industrial Relations Research Association.

———. 1957. "The Impact of Collective Bargaining on the Wage Structure in the United States." In John Dunlop, ed., *The Theory of Wage Determination*, 194–221. London: Macmillan.

Reynolds, Lloyd, and Joseph Shister. 1949. *Job Horizons*. New York: Harper.

Reynolds, Lloyd, and Cynthia Taft. 1956. *The Evolution of Wage Structure*. New Haven: Yale University Press.

Robinson, Joan. 1933. *Economics of Imperfect Competition*. London: Macmillan.

Ross, Arthur. 1948. *Trade Union Wage Policy*. Berkeley: University of California Press.

———. 1957. "The External Wage Structure." In George Taylor and Frank Pierson, eds., *New Concepts in Wage Determination*, 173–205. New York: McGraw–Hill.

———. 1958. "Is There a New Industrial Feudalism?" *American Economic Review* 48 (December): 903–920.

Ross, Arthur, and William Goldner. 1950. "Forces Affecting Interindustry Wage Structure." *Quarterly Journal of Economics* 64 (May): 254–261.

Samuelson, Paul, and William Nordhaus. 1985. *Economics*. 12th edition. New York: McGraw-Hill.

Segal, Martin. 1986. "Post-Institutionalism in Labor Economics: The Forties and Fifties Revisited." *Industrial and Labor Relations Review* 39 (April): 388–403.

Shister, Joseph. 1950. "Labor Mobility: Some Institutional Aspects." In Industrial Relations Research Association, *Proceedings of the Third Annual Meeting*, 42–59. Madison, Wis.: Industrial Relations Research Association.

————. 1956. *Economics of the Labor Market*. 2d edition. New York: Lippincott.

Shultz, George. 1951. *Pressures on Wage Decisions: A Case Study of the Shoe Industry*. New York: John Wiley.

————. 1962. "A Nonunion Market for White Collar Labor." In National Bureau of Economic Research, *Aspects of Labor Economics*, 107–155. Princeton: Princeton University Press.

Simon, Herbert. 1962. "New Developments in the Theory of the Firm." *American Economic Review* 52 (May): 1–15.

Smith, Robert, and Ronald Ehrenberg. 1983. "Estimating Wage-Fringe Trade-Offs: Some Data Problems." In Jack Triplett, ed., *The Measurement of Labor Cost*, 347–367. Chicago: University of Chicago Press.

Stigler, George. 1947. "Professor Lester and the Marginalists." *American Economic Review* 37 (March): 154–157.

————. 1949. *Five Lectures on Economic Problems*. London: Longmans, Green.

Stigler, George, and Gary Becker. 1977. "De Gustibus Non Est Disputandum." *Americn Economic Review* 67 (March): 76–90.

Taft, Philip. 1950. "Commons-Perlman Theory: A Summary." In Industrial Relations Research Association *Proceedings of the Third Annual Meeting*, 140–145. Madison, Wis.: Industrial Relations Research Association.

Thurow, Lester. 1975. *Generating Inequality*. New York: Basic Books.

————. 1983. *Dangerous Currents*. New York: Random House.

Viscusi, W. Kip. 1980. "Unions, Labor Market Structure, and the Welfare Implications of the Quality of Work." *Journal of Labor Research* 1 (Spring): 175–192.

Wallace, Marc, and Charles Fay. 1983. *Compensation Theory and Practice*. Boston: Kent.

Wilcock, R.C., and I. Sobel. 1958. *Small City Job Markets*. Urbana, Ill.: University of Illinois, Institute of Labor and Industrial Relations.

Yoder, Dale. 1933. *Labor Economics and Labor Problems*. 1st edition. New York: McGraw–Hill.

6

Does the New Generation of Labor Economists Know More Than the Old Generation?

Richard B. Freeman

Of course we do. Human capital lifetime optimization models with Hamiltonians. Log-earnings equations at the overtaking age. Longitudinal data. State dependence and heterogeneity in unemployment durations. Efficient labor contracts. NAIRU and natural rates of unemployment. Search theory and reservation wages. Cobweb and rational expectations market adjustments. Implicit contracts. Unobservables. Just open any major labor economics journal (the *Journal of Labor Economics*, for example) and the answer is transparent. Why, the 1950s crowd would have trouble following the invigorating modern discussion of how labor markets operate, much less doing the fundamental research.

Of course we do. Science always progresses, doesn't it? And surely economics is a science. In natural sciences, citations are invariably to articles in the last five years[1] and so too are citations in labor economics. Indeed, my count of citations from the most recent editions of three major labor journals yields a proportion of citations to articles within five years of 67 percent, 54 percent, and 52 percent.[2] Measuring advances in knowledge by the recentness of citations, we must be making as much progress as any of the natural sciences.

Of course we do. The athletes of today are faster, stronger, better fed, and better trained than those of the 1950s; why not labor economists? Put one of those old-timers—Joe Louis, Sugar Ray Robinson, Rocky Marciano—in the ring with a modern champion, and he wouldn't have a chance. Put one of those old scholars—John Dunlop, Clark Kerr, Richard Lester, or Lloyd Reynolds—in with a modern computer whiz, and it would be no contest.

Joe Louis? Sugar Ray Robinson? Rocky Marciano?

John Dunlop? Clark Kerr? Richard Lester? Lloyd Reynolds?

What did the other generation know about the operation of labor markets back then? How does it compare to what we know today? How did they discover what they discovered? How does it compare to our modern methodologies? How much progress have we made on the topics that interested them?

To answer these questions, I have reviewed a significant proportion of the works of Dunlop, Kerr, Lester, and Reynolds (DKLR) and have contrasted their analyses and findings to those in the modern (1970s–1980s) literature.

The first thing one notices in such a contrast is the difference in methodology. DKLR and their contemporaries built their picture of the labor market from: detailed knowledge of specific cases, often as a result of personal activity on a war labor board or related public agency; survey analyses of local labor markets, with *both* employers and workers covered by the surveys; carefully reasoned study of simple tabulations, cross-tabulations, and occasional correlation coefficients. Aside from the lack of sophisticated econometric manipulations and mathematical theorizing, the most striking difference between their work and modern analyses is the reliance on informed priors, based on personal observation and common economic sense rather than on econometric tests of competing explanations of behavior (including in some cases, explanations that defy both personal observation and common sense).

A second important difference between DKLR and modern labor economists relates to the use of competitive theory in interpreting empirical results. A large proportion (though not all) of modern labor economists regard their basic task as explaining whatever one observes in terms of competitive theory. Indeed, we ooh and ah at our peers who devise the most clever (far-fetched?) explanation for any regularity that, on the face of it, is inconsistent with the competitive model. When no one can devise a "good" explanation, some go so far as to question the fact (unemployment is voluntary rather than real) or put it into some sort of intellectual coventry. By contrast, the older generation of labor economists agreed uniformly that the labor market could not be understood as operating according to competitive principles:

> The labor market is by nature an imperfect instrument . . . all kinds of wage distortions exist even under nonunion conditions (Reynolds and Taft 1956: 168).

> The automatic pricing mechanism as model or institution in the labor market is dead (Dunlop 1944: 228).

> Actual wage facts seem contrary to what one might expect according to competitive theory (Lester 1948: 152).

> It (a competitive market-determined wage structure) is a useful norm for theoretical speculations but an unusable departure point for empirical studies" (Kerr 1977: 46).

The third thing one notices is a difference in the weight placed on different topics. DKLR were concerned largely with firm behavior, demand and wage setting, and broad industrial relations issues, whereas today's labor economists, schooled in human capital theory and adept at analyzing large computerized data sets, are more concerned with labor supply issues and a wide variety of forms of individual behavior that seemingly go beyond the labor market (demography, crime, and so on). Any comparision of what they "knew" and we "know" must as a result differentiate carefully between the topics of concern to them and the topics of concern to us. As the older generation did not work on "our" topics, I will limit my inquiry to whether or not we know more now on the four broad areas on which they focused their research: *Wage determination*, including wage adjustments to economic shocks and the structure of wages; the impact of *collective bargaining* on wages and employment; *labor mobility* and *firm hiring practices*; and the *interrelation among wages, employment, and unemployment*. Since the broad picture of the labor market depicted by DKLR and their generation has been ably synthesized by Segal (1986), I forgo developing my own synthesis and focus on the specific empirical findings which underlie the older generation's picture of how the labor market works. My strategy is to summarize the empirical findings of DKLR, focusing on the results of the analyst(s) whose work concentrated on the particular area, and then to compare those findings with modern work. While I make no pretense to having obtained a complete listing of relevant studies, I believe the comparisons provide a reasonably accurate picture of what they knew and what we know on the relevant topics.

To provide a brief overview, the main conclusion I reach is that while, labor economists are more knowledgeable of labor supply issues than the older generation, we do not know more about firm behavior, labor demand, and the overall functioning of markets. Most ensuing research has supported the empirical generalizations of DKLR, and while we put more mathematical theory and econometrics into our analyses, more math and econometrics does not signify greater understanding of the economic fundamentals.

I conclude the essay with some speculations as to why we have not made the kind of progress in surpassing our scientific elders, save in technique, as is the case in other scientific endeavors.

Specific Findings of DKLR on Market Wage Determination

The issue of wage determination was central to the analyses of DKLR. Dunlop's famous maiden paper was on the relation between money wages and real wages, and he later contributed important analyses on wage structure and the relation of wage changes to productivity and price changes. Reynolds dealt with wage structure issues at length in the book with Cynthia Taft; Kerr examined labor's share of income, while Lester focused on wage differentials among plants.

Table 6–1 gives what I believe to be the central findings of the four analysts on the structure of wages at a moment in time and on changes in the wage

Table 6–1
Comparison of Older Generation and Modern Findings on Wage
Determination and Wage Structures

Results of Older Generation	Modern Results and Partial List of References
1. Wages differ significantly across industries for reasons beyond competitive forces. Therefore the product market as well as the labor market affects wages. (Dunlop 1957; Reynolds and Taft 1956)	Industrial wage differentials remain significant when controlling for differences in human capital, including occupation, geographical locale, and work conditions, and remain in longitudinal as well as cross-section analyses. (Krueger and Summers 1986a, b; Dickens and Katz 1986a, b)
2. Wages differ significantly across plants, even within the same industry. (Reynolds 1951; Lester 1946a, 1946b)	A sizeable proportion of wage variation within industry is due to employer-based differences. Characteristics of establishments studied in the 1940s and 1950s (size, union affiliation, principal product, technology, and principal pay method), but not growth, can account for at least one-half of measured establishment effects. (Groschen 1986; Osterman 1982; MacKay et al. 1971; Nolan and Brown 1983; Brown et al. 1984)
3. Wages differ by firm size for reasons beyond competitive forces (Lester 1948)	Plant or establishment size and firm size are a major determinant of wages, holding fixed diverse human capital characteristics and other factors. (Brown and Medoff 1985; Dunn 1980, 1984; Groschen 1986; Mellow 1982; Personick and Barsky 1982; Miller 1981; Masters 1969)
4. Wage rates show some tendency to increase most (least) in industries in which output, employment, and productivity increase most (least); but wages and productivity diverge significantly in the short run. (Dunlop 1948; Kerr 1977)	Holding fixed diverse human capital and related variables, industries with rising product prices and physical productivity have relatively rising wages, counter to the standard competitive model of the industry wage structure. (Bell and Freeman 1985; Kaufman and Stephan 1987; OECD 1985)
5. Real wages rise when money wages rise, while a reduction in money wages is sometimes associated with a reduction in real wages. (Dunlop 1938)	No clear conclusion about real wages over the cycle. (Geary and Kennan 1982; Grubb, Layard, and Symons 1984; Bruno and Sachs 1985)
The structure of wages narrows in full employment and widens in recessions. (Dunlop 1939)	Wage differentials by industry, education, and age are countercyclical. (Wachter 1970; Freeman 1971)
6. Labor's share of national income is countercyclical. (Dunlop 1944; Kerr 1977)	Profits are the variable portion of GNP, with labor's share rising in recession and falling in booms.

structure over time at both aggregate and less aggregate levels. To begin with, one of the major conclusions which led the DKLR generation of labor economists to reject the competitive model of the labor market was the finding of significant wage differences among workers doing seemingly similar work across industries and among plants within an industry in particular local labor markets (lines 1–3). For a long time, modern labor economists ignored these results. Concerned with estimating the return to investment in human capital in the context of the by-now standard log earnings equation model, many modern labor economists have excluded industry dummy variables from wage analyses on the argument that part of the return to investing in skills is mobility into high-wage industries. The absence of readily available data sets with plant or firm information has discouraged investigation of differences among workers among plants. It is not that human capital analyses have challenged the older findings. They have not. They have rather excluded them from the area of active research concern.

More recently, younger economists interested in wage determination from a broader perspective have reexamined the role of the industry, establishment, and firm in wage determination, with empirical findings totally supportive of the results of the older generation. First, in separate but similar analyses of industry wage structures, Krueger and Summers and Dickens and Katz have analyzed the existence of industry wage differentials and found that no matter what other variables are entered in equations, those differentials were significant and sizeable. Work by Groschen, among others, has confirmed one of the chief findings of Lester's and Reynolds's work—that there are significant wage differentials among plants—and found that these differentials tend to be stable over time. Finally, Brown and Medoff have found that there are significant wage differentials by size of firm that cannot be readily explained by standard competitive theory.

While all the modern analysts, like the older generation, have tried to build competitive stories to explain industry and plant differentials, the broad conclusion they have reached also mimics that of the older generation— namely, that competitive theory cannot explain the observed phenomenon and that labor market analysis must change, accordingly, if it is to deal with the real world.

Turning to changes in wages over time, in an important paper in the 1948 volume in honor of Hansen, Dunlop argued that the wage structure was significantly affected by changes in productivity advances. In later work, he stressed the importance of product prices in wage determination, as well. While Salter (1966) found no such pattern of productivity advances leading to relative wage increases, more recent work has confirmed Dunlop's original insight, though in a modified multivariable context: productivity changes and wage changes by industry are uncorrelated by themselves but are correlated once price changes are held fixed. Alternatively, changes in value productivity rather than physical productivity alter the relative wage of industries.

With respect to cyclical movements in wages, Dunlop's original claim that real wages rise when money wages rise and thus tend to be procyclical rather than countercyclical, as predicted by marginal productivity analysis of a fixed labor demand curve, remains a point of debate in the economics literature. As indicated in line 5, some have presented evidence suggesting that real wages and employment are independent over the cycle, while others have argued the contrary. In part, as Bruno and Sachs note, the issue relates to country, with the United States seemingly more consistent with Dunlop's finding and Western Europe more consistent with the neoclassical pattern. In part, it may also hinge on whether one is concerned with product wages or wages in terms of consumer goods and thus the particular wage deflators used for analyses (consumer prices with/without adjustments for exchange rate fluctuations; value added deflators; or producer prices)—issues which, interestingly enough, took up much of Dunlop's article. Finally, the differences in results and continued debate may also reflect actual differences in the behavior of real wages among cycles, depending on the nature of business fluctuations (Malinvaud 1977; Bruno and Sachs 1985).

There is, by contrast, general agreement that Dunlop's second claim about wages over the cycle—that wage differentials widen in recessions and narrow in booms—is correct. Such a countercyclical pattern has been found in industry, education, and age differentials.

Finally, the finding that labor's share is also countercyclical, stressed by Kerr (1957) and reported by Dunlop (1944) has also been confirmed in modern work, though issues of labor's share have not been of much concern to American labor economists.

Collective Bargaining

When DKLR were doing their basic empirical research, trade unionism was growing in the United States (from 5 percent of the private sector work force in 1933 to approximately 40 percent in 1956) and the effect of unions on wage determination, the web of rules that govern labor relations, and the overall functioning of the labor market were major issues in economic analysis. There were those who believed unions would prove disastrous to the competitive system (Lindblom 1949, Chamberlain 1958, Simons 1944, Haberler 1959) as well as those with favorable attitudes. The DKLR generation provided careful empirical analyses of the actual effects of unions, contrasting the economic outcomes "between the bargained wage structure and that which actually exists in imperfect non-union labor markets . . . [not] with a hypothetical structure which might exist under perfect competition" (Reynolds and Taft 1956: 168). Together with their contemporary at Chicago, H. Gregg Lewis, they portrayed a union movement that had significant but limited effects on wages under ordinary circumstances. In addition, they stressed that unions had diverse other effects on the labor market, some positive, some negative, and made an effort to model the union as an institution, with Dunlop pushing the importance of economic factors on union policies in his famous debate with Ross and the California school. Kerr noted the different organizations encompassed under unionism, pointing out that "the type of union and the character of the environment together determine the impact of the union" (Kerr 1977: 145). Reynolds made the point that the new industrial unions had their principal impact on wages "through direct negotiations with the employer under threat of strike action" (Reynolds and Taft 1956: 168) rather than through control of labor supply.

Table 6–2 turns to the findings of DKLR with the respect to the impact of collective bargaining on the labor market. As can be seen, most of the nine propositions which I have garnered from their work has been supported in ensuing research.

First, a growing body of evidence based on computer analysis of CPS and establishment-based surveys shows that unions substantially reduce differentials by standard rate policies and indicate that wage differentials across plants are also lowered, though not by as much as the DKLR generation seems to have thought (lines 1 and 2).

Second, modern analyses also show that unions have a greater impact on fringes than on direct pay and have gone on to offer various "collective goods" and "median voter" explanations of this impact (line 3).

Third, while the issue of union impacts on labor's share of output has, as noted, not been seriously investigated of late, Bruno and Sachs have attributed some of the 1970s rise in labor's share of GNP in Europe to European union activity, consistent with Kerr's claim that while United States unions have not raised labor's share, European unions have. No one has addressed the issue, on which Kerr speculates, of why some union movements augment labor's share (possibly at the expense of employment) while others do not.

The final wage issues dealt with in table 6–2 relate to the overall inflationary impact of union settlements and to the effect of unions on industry and occupation wage structures. At a time when some observers believed unions were a threat to the competitive system, DKLR argued that unionism, while important, had much more limited effects than the alarmists believed. This argument has been confirmed by the plethora of studies reviewed by H.G. Lewis (1986). Estimates of the monopoly loss of output due to union wage gains have, moreover, suggested that efficiency losses associated with unionism are slight, with some modern later economists going so far as to suggest that the losses are nil, as unions and management reach efficient contracts. On

Table 6–2
Comparison of Older Generation and Modern Findings on Effects of Collective Bargaining

Results of Older Generation	Modern Results and Partial List of References
Wage findings	
1. Unionism reduces personal differentials via standard rates which attach pay to jobs, not to the man. (Reynolds and Taft 1956: 171)	Freeman (1980d) Freeman and Medoff (1984)
2. Unionism reduces wage differentials across plants (Reynolds and Taft 1956: 365; Lester 1948)	Groschen (1986) Freeman (1980d)
3. Fringes are higher the higher the wages, and are greater in union then in nonunion settings. (Reynolds 1957: 65)	All else the same, the union/monopoly hourly fringe differential is between 20% and 30%. The fringe share of compensation is higher at a given level of compensation. (Duncan 1976; Freeman 1981b; Goldstein and Pauly 1976; Leigh 1979; Solnick 1978; Viscusi 1980)
4. Trade unionism in the United States has no important effect on labor's share, whereas in other countries it has. (Kerr 1977: 115, 125)	Labor's share in European countries has risen partly as a result of real wage policies of unions. (Bruno and Sachs 1985)
5. Effect of unions on wage changes does not threaten the competitive system. (Kerr 1977; Dunlop 1944)	Union wage effects differ over time but range from 10–25%(Lewis 1986). The allocative costs are slight (Rees 1963). Unions may establish efficient contracts (Abowd 1985; Ashenfelter and Brown 1986).
6. Unionism has little impact on occupational or industrial differentials. (Reynolds and Taft 1956: 191, 365; Kerr 1977: 155)	Nonunion wage structures by industry are hightly correlated with union wage structures (Dickens and Katz 1986a, b; Kreuger and Summers 1986a, b. Unions reduce white-collar/blue-collar premium (Freeman 1980d).
Nonwage Rules	
7. Unionized plants have greater reliance on seniority and rely extensively on temporary layoffs, recalling workers by seniority. (Reynolds 1951: 54–55)	Seniority independent of productivity is rewarded substantially more in promotion decisions among union members than among otherwise comparable nonunion employees (Halasz 1980; Medoff and Abraham 1981b; Yanker 1980).
	There is much more cyclical labor adjustment through temporary layoffs in unionized manufacturing firms than in otherwise comparable firms that are nonunion (Blau and Kahn 1981; Medoff 1979).
	Terminations are more likely to be on a last-in/first-out basis among employees, ceteris paribus (Blau and Kahn 1981, 1983; Medoff and Abraham 1981b).

Table 6–2 continued.

Results of Older Generation	Modern Results and Partial List of References
8. Unionism creates "walls around enterprises," with lower quits and greater tenure (Reynolds 1951: 55, 148). Unions reduce interplant mobility in part through grievance procedures (Reynolds 1951: 254).	The quit rate is much lower for unionized workers than for similar workers who are nonunion. (Blau and Kahn 1981, 1983; Block 1978; Farber OLS results, 1980; Freeman 1978, 1980a, 1980b; Kahn 1977; Leigh 1979)
9. Unions are concerned with employment of members to a sufficiently important extent as to trade off wages for employment. (Dunlop 1944)	Unions have no noticeably negative impact on employment (Pencavel and Hartsog). Unions weigh employment heavily in wage determination (Farber 1978; Carruth and Oswald 1986; Dertouzos and Pencavel 1981; Pencavel 1984).

the wage structure side, recent work which has used Census of Population and Current Population Survey data to examine industry wage structures has found the structures for union and nonunion workers to be remarkably alike, supporting the DKLR claim that unionism has no great impact on the industry wage structure. On the other hand, the DKLR focus on the wages of manual workers led them to understate the effect of unions on the occupational wage structure. While modern studies support the conclusion that unions have no clear impact on occupational wage differences among blue-collar workers, they show that unions raise blue-collar wages relative to white-collar wages, reducing occupational premium along this dimension.

DKLR stressed throughout their work that unions did much more than raise wages in the labor market, just as they stressed that any labor market contract involved a web of rules and social relations. While this theme was for some time neglected in modern work, it has once again moved to the fore. Lines 7–9 of table 6–2 summarize the claims of the older generation with respect to some important non-wage effects of unions: seniority and layoff policies under unionism, quit behavior, and employment. Again, we have a general confirmation of results. Indeed, on the key issue of the extent to which unions weigh employment in their negotiations, several studies have found that workers are risk-averse and take account of employment as well as wage gains.

Finally, as I noted in my 1984 review of Reynolds's *The Structure of Labor Markets*, there is one interesting aspect to the agreement between the work of the 1950s and that of the 1970s–1980s. Taking the sixth edition of Reynolds's textbook on labor economics, we find him backtracking on two of the points in table 6–2, writing: "It is questionable whether collective bargaining has produced a major change in the pattern of labor turnover" (1974: 568), and that "the specific influence of unionism (on fringes) is hard to determine" (1974: 216–17). These apparent reversals of his views regarding the impact of unions on turnover (point 8 in table 6–2, and on fringes (point 3) resulted from cross-section industry regressions which found either statistically insignificant or widely divergent coefficients on unionism (in the case of quits, the results were those of Burton and Parker (1969), Stoikov and Raimson (1968), and Pencavel (1970); in the case of fringes, the results were those of Rice (1966). Modern work with data tapes on thousands of individuals and establishments has disproven the industry regressions. The implication is that the surveys, interviews, and informed judgments of the earlier period yielded more reliable results than did efforts to infer union effects from cross-industry regressions, as was common in the 1960s. We should be less willing to surrender conclusions based on case analyses and interviews to aggregative regression analyses than was Reynolds.

Given their knowledge of institutions, one might have expected the DKLR generation to have foreseen the problem of declining private sector unionism that has characterized the 1970s and 1980s, but, like other economists, they were not particularly good seers. In his book, *As Unions Mature*, Lester did not remotely anticipate a reversal in union fortunes, while in *Labor and the American Economy* (with D. Bok), Dunlop did not foresee anything like the current problems facing the union movement.

Mobility and Firm Hiring Practices

The older generations' work on labor supply and mobility made extensive use of survey and interview data, with Reynolds's *The Structure of Labor Markets* perhaps the most significant piece based on worker interviews and Lester's various surveys of firm practices perhaps the most significant work based on data from firms. In table 6–3, I have paired the findings from the worker and firm studies, under four broad groupings: internal labor markets, correlates of individual mobility, the role of information in the job market, and the process of job search.

With respect to internal labor markets, the conceptual piece by Kerr, "The Balkanization of Labor Markets," offes the broadest statement of the results from the entire spectrum of studies in the period, and I have quoted from it in line 1. Lester's surveys found that the internal market was strong in nonunion as well as in union companies, with large nonunion firms employing the same set of rules as union firms—results confirmed by Foulkes (1980) and Abraham and Medoff (1983). An important aspect of the finding that most workers work in internal markets is that this implies that the bulk of the labor force is effectively "inframarginal," and thus unlikely to respond to outside economic incentives in the simple manner represented in the neoclassical labor supply schedule .

Table 6–3
Comparison of Older Generation and Modern Findings on Mobility and Firm Hiring Practices

Results of Older Generation	*Modern Results and Partial List of References*
Internal Markets	
1. "There is an internal submarket to which persons outside the plant have little or no access." (Kerr 1977: 28)	Internal labor markets exist, and are important in determining wages and mobility. (Doeringer and Piore 1971; Abraham and Medoff 1983)
2. "Non-union firms seem to follow, more or less closely, the hiring, seniority, and promotional patterns prevailing in similar unionized plants." (Lester 1954: 35)	Large nonunion firms have essentially the same personnel practices as union firms. (Foulkes 1980; Abraham and Medoff 1983)
3. "Even in good years . . . something like 80 percent of manual workers . . . were not available to other firms." (Reynolds 1951: 83) Management believed that perhaps four-fifths of the employees (were) rather firmly attached to the company . . . employees with one to three years of seniority rarely leave." (Lester 1954: 59–60)	U.S. workers, like those in Japan, tend to stay with the same company for the bulk of their working life (except for job-shopping when they enter the market). (Hall 1982; Hashimoto and Raisian 1985)
Correlates of Mobility	
4 "Propensity to change employers diminishes rapidly with increasing length of service." (Reynolds 1951: 35) "Attractiveness of alternative employment may be greatly reduced by the need to start . . . on the least desirable job and work shift." (Lester 1954: 36) "Unskilled workers change jobs more frequently than the semi-skilled, and those in turn move more frequently than skilled workers." (Reynolds 1951: 35)	Empirical studies show a strong negative relation between quit rates and job tenure. (Freeman 1980a; Leigh 1979; Jovanovic and Mincer 1978; Parsons 1979; Blau and Kahn 1981, 1983) Craft workers accrue more tenure than operatives, who accrue more tenure than laborers; workers with more "specific" human capital quit less and are laid off less. (Parsons 1972; Pencavel 1972; Freeman 1980b)
5. "Satisfactorily employed workers are almost entirely uninterested in . . . other companies." (Reynolds 1951: 85)	Job satisfaction is a key determinant of quit rates. (Mandelbaum 1980; Freeman 1978)
6. "The minority of very mobile people accounted for a dispropor-tionate share of the total move-ment." (Reynolds 1951: 27–28)	Substantial core of United States labor force is employed in long-term jobs. Unemployment largely due to small minority. (Hall 1980; Clark and Summers 1979; Akerlof and Main 1980)

Table 6–3 continued.

Results of Older Generation	Modern Results and Partial List of References
7. "Inter-plant movement typically involves a reduction in the workers' earnings." (Reynolds 1951: 242)	Young workers gain from mobility; older workers roughly hold their own; gains/losses depend on the reason for the change. (Borjas and Rosen 1980; Bartel and Borjas 1978)
Information in the Job Market	
8. "Workers had only a vague and frequently inaccurate idea of wages in other plants." "Workers are poorly informed about the job opportunities." (Reynolds 1951: 45, 84)	College students have good information on wages for occupations (Freeman 1971); young people are fairly realistic about wage expectations and well informed about the going hourly pay for the kinds of jobs open to them. (Perrella 1971)
9. "A majority (56%) of workers replied they got their information (about jobs) from friends or relatives." (Reynolds 1951: 84) "Gate hiring and internal recruitment are the two methods (used) for the bulk of new hires." (Lester 1954: 38)	Personal contact is the predominant method of finding out about jobs (56%); better jobs found through contacts. (Rees and Gray 1979; Granovetter 1974) Persons with contacts more likely to be hired by companies. (Freeman 1981; Schmensen 1979)
10. "The only way to judge (a job) accurately is to work on it a while. After a few weeks or months of work, one can tell whether a job is worth keeping." (Reynolds 1951: 22)	Empirical analysis indicates that there is a strong impact on workers' quitting of . . . aspects of employment for which learning on the job is likely to be of importance. (Viscusi 1979a, 1979b) Theoretical analysis stresses role of quitting as means to obtain optimal job match. (Mortenson 1975; Jovanovic 1979)
Results on Process of Job Search	
11. "(The worker) evaluates jobs one at a time, on the basis of his minimum standards, instead of trying to compare each job with the full array of possible alternative 'good' jobs; he takes it without worrying over whether a 'better' job may be available somewhere else." (Reynolds 1951: 85)	Rational search strategy is to search for jobs, taking the job which meets the "reservation wage." (Burdett 1978; Johnson 1978; Keiffer and Neumann 1979; Lippman and McCall 1976, 1980)
12. "The usual pattern is to quit an unsatisfactory job, spend some time in unemployment, then locate a new job." "Most workers (80%) change jobs without any unemployment." (Kerr 1942: 157)	Majority of all quitters experience no unemployment between jobs. (Mattila 1974)

Table 6–3 continued.

Results of Older Generation	Modern Results and Partial List of References
13. "Much the best results were obtained by those who had lined up a new job before leaving the old one." (Reynolds 1951: 215)	Analyses show employed search more productive than unemployed search. (Mattila 1974; Black 1980; Kahn and Low 1982)
14. Reservation wages depend on: "workers' earnings on his last job; period of unemployment . . . with a strong inverse relation," "The level of (UI) benefit payments seems clearly to influence the minimum supply price." (Reynolds 1951: 109, 110)	Asking wage of workers falls modestly with length of unemployment. (Kasper 1967; Barnes 1975; Sandell 1980; Stephenson 1976). Level of UI influences wage changes after unemployment. (Ehrenberg and Oaxaca 1976; Grubel, Maki, and Sax 1975)

In the area of correlates of individual mobility, there has been considerable modern work, in large part because of the availability of large-scale longitudinal data sets. While clothed in quite different statistical methodology than the older work, these analyses have verified most of the points listed in the table. Seniority, whether for reasons of heterogeneity or state dependence, is generally the most powerful determinant of quit and separation rates. As a result of the reduction in turnover with seniority, it is now generally accepted that a large proportion of mobility and unemployment is due to the behavior of a minority, contrary to the earlier assertion (Feldstein 1973; Hall 1976) that high turnover of the work force is the key to understanding unemployment. Modern analyses of tenure and quit rates also show that mobility is greatest among the less skilled and least among the more skilled manual workers (construction excluded). Not surprisingly, moreover, job satisfaction turns out to be a major determinant of quit behavior, indicating that "the effective labor supply" does not include the satisfied. The only claim with which modern work disagrees is Reynolds's assertion that workers typically lose, rather than gain, from switching firms—a result reached on the basis of evidence of workers reporting gross weekly earnings on new jobs compared to their previous jobs. This may have been an artifact of the period, city, or group studied; Kerr's analysis of Seattle showed substantial wage gains. Modern work dealing with wage changes and mobility show gains for young workers, roughly no change for older male workers, but with noticeable difference depending on the reason for change. In addition, at least one model (Borjas and Rosen 1980) suggests that workers who change do better than they would have done by staying on their job.

Turning to the role of information in mobility, the conclusions of DKLR concerning the importance of informal channels of recruitment and of personal contacts in obtaining job market information have been verified in numerous surveys, with analyses of hiring showing that companies prefer workers with relatives or friends in the firm. Moreover, both empirical analyses and diverse models of workers' acquisition of information, most notably Viscusi's Bayesian search models, have put great stress on the importance of actually trying a job in order to obtain accurate information about it.

By contrast, modern work disagrees with a major result of the older generation's view of labor market information: that workers have only vague and inaccurate information about wages. While the specific issue with which Reynolds and others dealt (that is, knowledge by workers of job opportunities in other plants) has not been the subject of major modern study, the general picture of information in the market that emerges from the modern work is quite different. Comparisons of unemployed individuals' expectations of wages available in the market as a whole show striking similarity to actual wages, while my 1971 survey of college students—motivated in large measures by Reynolds's evidence on manual workers—found that students had quite good information about earnings among occupations. Of all the DKLR generalizations, that of the poorly informed worker is the least accepted today.

With respect to job search and selection, Reynolds' *The Structure of Labor Markets*—the main piece dealing with the topic—pointed out that workers choose among jobs by comparing each to a "minimum standard." While Reynolds seemed to believe that this was not rational, modern models of optimizing search behavior have shown that an appropriate strategy is in fact to compare offers to a reservation wage, accepting the first job with wages above the reservation level.

Modern work diverges from older work in other aspects of mobility behavior as well. For one, modern studies reject Reynolds's conclusion regarding the importance of unemployment in the search procedure—a finding based on his study of New Haven (which some of us who have lived there know cannot be representative)—and support Kerr's contrary finding for Seattle that the sequence of job mobility from employment to unemployment to a new job is less prevalent than job changing from one employer to another. Recent work also finds unemployment to have a much smaller impact on reservation wages than Reynolds obtained with his sample, where "for people unemployed less than three months, the median expected wage (was) over 90 percent of the last previous wage. For people unemployed three to six months, the figure dropped to 60 percent" (1951: 109). On the other hand, several studies have found, consistent with Reynolds, that workers who have a job lined up beforehand are likely to do better than those who do not. Finally, studies of job satisfaction have tended to yield results of a comparable nature to Reynolds's regarding the importance of money income and various nonpecuniary factors in individual's evaluation of the workplace.

Overall, the findings of the DKLR generation with respect to the importance of internal markets, correlates of mobility, and the importance of informal channels of information in the job market have been supported by later work, the primary exceptions relating to worker information, some aspects of job search, and their interpretation of search behavior. Where modern work has gone far beyond the older generation has been in extending analyses to white-collar labor markets, to issues of education and human capital, and to the broader impact of labor market incentives on diverse forms of behavior beyond the interfirm mobility question on which the older generation focused. Here, at least, I think it is safe to say, yes, we do know more than they did.

Interrelation of Wages and Employment and Functioning of Labor Markets

The key to the broad picture of the labor market as seen by the DKLR generation—to what Martin Segal has aptly called the "post-institutional model"—rests with their view that wage rates are only modestly affected by labor market conditions (within boundaries), and thus that the classical market view that wages represent an equilibrium intersection of labor supply and demand is too great an abstraction to be useful for analysis of short- or medium-term problems. As Dunlop (1944) put it, "The labor market is not a bourse; wage rates are typically quoted prices."

In my view, there are three components to this "model." First, the supply side of the labor market sets "surprisingly wide" limits to wage differentials, *permitting* firms to pay above market rates. Second, some firms adopt high wage policies for reasons beyond attracting and holding the desired labor force. Third, as a result of permissive supply and wage policies (including those of unions), there is a partial divorce of wage setting from labor market conditions, with such nonneoclassical factors as product market conditions and ability to pay affecting worker compensation.

One striking consequence of this view, which takes on particular importance in light of macroeconomic research, is the denial of the existence of what has come to be called a stable Phillips curve (see line 2 of table 6–4). I vividly remember John Dunlop pounding the table against the Phillips curve in a graduate labor economics course: he, Reynolds, Kerr, Lester, and others who based their assessment on firsthand knowledge of wage setting came away with a very different picture of the role of unemployment than that given by 1960s macroeconomists enamored of the Phillips curve. Recent developments and research have supported their assessment about the fragility of the relation between unemployment and wage changes.

Another consequence of the view that wages in many firms are administered prices set above "competitive rates" is that there need be no relation between changes in wages and changes in unemployment: GM and IBM,

Table 6–4
Findings on the Interrelation Among Wages, Employment, and Unemployment

Results of Older Generation	Modern Results and Partial List of References
1. "Wage policy is determined by the employed rather than by the unemployed." (Dunlop 1944: 69) Decline in product prices and not unemployment constitute the effective downward pressure on wage structures. (Dunlop 1944, 1957) The level of unemployment has nothing directly to do with the time at which wage increases begin or with the need of advance; this is determined mainly by the commodity pricing mechanism." (Reynolds 1951: 23) "The wage market and the job market are substantially disjointed and sometimes do go their separate ways." (Kerr 1977: 42–43) "A significant gulf exists between company wage policies or practices and economists' wage theories." (Lester 1954: 45)	The Phillips curve relating wage changes to unemployment is not stable over time. Price changes are a critical determinant of many wage changes (Wachter 1970; Eckstein 1969; Medoff and Abraham 1981a; Santomero and Seater 1978) It is "the labor utilization rate that is important for negotiations, rather than the labor utilization rate within the economy." (Gregory 1986; Solow 1980; Okun 1981)
2. "There was virtually no correlation between the rate of wage increase and the rate of change of employment in individual companies." (Reynolds 1951: 223) "Impediments to intercompany movement tend to make for zones of no reaction between wages and mobility." (Lester 1954: 86) "Movement and potential movement of labor seems inadequate to prevent large and persistent differences in aggregate job attractiveness." (Reynolds 1951: 246)	Industry wage and employment changes only slightly related. (OECD 1966; Freeman 1980c; Ulman 1965) Labor supply curves by industry are relatively elastic; variations of changes in employment exceeds variation in changes in wages. (Implicit in Salter 1966; Kendrick 1961; Freeman 1980c) There are "good" and "bad" jobs; compensating differentials do not equate the values of jobs. (Brown 1980; Doeringer and Piore 1971; Bluestone et al. 1973)

petroleum refining and steel, can attract labor without raising wages—a finding corroborated in various studies of industry wages and employment. While one can interpret the weak correlation between changes in employment and wages as reflecting the operation of competitive labor markets in which firms face infinitely elastic labor supply curves or of simultaneous shifts of supply and demand schedules, such interpretations would be inconsistent with the finding of persistent plant and industrial wage differentials between apparently similar workers and jobs. Such differentials are the key inconsistency between the evidence presented by DKLR and confirmed by modern analysts and the standard competitive market theory, a point which Segal (1986) has emphasized.

Conclusions and Speculations

To summarize matters: On the issues of wage determination, collective bargaining, and the interrelation among employment, wages, and unemployment, which were the principal concerns of the older generation of labor economists, their empirical findings have, with rare exception, been corroborated by modern analysts using sophisticated econometric tools. In one sense, modern human capital earnings models have turned out to be largely "orthogonal" to the older analyses, adding a supply dimension to our view of labor markets without rejecting the older demand results. Moreover, modern efforts to explain away the key findings of the older generation in terms of competitive market behavior have not succeeded, even in the eyes of some of those offering such explanations (see Krueger and Summers 1986a, b; Dickens and Katz 1986a, b). With respect to supply-side issues, which were of less concern to the older generation (save for Reynolds), the basic finding that labor supply has a largely passive effect on wage determination has been accepted in most respects, although observed job search and labor mobility has been interpreted as reflecting a more rational form of behavior. Only in issues which attracted little attention from the older generation—investment in human capital, economics of discrimination, dynamics of unemployment, to name a few topics—have we clearly surpassed our elders.

From one perspective, corroborating the results of the older generation on *their* issues is encouraging, as it indicates that neither the passage of time nor development of new techniques and data sets gives the profession a dramatically different picture of the labor market. That is not, however, the perspective from which I see our confirmation—our rediscovery—of the older results. In advancing science, one does not reconfirm or rediscover the facts of the previous generation; one builds on their analyses to obtain additional fact and new and deeper understanding about the way the world works. We should know a *lot* more about the labor market than the older generation, not only on issues they rarely addressed but on their central issues as well. But, despite our considerably more powerful tools of analysis, we don't know more than they do.

Why? Does our failure to make greater progress surpassing the older generation lie in the nature of our science? In our methods and approaches? In the structure of rewards given economists?

Without a detailed comparison of the sociology (epistemology?) of economics with that of other sciences, which goes far beyond the confines of this essay, one can offer no more than speculations on these fundamental questions.

My speculation is that part of the problem resides in the nature of empirical economics, which is endemic to our endeavor, but that part of the problem also resides in the way in which we have proceeded in recent years.

The basic problem with accruing knowledge about how labor markets (other aspects of economies) work is that economic events are on-going, with the world continually performing "experiments" for us under ever-changing conditions. Since the economic environment always changes (at the minimum because agents have additional past history from which to form expectations), there is a sense in which we always have to "replicate" the findings of older generations to see if they hold up under modern conditions. Unlike physical scientists who can take certain "facts" as given and build on them, we must make sure that patterns and relations found in the past hold under different environments. Because we cannot perform controlled experiments and, in one sense, are not terribly interested in the results of such experiments (we want to discover robust relations—ones which hold under many possible conditions— more than we want to discover ceterus paribus relations), our stock of knowledge can depreciate in ways unknown to scientists who conduct controlled experiments. The continued way in which macroeconomic developments overturn accepted doctrine is a case in point, with the history of the Phillips curve (here Monday, gone Tuesday, back Wednesday) indicating the problem in interpreting wage and unemployment relations. From this perspective, corroboration of the main findings of the older generation in today's economic world is no mean accomplishment. We do "know" more than the older generation, for we know that their findings on the labor market hold not only under the conditions of the 1930s, 1940s, and 1950s but also under the conditions of the 1960s, 1970s, and 1980s. We know, for example, that even with computerized personnel departments and economies that have avoided anything like the Great Depression or a World War II boom, interplant differentials are as large and inexplicable in simple competitive terms as they were in the postwar reconstruction years when DKLR did much of their detailed empirical work. Our progress in surpassing the previous generation is slow in part because we are obligated by the nature of economic evidence to verify in "modern times" what they found in older days.

Our progress is also slow, however, because of a pronounced tendency to neglect the work of those who came before us. How many graduate students read older empirical work? How many *can* read studies that are not presented with formal models and described in "regressionese"? How many believe results that are not written with the newest mathematical jargon and put through the latest econometric sieve? One sure way to depreciate our stock of knowledge, and thus reduce the likelihood that we "know" more than our predecessors, is to ignore their work.

Third, I fear that in part our failure to make greater advance with more powerful techniques is itself due to our inamorata with those techniques—a devotion to mastering and demonstrating our mastery of techniques as opposed to studying our subject itself—that a Marxist (we all have heard of them) might call "techniques fetishism." In econometrics, there is of course some justification for assessing old facts with new techniques because our "experiments" are imperfect, but in light of the past two decades, experience with structural equations, corrections for sample selection, and the like, it is clear that fancier techniques are not the way to increase knowledge rapidly. In theory, I find the justification for techniques fetishism even weaker, for all too often what happens is that old principles are restated in new mathematical language. This is not to say that advances in techniques cannot be useful and fun. Some are useful. Some are fun. To some people. With a limited amount of research resources, however, the extent to which ours are devoted to techniques as opposed to discovery has, I believe, slowed progress. Valuing mathematical elegance and consistency, we surpass our predecessors in mathematical elegance and consistency, but not necessarily in understanding.

Does the new generation of labor economists know more than the older generation? On their issues, perhaps not. But that does not, I warn you, mean that when we disagree with them you should believe what they say. According to Edward Leamer's (1975) theory of random access-biased memory, quite the contrary. John Dunlop may have a storehouse of knowledge on a particular issue—dozens of specific cases that he can marshal like soldiers in an argument—while Richard Freeman may know only one fact. But as a result, Dunlop will *always* be able to recall instances consistent with whatever point he is making, and thus (inadvertently, of course) give a biased picture of the world. Freeman's one example is, by contrast, unbiased. Now, if we could model the access-biased memory path . . . and develop a multivariate statistical correction procedure for memory selection bias . . . or teach Freeman something more.

Notes

1. See Derek de Solla Price, *Science Since Babylon* (New Haven, Conn.: Yale University Press, 1975) and *Little Science, Big Science* (New York: Columbia University Press, 1965).

2. *Industrial Labor Relations Review*, July 1986, 67 percent; *Journal of Labor Economics*, July 1986, 54 percent; *Journal of Human Resources*, Winter 1986, 52 percent.

References

Abowd, John. 1985. "Collective Bargaining and the Division of the Value of the Enterprise." Chicago: University of Chicago, unpublished.

Abraham, Katherine, and James Medoff. 1983. "Length of Service, Terminations, and the Nature of the Employment Relation." Cambridge, Mass.: National Bureau of Economic Research, Working Paper 1086.

Akerloff, Ga.A., and B.G.M. Main. 1980. "Unemployment Spells and Unemployment Experience." *American Economic Review* 70 (December): 885–893.

Alexander, Kenneth. 1961. "Market Practices and Collective Bargaining in Automotive Parts." *Journal of Political Economy* 69 (February): 15–29.

Barnes, W.F. 1975. "Job Search Models, the Duration of Unemployment, and the Asking Wage: Some Empirical Evidence." *Journal of Human Resources* 10 (Spring): 230–240.

Barron, J., and S. McCafferty. "Job Search, Labor Supply and the Quit Decision." *American Economic Review* 67 (September): 683–691.

Bartel, Ann, and George Borjas. 1978. "Wage Growth and Job Turnover: An Empirical Analysis." Cambridge, Mass.: National Bureau of Economic Research, Working Paper 259.

Behman, Sara. 1978. "Interstate Differentials in Wages and Unemployment." *Industrial Relations* 17 (May): 168–188.

Bell, Linda, and Richard Freeman. 1985. "Does a Flexible Industry Wage Structure Increase Employment?: The U.S. Experience." Cambridge, Mass.: National Bureau of Economic Research, Working Paper 1604.

Black, M. 1980. "Pecuniary Implications of On-The-Job Search and Quit Activity." *The Review of Economics and Statistics* 62 (May): 222–229.

Blau, Francine, and Lawrence Kahn. 1981. "Race and Sex Differences in Quits by Young Workers." *Industrial and Labor Relations Review* 34 (July): 563–577.

———. 1983 "Unionism, Seniority, and Turnover." *Industrial Relations* 22 (Fall): 362–373.

Block, Richard. 1978. "The Impact of Seniority Provisions on the Manufacturing Quit Rate." *Industrial and Labor Relations Review* 31 (July): 474–488.

Bluestone, Barry, W.M. Murphy, and Mary Stevenson. 1973. "Low Wages and the Working Poor." Ann Arbor: The Institute of Labor and Industrial Relations, University of Michigan, Policy Paper 22.

Borjas, George. 1979. "Job Satisfaction, Wages and Unions." *Journal of Human Resources* 14 (Winter): 21–40.

———. 1981. "Job Mobility and Earnings Over the Life Cycle." *Industrial and Labor Relations Review* 34 (April): 365–376.

Borjas, George, and Sherwin Rosen. 1980. "Income Prospects and Job Mobility of Younger Men." *Research in Labor Economics* 3: 159–181.

Borjas, George, and Ann Bartel. 1977. "Middle-Age Job Mobility: Its Determinants and Consequences." In Seymour Wolbein, ed., *Men in the Preretirement Years*, 39–97. Philadelphia: Temple University Press.

Brown, Charles. 1980. "Equalizing Differences in the Labor Market." *Quarterly Journal of Ecomonics* 62 (November): 529–538.

Brown, Charles, and James Medoff. 1985. "The Employer Size Wage Effect." Cambridge: Harvard University, unpublished.

Brown, J. 1962. "Expected Ability to Pay and the Interindustry Wage Structure in Manufacturing." *Industrial and Labor Relations Review* 16 (October): 45–62.

Brown, W., J. Hayles, B. Hughes, and T. Rowe. 1984. "Production and Labor Markets in Wage Determination: Some Australian Evidence," *British Journal of Industrial Relations* 22 (July): 169–178.

Browne, Lynn. 1978. "Regional Unemployment Rates—Why Are They So Different?" *New England Economic Review*, November/December: 35–53.

Bruno, Michael, and Jeffry Sachs. 1985. *The Economics of Worldwide Stagflation.* Oxford: Basil Blackwell.

Bunting, R. 1962. *Employer Concentration in Local Labor Markets.* Chapel Hill, N.C.: University of North Carolina Press.

Burdett, Kenneth. 1978. "A Theory of Employee Job Search and Quit Rates." *American Economic Review* 68 (March): 212–220.

Burton, John, and J. Parker. 1969. "Inter-Industry Variation in Voluntary Job Mobility." *Industrial and Labor Relations Review* 23 (January): 199–216.

Carruth, Alan, and Andrew Oswald. 1985. "Miners' Wages in Post-War Britain: An Application of a Model of Trade Union Behavior." *Economic Journal* 95 (December): 1003–1020.

———. 1986. "A Test of a Model of Union Behavior: The Coal and Steel Industries in Britain." *Oxford Bulletin of Economics and Statistics* 48 (February): 1–18.

Chamberlain, Edwin. 1958. "The Economic Analysis of Labor Union Policies." *In Labor Unions and Public Policy.* Washington, D.C.: American Enterprise Institute.

Clark, Kim, and Richard Freeman. 1980. "How Elastic is the Demand for Labor? *Review of Economics and Statistics* 47 (November): 509–520.

Clark, Kim, and Lawrence Summers. 1979. "Labor Market Dynamics and Unemployment: A Reconsideration." *Brookings Papers on Economic Activity*, Vol. 1, pp. 13–60.

Cohen, H. 1972. "Monopsony and Discriminating Monopsony in the Nursing Market." *Applied Economics* 4: 39–48.

Dertouzos, James, and John Pencavel. 1981. "Wage and Employment Determination Under Trade Unionism: The International Typographical Union." *Journal of Political Economy* 89 (December): 1162–1181.

Dickens, William, and L.F. Katz. 1986a. "Interindustry Wage Differences and Industry Characteristics." In K. Lang and J. Leonard, eds., *Unemployment and the Structure of Labor Markets.* London: Basil Blackwell, forthcoming.

———. 1986b. "Interindustry Wage Differences and Theories of Wage Determination." Cambridge, Mass.: National Bureau of Economic Research, Working Paper 2014.

Doeringer, Peter, and Michael Piore. 1971. *International Labor Markets and Manpower Analysis.* Lexington, Mass.: Lexington Books.

Duncan, Greg. 1976. "Earnings Functions and Nonpecuniary Benefits." *Journal of Human Resources* II (Fall): 462–483.

Dunlop, John. 1938. "The Movement of Real and Money Wage Rates." *Economic Journal* 48 (September):413–434.

———. 1939. "Cyclical Variations in Wage Structure." *Review of Economics and Statistics* 21 (February):30–39.

———. 1944. *Wage Determination Under Trade Unions*, New York: Augustus Kelley.

———. 1948. "Productivity and the Wage Structure." In *Income, Employment and Public Policy, Essays in Honor of Alvin H. Hansen*, 341–362. New York: W.W. Norton.

———. 1957. "The Task of Contemporary Wage Theory." In George Taylor and Frank Pierson, eds., *New Concepts in Wage Determination*, 117–139. New York: McGraw–Hill.

Dunn, Lucia F. 1980. "The Effects of Firm and Plant Size on Employee Well-Being." In J. Siegfried, ed., *The Economics of Firm Size, Market Structure and Social Performance*, 348–358. Washington, D.C.: Federal Trade Commission.

———. 1984. "The Effects of Firm Size on Wages, Fringe Benefits and Worker Disutility." In H. Goldschmid, ed., *The Impact of the Modern Corporation*, 5–58. New York: Columbia University Press.

Eckstein, Otto. 1969. "Money Wage Determination Revisited." *Review of Economic Studies* 35 (April):133–143.

Ehrenberg, Ronald, and Ronald Oaxaca. 1976. "Unemployment Insurance, the Duration of Unemployment, and Subsequent Wage Growth." *American Economic Review* 65 (December):754–766.

Farber, Henry. 1978. "Individual Preferences and Union Wage Determination: The Case of the United Mine Workers." *Journal of Political Economy* 68 (October): 923–942.

———. 1980. "Unionism, Labor Turnover and Wages of Young Men." *Research in Labor Economics* 3:33–53.

———. 1986. "The Analysis of Union Behavior." In O. Ashenfelter and R. Layard, eds., *Handbook of Labor Economics*. Amsterdam: North Holland, forthcoming.

Feldstein, Martin. 1973. "The Economics of the New Unemployment." *The Public Interest* 33 (Fall):3–42.

Foulkes, Fred. 1980. *Personnel Policies in Large Nonunion Companies*. Englewood Cliffs, N.J.: Prentice–Hall.

Freeman, Richard. 1971. *The Labor Market for College Trained Manpower*. Cambridge: Harvard University Press.

———. 1978. "Job Satisfaction As An Economic Variable." *American Economic Review* 68 (May):135–141.

———. 1980a. "The Exit-Voice Trade-Off in the Labor Market: Unionism, Job Tenure, Quits and Separations." *Quarterly Journal of Economics* 94 (June):643–676.

———. 1980b. "The Effect of Unionism on Worker Attachment to Firms." *Journal of Labor Research* 1 (Spring):29–62.

————. 1980c. "An Empirical Analysis of the Fixed Coefficient Manpower Requirements Model, 1960–1970." *Journal of Human Resources* 15 (Spring): 176–199.

————. 1980d. "Unionism and the Dispersion of Wages." *Industrial and Labor Relations Review* 34 (October): 3–23.

————. 1981a. "Changing Market for Young Persons: Who Gets Hired? A Case Study of the Market for Youth." Washington D.C.: Department of Labor, Final Report Grant No. 21–25–78–19.

————. 1981b. "The Effect of Trade Unionism on Fringe Benefits." *Industrial and Labor Relations Review* 34 (July):489–509.

————. 1982. "Union Wage Practices and Wage Dispersion Within Establishments." *Industrial and Labor Relations Review* 36 (October):3–21.

————. 1984. "The Structure of Labor Markets: A Book Review Three Decades Later." In Gustav Ranis, et al., ed., *Comparative Economic Perspectives*, Boulder, Colo.: Westview. 201–226.

Freeman, Richard, and James Medoff. 1981. "The Impact of Collective Bargaining: Illusion or Reality." In Jack Stieber, et al., eds., *U.S. Industrial Relations 1950–1980: A Critical Assessment*, 47–97. Madison, Wis.: Industrial Relations Research Association.

————. 1984. *What do Unions Do?* New York: Basic Books.

Geary, P.T., and John Kennan. 1982. "The Employment–Real Wage Relationship: An International Study." *Journal of Political Economy* 90 (August): 854–871.

Goldstein, G., and M. Pauly. 1976. "Group Health Insurance as a Local Public Good." In R. Rosett, ed., *The Role of Health Insurance in the Health Services Sector*, 73–110. New York: National Bureau of Economic Research.

Granovetter, Mark. 1974. *Getting a Job: A Study of Contacts and Careers*. Cambridge: Harvard University Press.

Green, J., and C. Kahn. 1983. "Wage Employment Contracts." *Quarterly Journal of Economics* 98, Supplement: 173–187.

Greenberg, David. 1968. "Deviations from Wage-Fringe Standards." *Industrial and Labor Relations Review* 22 (January): 197–209.

Gregory, R. 1986. "Wage Policy and Unemployment in Australia." *Econometrica*, Supplement: S53–S74.

Gronau, Reuben. 1971. "Information and Frictional Unemployment." *American Economic Review* 61 (June):290–301.

Groschen, Erica. 1986. *Sources of Within Industry Wage Dispersion: Do Wages Vary By Employers?* Cambridge, Harvard University, unpublished Ph.D dissertation.

Grubb, David, Richard Layard, and James Symons. 1984. "Wages, Unemployment, and Incomes Policy." London: Centre for Labour Economics, Discussion Paper 168.

Grubel, H., D. Maki, and S. Sax. 1975. "Real and Insurance Induced Unemployment in Canada." *Canadian Journal of Economics* 8 (May):174–191.

Haberler, Gottfried. 1959. "Wage Policy and Inflation." In Philip Bradley, ed., *The Public Stake in Union Power*, 63–85. Charlottesville, Va.: University of Virginia Press.

Halasy, P. 1980. "What Lies Behind the Slope of the Age-Earnings Profile?" Cambridge: Harvard University, Senior Honors Thesis.

Hall, Robert. 1970. "Why is the Unemployment Rate so High at Full Employment?" *Brookings Papers on Economic Activity*, Vol. 3:709–764.

———. 1982. "The Importance of Lifetime Jobs in the U.S. Economy." *American Economic Review* 72 (September):716–724.

Hamermesh, Daniel. 1976. "Econometric Studies of Labor Demand and Their Application to Policy Analysis." *Journal of Human Resources* 11 (Fall):507–528.

———. 1977. "Economics of Job Satisfaction and Worker Alienation." In O. Ashenfelter and W. Dates, eds., *Essays in Labor Market and Policy Analysis*, 53–72. Princeton: Princeton University Press.

Hashimoto, Masinori, and John Raisian. 1985. "Employment Tenure and Earnings in Japan and the U.S." *American Economic Review* 75 (September):721–735.

Haworth, C., and D. Rasmussen. 1971. "Human Capital and Inter-Industry Wages in Manufacturing." *Review of Economics and Statistics* 53 (November):376–379.

Johnson, William. 1978. "A Theory of Job Shopping." *Quarterly Journal of Economics* 92 (May):261–278.

Jovanovic, B. 1979. "Firm Specific Capital and Turnover." *Journal of Political Economy* 87 (December):1246–1260.

Jovanovic, B., and Jacob Mincer. 1978. "Labor Mobility and Wages." New York: Columbia University, unpublished paper.

Kahn, Lawrence. 1977. "Union Impact: A Reduced Form Approach." *The Review of Economics and Statistics* 59 (November):503–507.

Kahn, Lawrence, and Stuart Low. 1982. "The Relative Effects of Employed and Unemployed Job Search," *Review of Economics and Statistics* (May):234–241.

Kasper, H. 1967. "The Asking Wage of Labor and the Duration of Unemployment." *Review of Economics and Statistics* (May):165–172.

Kaufman, Bruce E., and Paula E. Stephan. 1987. "Determinants of Interindustry Wage Growth in the Seventies." *Industrial Relations* 26 (Spring):186–94.

Keiffer, N., and G. Neumann. 1979. "An Empirical Job Search Model with a Test of a Constant Reservation Wage Hypothesis." *Journal of Political Economy* 87 (February):89–107

Kendrick, John. 1961. *Productivity Trends in the U.S.* New York: National Bureau of Economic Research.

Kerr, Clark. 1942. *Migration to the Seattle Labor Market Area: 1940–1942.* Seattle: University of Washington Press.

———. 1977. *Labor Markets and Wage Determination.* Berkeley: University of California Press.

Kreuger, Alan, and Lawrence Summers. 1986a. "Reflections on the Interindustry Wage Structure." Cambridge: Harvard University, Working Paper 1968.

———. 1986b. "Efficiency Wages and the Interindustry Wage Structure." Cambridge: Harvard Institute of Economic Research, Discussion Paper 1247.

Landon, John, and Robert Baird. 1971. "Monopsony in the Market for Public School Teachers." *American Economic Review* 61 (December):966–971.

Landon, John, and William Pierce. 1971. "Discrimination, Monopsony, and Union Power in the Building Trades: A Cross-Sectional Approach." In Industrial Relations Research Association, *Proceedings of the Twenty-Fourth Annual Winter Meeting*, 254–261. Madison Wis.: Industrial Relations Research Association.

Leamer, Edward. 1975. "Explaining New Results as Access Biased Memory." *Journal of American Statistical Association* 70:85–93.

Leigh, Duane. 1978. "Racial Discrimination and Labor Unions: Evidence From the NLS Sample of Middle-Aged Men." *Journal of Human Resources* 13 (Fall):568–577.

———. 1979. "Unions and Non-Wage Racial Discrimination." *Industrial and Labor Relations Review* 32 (July):439–450.

Lester, Richard. 1945. "Trends in Southern Wage Differentials Since 1890." *Southern Economic Journal* II (April):317–344.

———. 1946a. "Shortcomings of Marginal Analysis for Wage-Employment Problems." *American Economic Review* 36 (February):63–72.

———. 1946b. "Wage Diversity and Its Theoretical Implications." *Review of Economics and Statistics* 28 (August):152–159.

———. 1948. *Company Wage Policies: A Survey of Patterns and Experience*. Princeton: Princeton University, Industrial Relations Section.

———. 1952. "A Range Theory of Wage Differentials." *Industrial and Labor Relations Review* 5 (July):483–500.

———. 1954. *Hiring Practices and Labor Competition*. Princeton: Princeton University, Industrial Relations Section.

———. 1958. *As Unions Mature*. Princeton: Princeton University Press.

Levinson, Harold. 1960. "Pattern Bargaining: A Case Study of the Automobile Workers." *Quarterly Journal of Economics* 74 (May):296–317.

Lewis, H. Gregg. 1986. *Union Relative Wage Effects: A Survey*. Chicago: University of Chicago Press.

Lindblom, Charles. 1949. *Unions and Capitalism*. New Haven: Yale University Press.

Lippman, S.A., and J.J. McCall. 1976. "The Economics of Job Search: A Survey: *Economic Inquiry* 14 (September):155–189.

———. 1980. *Studies in the Economics of Search*. Amsterdam: North Holland.

Mackay, D.T., B. Boddy, J. Brack, J.A. Diack, and N. Jones. 1971. *Labour Markets Under Different Employment Conditions*. London: Allen and Unwin.

Malinvaud, Edward. 1977. *The Theory of Unemployment Reconsidered*. Oxford: Basil Blackwell.

Mandelbaum, D. 1980. *Responses to Job Satisfaction Questions into Why Workers Change Employers*. Cambridge: Harvard University, unpublished undergraduate thesis.

Marston, Steven. 1980. "Anatomy of Persistent Local Unemployment." Draft paper prepared for the National Commission for Employment Policy Conference.

———. 1981. "Two Views of the Geographic Distribution of Unemployment." Ithaca: Cornell University, Working Paper 255.

Masters, Stanley. 1969. "An Interindustry Analysis of Wages and Plant Size." *Review of Economics and Statistics* 51 (August):341–345.

Mattila, J. 1974. "Job Quitting and Frictional Unemployment." *American Economic Review* 64 (March):235–239.

Medoff, James. 1979. "Layoffs and Alternatives Under Trade Unions in United States Manufacturing." *American Economic Review* 69 (June):380–395.

Medoff, James, and Katherine Abraham. 1980. "Experience, Performance, and Earnings." *Quarterly Journal of Economics* 69 (December):703–736.

———. 1981a. "Unemployment, Unsatisfied Demand for Labor, and Compensation Growth in the U.S., 1956–1980." Cambridge: Harvard Institute of Economic Research, Working Paper 848.

———. 1981b. "The Role of Seniority at U.S. Work Places: A Report on Some New Evidence." Cambridge: Harvard University, unpublished paper.

———. 1981c. "Are Those Paid More Really More Productive? The Case of Experience." *Journal of Human Resources* 16 (Spring):186–216.

Medoff, James, and J.A. Fay. 1985. "Labor and Output over the Business Cycle." *American Economic Review* 75 (September):638–655.

Mellow, Wesley. 1982. "Employer Size and Wages. *Review of Economics and Statistics* 64 (August):495–500.

Miller, E. 1981. "Variation of Wage Rates With Size of Establishment." *Economics Letters* 8 (No. 3):281–286.

Mincer, Jacob. 1974 *Schooling, Experience and Earnings*. New York: National Bureau of Economic Research.

Mortenson, Dale. 1975. "The Turnover Implications of Learning About Attributes on the Job." Evanston, Ill. Northwestern University Discussion Paper.

Nolan, Peter, and William Brown. 1983. "Competition and Work Place Wage Determination." *Oxford Bulletin of Economics and Statistics* 45 (August):269–288.

Organization for Economic Cooperation and Development. 1966. *Wages and Labor Mobility*. Paris.

———. 1985. *Employment Outlook*. (September). Paris.

Oi, Walter. 1983. "Heterogeneous Firms and the Organization of Production." *Economic Inquiry* 21 (April):147–175.

Oi, Walter, and John Raisian. 1985. "Impact of Firm Size on Wages and Salaries." Unpublished paper.

Okun, Arthur. 1981. *Prices and Quantities: A Macroeconomic Analysis*. Washington, D.C.: The Brookings Institute.

Osterman, Paul. 1982. "Employment Structures Within Firms." *British Journal of Industrial Relations* 20 (November):349–361.

Parsons, Donald. 1972. "Specific Human Capital: An Application to Quit Rates and Layoff Rates." *Journal of Political Economy* 80 (November/December): 1120–1143.

———. 1973. "Quit Rates Over Time: A Search and Information Approach." *American Economic Review* 63 (June):390–401.

———. 1979. "Models of Labor Turnover." *Research in Labor Economics*. Greenwich, Conn.: JAI Press.

Pencavel, John. 1970. *An Analysis of the Quit Rate in American Manufacturing*. Princeton: Princeton University Press.

———. 1972. "Wages, Specific Training and Labor Turnover in U.S. Manufacturing Industries." *International Economic Review* 13 (February):53–64.

————. 1984. "The Trade-Off Between Wages and Employment in Trade Union Objectives." *Quarterly Journal of Economics* 99 (May):215–232.

Pencavel, John, and Catherine Hartsog. 1984. "Reconsideration of the Effects of Unionism on Relative Wages and Employment in the United States, 1920–1980." *Journal of Labor Economics* 2 (April):193–232.

Perrella, U.C. 1971. "Young Workers and Their Earnings." *Monthly Labor Review*, July:3–11.

Personick, M.E., and C.B. Barsky. 1982. "White Collar Pay Levels Linked to Corporate Work Force Size." *Monthly Labor Review*, May:23–28.

Peterson, D. 1972. "Economics of Information and Job Search: Another View." *Quarterly Journal of Economics* 86 (February):127–131.

Phelps, Edmund. 1968. "Money-Wage Dynamics and the Labor Market Equilibrium." *Journal of Political Economy* 76 (July/August):678–711.

Quinn, R., and G. Staines. 1978. *The 1977 Quality of Employment Survey*. Ann Arbor: University of Michigan.

Rees, Albert. 1963. "The Effects of Unions on Resource Allocation." *Journal of Law and Economics* 6 (October):69–78.

Rees, Albert, and W. Gray. 1979. "Family Effects in Youth Employment." Cambridge, Mass.: National Bureau of Economic Research, Working Paper 396.

Reya, A.M. 1978. "Geographical Differences in Earnings and Unemployment Rates." *Review of Economics and Statistics* 60 (May):201–08.

Reynolds, Lloyd. 1951. *The Structure of Labor Markets*. New York: Harper.

————. 1974. *Labor Economics and Labor Relations*, 6th edition. Englewood Cliffs, N.J.: Prentice–Hall.

Reynolds, Lloyd, and Cynthia Taft. 1956. *The Evolution of Wage Structure*. New Haven: Yale University Press.

Rice, R. 1966. "Skill, Earnings and the Growth of Wage Supplements." *American Economic Review* 54 (May):583–593.

Salter, W.E.G. 1966. *Productivity and Technological Change*. Cambridge, England: Cambridge University Press.

Sandell, Steven. 1980. "Job Search By Unemployed Women: Determinants of the Asking Wage." *Industrial and Labor Relations Review* 33 (April):368–378.

Santomero, A.A., and Seater, J.J. 1978. "The Inflation–Unemployment Trade-Off: A Critique of the Literature." *Journal of Economic Literature* 16 (June):499–544.

Schmensen, J.M. 1979. "A Comparison of Hiring and Performance in a Low Wage Labor Market." Cambridge: Harvard University, Senior Honor Thesis.

Schultz, Charles. 1971. "Has the Phillips Curve Shifted? Some Additional Evidence." *Brookings Papers on Economic Activity*, Vol. 2, pp. 452–467.

Scully, Gerald. 1974. "Pay and Performance in Professional Baseball." *American Economic Review* 64 (December):915–930.

Segal, Martin. 1986. "Post-Institutionalism in Labor Economics: The Forties and Fifties Revisited." *Industrial and Labor Relations Review* 39 (April):388–403.

Seltzer, G. 1961. "The United Steelworkers and Unionwide Bargaining." *Monthly Labor Review*, (February):129–136.

Simons, Henry. 1944. *Economic Policy for a Free Society*, Chicago: University of Chicago Press.

Solnick,T. 1978. "Unionism and Fringe Benefit Expenditure." *Industrial Relations* 17 (February):102–107.

Solow, Robert. 1980. "On Theories of Unemployment." *American Economic Review* 70 (March):1–11.

Stephenson, S. 1976. "The Economics of Youth Job Search Behavior." *Review of Economics and Statistics* 58 (February):104–111.

Stigler, George. 1961. "The Economics of Information." *Journal of Political Economy* 69 (June):213–225.

Stoikov, V., and R. Raimson. 1968. "Determinants of the Differences in Quit Rates Among Industries." *American Economic Review* 58 (December):1283–1298.

Ulman, Lloyd. 1965. "Labor Mobility and the Industrial Wage Structure in the Post-War United States." *Quarterly Journal of Economics* 67 (February):73–97.

Viscusi, W. Kip. 1979a. *Employment Hazards: An Investigation of Market Performance.* Cambridge: Harvard University Press.

———. 1979b. "Job Hazards and Worker Quit Rates: An Analysis of Adaptive Worker Behavior." *International Economic Review* 20 (February):29–58.

———. 1980. "Labor Market Structure and the Welfare Implication of the Quality of Work." *Journal of Labor Research* 1 (Spring):175–192.

Wachter, Michael. 1970. "Cyclical Variation in the Interindustry Wage Structure." *American Economic Review* 60 (March):75–84.

Yanker, R.H. 1980. "Productivity Versus Seniority: What Is the Determining Factor in Regard to Wages and Promotion?" Cambridge: Harvard University Senior Honors Thesis.

Selected Bibliographies*

John T. Dunlop

1938   "The Movement of Real and Money Wage Rates." *Economic Journal* 48 (September): 413–34.

1939   "Cyclical Variations in Wage Structure." *Review of Economics and Statistics* 21 (February): 30–39.

1939   "Price Flexibility and the 'Degree Monopoly.'" *Quarterly Journal of Economics* 53 (August): 522–34.

1939   "Trends in the 'Rigidity' of English Wage Rates." *Review of Economic Studies* 53 (August): 189–99.

1941   "Real and Money Wage Rates—A Reply." *Quarterly Journal of Economics* 54 (August): 683–91.

1942   "Bargaining Power and Market Structures." *Journal of Political Economy* 50 (February): 1–26. (With Benjamin Higgins).

1942   "Wage Policies of Trade Unions." *American Economic Review* 32 (March), Supplement: 290–301.

1944   "The Changing Status of Labor." In H. F. Williamson, ed., *The Growth of the American Economy*. New York: Prentice–Hall.

1944   *Wage Determination Under Trade Unions*. New York: Macmillan. Reprinted with new preface, 1950.

1946   "Fact-Finding in Labor Disputes." In *Proceedings of the American Academy of Social and Political Sciences*, May: 64–73.

1947   "American Wage Determination: Its Trend and Significance." In U.S. Chamber of Commerce, *Wage Determination and Liberalism*, 34–48.

1947   "A Review of Wage–Price Policy." *Review of Economics and Statistics* 29 (August): 154–160.

1947   "Wage–Price Relations at High-Level Employment", *American Economic Review* 37 (May): 243–53.

1947   "The Economics of Wage Dispute Settlement." *Law and Contemporary Problems*, May: 281–96.

1948   "The Development of Labor Organization." In R.A. Lester and J. Shister, eds., *Insights into Labor Issues*, 163–93. New York: Macmillan.

1948   "The Demand and Supply Functions of Labor," *American Economic Review* 38 (May): 340–50.

---

* Does not include publications outside of labor economics and industrial relations

1948   "Productivity and the Wage Structure." In *Income, Employment and Public Policy, Essays in Honor of Alvin Hansen*, 341–62. New York: W.W. Norton.

1948   "A National Labor Policy." In S.E. Harris, ed., *Saving American Capitalism*, 295–308. New York: Knopf.

1949   *Collective Bargaining: Principles and Cases*. Homewood, Ill.: Irwin. Revised edition with James J. Healy, 1953.

1949   "The Decontrol of Wages and Prices." In Colston Warne, ed., *Labor in Post-War America*, 3–24, 657–59. New York: Remsen.

1949   "Allocation of the Labor Force." *Proceedings of the Conference on Industry-Wide Collective Bargaining*, May 14, 1948, pp. 34–46. University of Pennsylvania Press, 1949.

1950   "Estimates of Unemployment: Some Unresolved Problems." *The Review of Economics and Statistics* 32 (February):77–79.

1950   "An Analytic Framework for Industrial Relations Research." *Industrial and Labor Relations Review* 3 (April): 383–93.

1950   *The Wage Adjustment Board*. Cambridge: Harvard University Press. (With Arthur Hill.)

1950   "Note: Jurisdictional Strike Statistics." *Review of Economics and Statistics* 32 (May): 51–54.

1950   "An Appraisal of Wage Stabilization Policies." in *Problems and Policies of Dispute Settlement and Wage Stabilization During World War II*, 155–86. Washington, D.C.: U.S. Department of Labor, Bureau of Labor Statistics, Bulletin 1009.

1952   "The Settlement of Emergency Disputes." In Industrial Relations Research Association, *Proceedings of the Fifth Annual Meeting*, 1–7. Madison, Wis.: Industrial Relations Research Association.

1954   "Research in Industrial Relations: Past and Future." In Industrial Relations Research Association, *Proceedings of the Seventh Annual Meeting*, 92–101. Madison, Wis.: Industrial Relations Research Association.

1955   "International Comparison of Wage Structures." *International Labour Review*, April: 347–63. (With Melvin Rothbaum.)

1955   "The Growth of the Relationship." In C.S. Golden and V.D. Parker, eds., *Causes of Industrial Peace Under Collective Bargaining*, 23–28. New York: Harper.

1955   "The Industrial Relations Function in Management, Some Views on its Organizational Status." *Personnel*, March: 1–10. (With Charles Myers.)

1955   "The Labor Problem in Economic Development, a Framework for a Reappraisal," (With Clark Kerr, Charles A. Myers, and F.H. Harbison.) *International Labour Review*, April, 3–19.

1956   "Structural Changes in the American Labor Movement and Industrial Relations System." In Industrial Relations Research Association, *Proceedings of the*

Ninth Annual Meeting, 12–32. Madison, Wis.: Industrial Relations Research Association.

1957 Ed., *The Theory of Wage Determination*. London: Macmillan.

1957 "The Task of Contemporary Wage Theory." In George Taylor and Frank Pierson, eds., *New Concepts on Wage Theory*, 117–39. New York: McGraw–Hill.

1958 "The American Industrial Relations System in 1975." In Jack Stieber, ed., *U.S. Industrial Relations—The Next Twenty Years*, 27–54. Lansing, Mich.: Michigan State University Press.

1958 *Industrial Relations Systems*. New York: Henry Holt.

1959 "Policy Problem: Choices and Proposals." In Charles Myers, ed., *Wages, Prices, Profits and Productivity*, 137–60. New York: American Assembly.

1959 "Sumner Slichter: The Man, the Scholar, and the Critic of His Times." In Industrial Relations Research Association, *Proceedings of the Twelfth Annual Meeting*, 2–7. Madison, Wis.: Industrial Relations Research Association.

1960 *Industrialism and Industrial Man, The Problems of Labor and Management in Economic Growth*. Cambridge: Harvard University Press. (With Clark Kerr, Frederick Harbison, and Charles Myers.)

1961 "Consensus and National Labor Policy" *Monthly Labor Review*, March: 228–33.

1961 "The Industrial Relations System in Construction." In Arnold Weber, ed., *The Structure of Collective Bargaining, Problems and Perspectives*, 255–77. Glencoe, Ill.: Free Press.

1961 Ed., *Potentials of the American Economy, Selected Essays of Sumner H. Slichter*. Cambridge: Harvard University Press.

1962 Ed., *Automation and Technological Change*. New York: Prentice–Hall, Inc., American Assembly.

1964 "Impact of Technological Change on Labour–Management Relations." In *Automation and Social Change*, 83–95. Ontario Economic Council.

1965 "Evaluation of Factors Affecting Productivity." In E.A.C. Robinson, ed., *Problems in Economic Development*, 350–62. London: Macmillan.

1966 Technological Change and Manpower Policy—The Older Worker." In Juanita M. Kreps, ed., *Technology, Manpower, and Retirement Policy*, 13–26. Cleveland, Oh.: World Publishing.

1966 "Job Vacancy Measures and Economic Analysis." In National Bureau of Economic Research, *The Measurement and Interpretation of Job Vacancies*, 27–47. New York: National Bureau of Economic Research.

1966 "Guideposts, Wages and Collective Bargaining." In George Shultz and Robert Aliber, eds., *Guidelines, Informal Controls, and the Market Place*, 81–96. Chicago: University of Chicago Press.

1967   "An Overall Evaluation and Suggestion for the Future." In Robert Gordon, ed., *Toward a Manpower Policy*, 355–72. New York: John Wiley.

1967   "The Function of the Strike." In John T. Dunlop and Neil Chamberlain, eds., *Frontiers of Collective Bargaining*, 103–21. New York: Harper and Row.

1967   "Two Views of Collective Bargaining," In Lloyd Ulman, ed., *Challenges to Collective Bargaining*, 168–80. Englewood Cliffs, N.J.: Prentice–Hall.

1968   "New Forces in the Economy." *Harvard Business Review*, March/April: 121–29.

1968   "Manpower in Construction: A Profile of the Industry and Projections to 1975." In J.T. Dunlop and D.Q. Mills, *The Report of the President's Committee on Urban Housing*, 239–68. Technical Studies, Vol. II.

1969   Ed., *Planning and Markets: Modern Trends on Various Economic Systems.* New York: McGraw–Hill. (With Nikolay Fedorenko.)

1969   "Industrial Relations Systems at Work." In Gerald Somers, ed., *Essays in Industrial Relations Theory*, 25–38. Ames, Iowa: Iowa State University Press.

1970   "Major Issues in New Sector Bargaining." In Seymour Wolfbein, ed., *Emerging Sectors of Collective Bargaining*, 11–22. Braintree, Mass.: Mark.

1970   "What's Ahead in Union Government?" In Joel Seidman, ed., *Trade Union Government and Collective Bargaining: Some Critical Issues*, 198–206. New York: Praeger.

1970   *Labor and the American Community*. New York: Simon and Schuster. (With Derek Bok.)

1971   "Postscript to 'Industrialism and Industrial Man.' " *International Labour Review*, June: 519–40.

1973   "Structure of Collective Bargaining." In Gerald G. Somers, ed., *The Next Twenty-five Years of Industrial Relations*, 10–18. Madison, Wis.: Industrial Relations Research Association.

1975   "Inflation and Incomes Policy: The Political Economy of Recent U.S. Experience." *Public Policy* 23 (Spring): 135–66.

1975   "Wage and Price Controls as Seen by a Controller." In Industrial Relations Research Association, *Proceedings of the Twenty-eighth Annual Winter Meeting*, 457–63. Madison, Wis.: Industrial Relations Research Association.

1977   Ed., *The Lessons of Wage and Price Control—The Food Sector.* Cambridge: Harvard University Press. (With Kenneth Fedor.)

1977   "Policy Decisions and Research in Economics and Industrial Relations." *Industrial and Labor Relations Review* 30 (April): 275–82.

1977   "Inflation and Income Policies: The Political Economy of Recent U.S. Experience." In Stuart Nagel, ed., *Policy Studies Annual Review*, 372–403. London: Sage.

1978   Ed., *Labor in the Twentieth Century.* New York: Academic Press. (With Walter Galenson.)

1978   "Past and Future Tendencies in American Labor Organizations." *Daedalus*, Winter: 79–96.

1979   "The Future of the American Labor Movement." In Seymour Lipset, ed., *The Third Century, America as a Post-Industrial Society*, 183–203. Stanford, Calif.: Hoover Institution.

1980   "The Changing Character of Labor Markets." In Martin Feldstein, ed., *The American Economy in Transition*, 396–402. Chicago: University of Chicago Press.

1981   "The Consensus: Process and Substance." In Michael Wachter and Susan Wachter, eds., *Toward a New U.S. Industrial Policy?* 497–500. Philadelphia: University of Pennsylvania Press.

1982   "Working Toward Consensus." *Challenge*, July/August: 26–34.

1983   "The Limits of Legal Compulsion." In James Perry and Kenneth Kraemer, eds., *Public Management, Public and Private Perspectives*, 158–65. Palo Alto,Calif.: Mayfield.

1983   "Involving Government as a Catalyst, Not as Regulator." In William Kilberg, ed., *The Dislocated Worker, Preparing America's Workforce*, 14–17. Washington, D.C.: Seven Locks Press.

1983   "The Negotiations Alternative in Dispute Resolution." *Villanova Law Review* 29 (No. 6): 1421–48.

1984   *Dispute Resolution, Negotiation and Consensus Building*. Dover, Mass.: Auburn.

1984   "Industrial Relations and Economics: The Common Frontier of Wage Determination." In Industrial Relations Research Association, *Proceedings of the Thirty-seventh Annual Winter Meeting*, 9–23. Madison, Wis.: Industrial Relations Research Association

1985   "Challenges to Management of Structural Adjustments." In Catherine Sterling and John Yochelson, eds., *Under Pressure, U.S. Industry and the Challenges of Structural Adjustment*, 209–18. Boulder, Colo.: Westview.

1986   "A Decade of National Experience." In Jerome Rosow, ed., *Teamwork: Joint Labor–Management Programs in America*, 12–25 New York: Pergamon.

1987   "The Legal Framework of Industrial Relations and the Economic Future of the United States." In Charles J. Morris, ed., *American Labor Policy: A Critical Appraisal of the National Labor Relations Act*, 1–15. Washington, D.C.: The Bureau of National Affairs, Inc.

Clark Kerr

1941   "Industrial Relations in Large-Scale Cotton Farming." In Pacific Coast Economic Association, *Proceedings of the Nineteenth Annual Conference*, 62–69. Eugene, Ore.: Koke-Chapman.

1942 *Migration to the Seattle Labor Market Area, 1940–1942*, Seattle, Wa.: University of Washington Press.

1948 "Multiple Employer Bargaining: The San Francisco Experience." In R.A. Lester and J. Shister, eds., *Insights into Labor Issues*, 25–61. New York: Macmillan. (With Lloyd Fisher.)

1949 "Short-Run Behavior of Physical Productivity and Average Hourly Earnings." *Review of Economics and Statistics* 31 (November): 299–309.

1950 "Framework for Analysis of Industrial Relations." *Industrial and Labor Relations Review* 3 (April): 410–11.

1950 "Labor Markets: Their Character and Consequences." *American Economic Review* 40 (May): 278-91.

1950 "Effects of Environment and Administration on Job Evaluation." *Harvard Business Review* 28 (May): 77-96. (With Lloyd Fisher.)

1952 "Governmental Wage Restraints—Their Limits and Uses in a Mobilized Economy." *American Economic Review* 42 (May): 369–84.

1953 "Industrialization and the Labor Force: A Typological Framework." In Robert Aronson and John Windmuller, eds., *Labor, Management and Economic Growth*, 137–47. Ithaca, N.Y.: Cornell University Press. (With Abraham Siegal.)

1954 "Trade Unionism and Distributive Shares." *American Economic Review* 44 (May): 279–92.

1954 "The Balkanization of Labor Markets." In *Labor Mobility and Economic Opportunity*, 92–110. New York: John Wiley.

1954 "The Interindustry Propensity to Strike—An International Comparison." In Arthur Kornhauser, ed., *Industrial Conflict*, 189–212. New York: McGraw–Hill. (With Abraham Siegel.)

1954 "Industrial Conflict and Its Mediation." *American Journal of Sociology* 60 (November): 230–245.

1955 "The Structuring of the Labor Force in Industrial Society: New Dimensions and Questions." *Industrial and Labor Relations Review* 8 (January): 151–68. (With Abraham Siegel.)

1955 "Industrial Relations and the Liberal Pluralist." In Industrial Relations Research Association, *Proceedings of the Seventh Annual Meeting*, 2–16. Madison, Wis.: Industrial Relations Research Association.

1957 "Wage Relationships—The Comparative Impact of Market and Power Forces." In John T. Dunlop, ed., *The Theory of Wage Determination*, 173–93. New York: Macmillan.

1957 "Labor's Income Share and the Labor Movement." In George Taylor and Frank Pierson, eds., *New Concepts in Wage Determination*, 260–98. New York: McGraw–Hill.

1957 *Unions and Union Leaders of Their Own Choosing*. New York: The Fund for the Republic.

1957   "Plant Sociology: The Elite and the Aborigines." In Mirra Komarovsky and Paul Lazarsfeld, eds., *Common Frontiers of the Social Sciences*, 281–309. Glencoe, Ill.: Free Press. (With Lloyd Fisher.)

1958   "The Prospect for Wages and Hours in 1975." In Jack Stieber, ed., *U.S. Industrial Relations: The Next Twenty Years*, 167–74. East Lansing, Mich.: Michigan State University Press.

1959   "The Impacts of Unions on the Level of Wages." In American Assembly, *Wages, Prices, Profits and Productivity*, 91–108. New York: Columbia University Press.

1960   *Industrialism and Industrial Man: The Problems of Labor and Management in Economic Growth*. Cambridge: Harvard University Press. (With John T. Dunlop, Frederick H. Harbison, and Charles A. Myers.)

1964   *Labor and Management in Industrial Society*. New York: Doubleday & Co., Inc.

1969   *Marshall, Marx and Modern Times: The Multi-Dimensional Society*. Cambridge and New York: Cambridge University Press.

1971   "Postscript to Industrialism and Industrial Man" (With John T. Dunlop, Frederick H. Harbison, Charles A. Myers). *International Labor Review* 103 (June): 519–40.

1977   *Labor Markets and Wage Determination: The Balkanization of Labor Markets and Other Essays*. Berkeley: University of California Press.

1978   "Industrial Relations Research: A Personal Retrospective." *Industrial Relations* 17 (May): 131–42.

1983   "The Intellectual Role of the Neorealists in Labor Economics." *Industrial Relations* 22 (Spring): 298–318.

1983   "A Perspective on Industrial Relations Research—Thirty-Six Years Later." Industrial Relations Research Association, *Proceedings of the Thirty-Sixth Annual Winter Meeting*, 14–21. Madison, Wis.: Industrial Relations Research Association.

1983   *The Future of Industrial Societies—Convergence or Continuing Diversity?* Cambridge, Mass.: Harvard University Press.

Richard A. Lester

1935   "Work Relief and Wage Rates." *American Federationist* 42 (July): 696–99.

1936   "Is Work Relief Economical?" *Social Science Review* 10 (June): 264–76.

1938   "Political Economy Versus Individual Economics." *American Economic Review* 28 (March): 55–64.

1939   "Overtime Wage Rates." *American Economic Review* 29 (December): 790–92.

1941   *Economics of Labor*. New York: Macmillan. 2d edition, 1964.

1943 "Effects of the War on Wages and Hours." *American Economic Review* 33 (March), Supplement: 218–37.

1943 "War Controls of Materials, Equipment, and Manpower." *Southern Economic Journal* 9 (January): 197–216.

1944 "Note on Wages and Labor Cost." *Southern Economic Journal* 10 (January): 235–38.

1945 "Trends in Southern Wage Differentials Since 1890." *Southern Economic Journal* 11 (April): 317–44.

1945 *Providing for Unemployed Workers in the Transition.* New York: McGraw–Hill.

1946 *Wages Under National and Regional Collective Bargaining, Experience in Seven Industries.* Princeton: Princeton University, Industrial Relations Section.

1946 "Diversity in North–South Wage Differentials and in Wage Rates within the South." *Southern Economic Journal* 12 (January): 238–62.

1946 "Effectiveness of Factory Labor: North–South Comparisons." *Journal of Political Economy* 54 (February): 60–75.

1946 "Shortcomings of Marginal Analysis for Wage-Employment Problems." *American Economic Review* 36 (March): 63–82.

1946 "Wage Diversity and Its Theoretical Implications," *Review of Economics and Statistics* 28 (August): 152–59.

1947 "Marginalism, Minimum Wages, and Labor Markets." *American Economic Review* 37 (March): 135–48.

1947 "Southern Wage Differentials: Developments, Analysis and Implications." *Southern Economic Journal* 13 (April): 152–59.

1947 "Reflections on the 'Labor Monopoly' Issue." *Journal of Political Economy* 55 (December): 13–36.

1948 "Absence of Elasticity Considerations in Demand to the Firm." *Southern Economic Journal* 14 (January): 285–89.

1948 Ed., Insights into Labor Issues. New York: Macmillan. (With Joseph Shister.)

1948 "Results and Implications of Some Recent Wage Studies." In R.A. Lester and J. Shister, eds., *Insights into Labor Issues*, 197–225. New York: Macmillan.

1948 *Constructive Labor Relations: Experience in Four Firms.* Princeton: Princeton University, Industrial Relations Section.

1948 *Company Wage Policies: A Survey of Patterns and Experience.* Princeton: Princeton University, Industrial Relations Section.

1948 "The Influence of Unionism Upon Earnings: Comment." *Quarterly Journal of Economics* 62 (November): 783–87.

1949 "Equilibrium of the Firm." *American Economic Review* 36 (March): 478–84.

1950 *Job Modifications Under Collective Bargaining: A Survey of Company Experience and Four Case Studies.* Princeton: Princeton University, Industrial Relations Section. (With Robert Aronson.)

1951   "Collective Bargaining Under Stabilization." In Emmanuel Stein, ed., *Proceedings of New York University Fourth Annual Conference on Labor*, 163–78. New York: Mathew Bender.

1951   *Compulsory Arbitration of Utility Disputes in New Jersey and Pennsylvania.* (with R.R. France). Princeton, N.J.: Princeton University, Industrial Relations Section.

1951   *Labor and Industrial Relations, A General Analysis.* New York: Macmillan.

1952   "A Range Theory of Wage Differentials." *Industrial and Labor Relations Review* 5 (July): 483–50.

1954   *Hiring Practices and Labor Competition.* Princeton: Princeton University, Industrial Relations Section.

1955   "The Nature and Level of Income Security for a Free Society." In J.E. Russell, ed., *National Policies for Education, Health, and Social Services*, 273–322. New York: Doubleday.

1955   *Adjustments to Labor Shortages: Management Practices and Institutional Controls in an Area of Expanding Employment.* Princeton: Princeton University, Industrial Relations Section.

1956   "Progress in Industrial Relations Research and Policy." In Industrial Relations Research Association, *Proceedings of the Ninth Annual Meeting*, 2–9. Madison, Wis.: Industrial Relations Research Association.

1957   "Reflections on Collective Bargaining in Britain and Sweden." *Industrial and Labor Relations Review* 10 (April): 375–401.

1957   "Economic Adjustments to Changes in Wage Differentials." In George Taylor and Frank Pierson, eds., *New Concepts in Wage Determination*, 206–35. New York: McGraw–Hill.

1958   "Revolution in Industrial Employment." *Labor Law Journal* 9 (June): 439–46.

1958   *As Unions Mature: An Analysis of the Evolution of American Unionism.* Princeton: Princeton University Press.

1960   "Employment Effects of Minimum Wages: Comment." *Industrial and Labor Relations Review* 13 (January): 254–64.

1960   "The Changing Nature of the Union." In Emmanuel Stein, ed., *Proceedings of New York University Fourteenth Annual Conference on Labor*, 19–30. New York: Mathew Bender.

1960   "Financing of Unemployment Compensation." *Industrial and Labor Relations Review* 14 (October): 52–67.

1960   "The Economic Significance of Unemployment Compensation, 1948–1959." *Review of Economics and Statistics* 42 (November): 14–19.

1960   "Alternative to the Strike." In George Taylor and Edward Shils, eds., *Industrial Relations in the 1960s—Problems and Prospects*, Vol. 2, 1–12. Philadelphia: University of Pennsylvania.

1961   "Implications of Labor Force Developments for Unemployment Benefits." *Quarterly Review of Economics and Business* 1 (May): 47–56.

1962   *The Economics of Unemployment Compensation*. Princeton: Princeton University, Industrial Relations Section.

1962   "Labor Policy in a Changing World." *Industrial Relations* 2 (October): 39–52.

1965   *Labor: Readings on Major Issues*. New York: Random House.

1966   *Manpower Planning in a Free Society*. Princeton: Princeton University Press.

1966   "Comment." In *The Measurement and Interpretation of Job Vacancies*, 115–20. New York: Columbia University Press.

1967   "The Role of Organized Labor." In Robert Gordon, ed., *Toward a Manpower Policy*, 317–32. New York: John Wiley.

1967   "Benefits as a Preferred Form of Compensation." *Southern Economic Journal* 33 (April): 488–95.

1967   "National Manpower Administration and Policies." In Solomon Barkin, ed., *International Labor*, 205–15. New York: Harper and Row.

1967   "Manpower in the American Scene." In John Coleman, ed., *The Changing American Economy*, 100–09. New York: Basic Books.

1967   "Pay Differentials by Size of Establishment." *Industrial Relations* 7 (October): 57–67.

1968   "Negotiated Wage Increases, 1951–1967." *Review of Economics and Statistics* 50 (May): 173–81.

1968   "The Uses of Unemployment Insurance." In W.G. Bowen, F.H. Harbison, R.A. Lester, and H.M. Somers, eds., *The Princeton Symposium on the American System of Social Insurance: Its Philosophy, Impact, and Future Development*, 153–76. New York: McGraw–Hill.

1969   "Some Investment-Like Aspects of Employment and Pay." *Monthly Labor Review*, November: 62–5.

1972   "Reflections on Manpower Planning." In Ivar Berg, ed., *Human Resources and Economic Welfare*, 15–34. New York: Columbia University Press.

1973   "Manipulation of the Labor Market." In Gerald Somers, ed., *The Next Twenty-five Years of Industrial Relations*, 47–55. Madison, Wis.: Industrial Relations Research Association.

1977   "Labor-Market Discrimination and Individualized Pay: The Complicated Case of University Faculty." In Leonard Hausman, et al., eds., *Equal Rights and Industrial Relations*, 197–233. Madison, Wis.: Industrial Relations Research Association.

1980   *Reasoning About Discrimination: The Analysis of Professional and Executive Work in Federal Antibias Programs*. Princeton: Princeton University Press.

1981   "Age, Performance, and Retirement Legislation." In Anne Somers and Dorothy Fabian, eds., *The Geriatric Imperative*, 77–88. New York: Appleton-Century-Crofts.

1984   *Labor Arbitration in State and Local Government: An Examination of Experience in Eight States and New York City.* Princeton: Princeton University, Industrial Relations Section.

1986   "Lessons from Experience with Interest Arbitration in Nine Jurisdictions." *Arbitration Journal* 41 (June): 34–37.

1986   *The Industrial Relations Section of Princeton University, 1922–1985.* Princeton: Princeton University, Industrial Relations Section.

Lloyd G. Reynolds

1935   *The British Immigrant: His Economic and Social Adjustment in Canada.* Toronto: Oxford University Press.

1938   "Competition in the Rubber Tire Industry." *American Economic Review* 28 (September): 459–68.

1940   "Cut-throat Competition." *American Economic Review* 30 (December): 736–47.

1941   *Labor and National Defense.* New York: Twentieth Century Fund.

1942   "Relations Between Wage Rates, Costs, and Prices." *American Economic Review* 32 (March): 275–89.

1944   *Trade Union Publications, 1850–1941: An Analysis, Bibliography, and Subject Matter Index.* Baltimore: Johns Hopkins University Press. (With Charles Killingsworth.)

1946   "The Supply of Labor to the Firm." *Quarterly Journal of Economics* 60 (May): 390–411.

1946   "Wage Differences in Local Labor Markets." *American Economic Review* 36 (June): 366–75.

1947   "Research on Wages." Social Science Research Council Memorandum No. 4. New York: Social Science Research Council.

1948   "Economics of Labor." In H.S. Ellis, ed., *A Survey of Contemporary Economics*, 255–87. New York: Blakiston.

1948   "Toward a Short-Run Theory of Wages." *American Economic Review* 38 (June):289–308.

1948   "Some Aspects of Labor Market Structure." In R.A. Lester and J. Shister, eds., *Insights into Labor Issues*, 267–302. New York: Macmillan.

1948   "Wage Bargaining, Price Changes, and Employment." In Industrial Relations Research Association, *Proceedings of the First Annual Meeting*, 35–50. Madison, Wis.: Industrial Relations Research Association.

1949   *Job Horizons: A Study of Labor Mobility.* New York: Harper. (With Joseph Shister.)

1949   *Labor Economics and Labor Relations.* 1st edition. Englewood Cliffs, N.J.: Prentice–Hall. (9th edition, 1986, with Stanley Masters and Colletta Moser.)

1949   "Bargaining Over General Wage Changes." In New York University, *Trends in Collective Bargaining and Labor Law*, 155–71. New York: New York University.

1951   *The Structure of Labor Markets.* New York: Harper.

1952   "Wages in the Business Cycle." *American Economic Review* 42 (May): 84–99.

1953   "The State of Wage Theory." In Industrial Relations Research Association, *Proceedings of the Sixth Annual Meeting*, 234–240. Madison, Wis.: Industrial Relations Research Association.

1955   "Research and Practice in Industrial Relations." In Industrial Relations Research Association, *Proceedings of the Eighth Annual Meeting*, 2–13. Madison, Wis.: Industrial Relations Research Association.

1956   *The Evolution of Wage Structure.* New Haven: Yale University Press. (With Cynthia Taft.)

1957   "The General Level of Wages." In George Taylor and Frank Pierson, eds., *New Concepts in Wage Determination*, 239–59. New York: McGraw–Hill.

1957   "The Impact of Collective Bargaining on the Wage Structure in the United States." In John Dunlop, ed., *The Theory of Wage Determination*, 173–93. London: Macmillan.

1959   "Roundtable on Economic Research." *American Economic Review* 49 (May): 576–80.

1959   "Wage Behavior and Inflation: An International View." In *Wages, Prices, Profits and Productivity*, 109–36. New York: The American Assembly.

1960   "Wage-Push and All That." *American Economic Review* 50 (May): 195–204.

1965   "Wages and Employment in a Labor-Surplus Economy." *American Economic Review* 55 (March): 19–39.

1965   *Wages, Productivity, and Industrialization in Puerto Rico.* Homewood, Ill.: Irwin. (With Peter Gregory.)

1969   "Objectives of Wage Policy in Developing Countries." In Anthony Smith, ed., *Wage Policy Issues in Economic Development*, 217–34. New York: St. Martin's Press.

1969   "Relative Earnings and Manpower Allocation in Developing Economies." *Pakistan Development Review.* Spring.

1973   "Labor in Less Developed Economies." In Gerald Somers, ed., *The Next Twenty-five Years of Industrial Relations*, 165–76. Madison, Wis.: Industrial Relations Research Association.

1987   *Economics of Labor.* (with Colletta H. Moser and Stanley H. Masters) Englewood Cliffs, N.J.: Prentice-Hall.

Index

About the Authors

John T. Dunlop received his Ph.D. degree in Economics in 1939 from the University of California, Berkeley, and since then has been Professor of Economics at Harvard University. Other positions held include President, Industrial Relations Research Association, 1960; Chairman, Construction Industry Stabilization Committee, 1971–74; Director and Chairman of Labor–Management Advisory Committee, Cost of Living Council, 1973–74; and U.S. Secretary of Labor, 1974–76.

Clark Kerr received his Ph.D. degree in Economics in 1939 from the University of California, Berkeley. From 1945 to 1973 he was Professor of Economics and Industrial Relations at Berkeley, and from 1973 to the present Professor Emeritus. Other positions held include President, Industrial Relations Research Association, 1954; President, University of California, 1958–67; and Chairman and Staff Director, Carnegie Council on Policy Studies in Higher Education, 1974–79.

Richard A. Lester received his Ph.D. degree in Economics from Princeton University in 1936, and from 1945 to the present has served at Princeton as Professor of Economics, Research Associate in the Industrial Relations Section, and Dean of the Faculty. Other positions held include Chairman of the Southern Textile Commission, National War Labor Board, 1943–45; President, Industrial Relations Research Association, 1956; Chairman, New Jersey Employment Security council, 1955–65; and Vice-Chairman, President's Commission on the Status of Women, 1961–63.

Lloyd G. Reynolds received his Ph.D. degree in Economics in 1936 from Harvard University, and since 1945 has been Professor of Economics at Yale University. Other positions held include Chief Economist, War Manpower Commission, 1942–43; President, Industrial Relations Research Association, 1955; and Director, Yale Economic Growth Center, 1961–67, 1975–76.

Bruce E. Kaufman received his Ph.D. degree in Economics in 1978 from the University of Wisconsin, Madison, and since 1977 has been Assistant and Associate Professor of Economics at Georgia State University. He is author of two books and a number of scholarly articles on a variety of labor subjects, including wage determination, models of union behavior, and strike activity.

Richard B. Freeman received his Ph.D. degree in Economics from Harvard University in 1969. Currently he is Professor of Economics at Harvard, visiting Professor at the London School of Economics, and Director of the Labor Studies Program at the National Bureau of Economic Research. He is author of numerous influential books and articles on the economics of education, discrimination, wage determination, and labor unions.